1983

University of St. F.
GEN 128 B52

W9-CNI-378

3 0301 00054264 3

HUME, HEGEL AND HUMAN NATURE

ARCHIVES INTERNATIONALES D'HISTOIRE DES IDEES
INTERNATIONAL ARCHIVES OF THE HISTORY OF IDEAS

103

CHRISTOPHER J. BERRY

HUME, HEGEL AND HUMAN NATURE

Directors: P. Dibon (Paris) and R. Popkin (Washington Univ. St. Louis)
Editorial Board: J. Aubin (Paris); J.F. Battail (Upsala); J. Collins (St. Louis Univ.); P. Costabel (Paris; A. Crombie (Oxford); I. Dambska (Cracow); H. de la Fontaine-Verwey (Amsterdam); H. Gadamer (Heidelberg); H. Gouhier (Paris); T. Gregory (Rome); T.E. Jessop (Hull); W. Kirsop (Melbourne); P.O. Kristeller (Columbia Univ.); Elisabeth Labrousse (Paris); A. Lossky (Los Angeles); J. Malarczyk (Lublin); J. Orcibal (Paris); Wolfgang Röd (München); J.P. Schobinger (Zürich); G. Sebba (Emory Univ., Atlanta); R. Schackleton (Oxford); J. Tans (Groningen).

HUME, HEGEL AND HUMAN NATURE

by

CHRISTOPHER J. BERRY

LIBRARY
College of St. Francis
JOLIET, ILL.

1982
MARTINUS NIJHOFF PUBLISHERS
THE HAGUE / BOSTON / LONDON

Distributors:

for the United States and Canada
Kluwer Boston, Inc.
190 Old Derby Street
Hingham, MA 02043
USA

for all other countries:
Kluwer Academic Publishers Group
Distribution Center
P.O. Box 322
3300 AH Dordrecht
The Netherlands

Library of Congress Cataloging in Publication Data

Berry, Christopher J.
    Hume, Hegel, and human nature.

    (Archives internationales d'histoire des
idées = International archives of the history of
ideas ; 103)
    Bibliography: p.
    Includes index.
    1. Hume, David, 1711-1776--Anthropology.
2. Hegel, Georg Wilhelm Friedrich, 1770-1831--
Anthropology. I. Title. II. Series: Archives
internationales d'histoire des idées ; 103.
B1499.M27B47   128   82-6346
ISBN 90-247-2682-4   AACR2

ISBN 90-247-2682-4 (this volume)
ISBN 90-247-2433-3 (series)

© *1982 by Martinus Nijhoff Publishers, The Hague. All rights reserved. No part of this publication may be reproduced, stored in a retrieval system, or transmitted in any form of by any means, mechanical, photocopying, recording, or otherwise, without the prior written permission of the publisher, Martinus Nijhoff Publishers, P.O. Box 566, 2501 CN The Hague, The Netherlands.*

PRINTED IN THE NETHERLANDS

128
B526

TO MY PARENTS

104,988

CONTENTS

PREFACE

This is both a modest and a presumptuous work. It is presumptuous because, given the vast literature on just one of its themes, it attempts to discuss not only the philosophies of both Hume and Hegel but also something of their intellectual milieu. Moreover, though the study has a delimiting perspective in the relationship between a theory of human nature and an account of the various aspects that make up social experience, this itself is so central and protean that it has necessitated a discussion of, amongst others, theories of history, language, aesthetics, law and politics.

Yet it is a modest work in that, although I do think I have some fresh things to say, the study does not propose any revolutionary new reading of the material. I am not here interested in the relative validity of the theories put forward — I do not 'take sides'. Nevertheless it is part of the modest intent that recourse to Hume and Hegel in arguments pertaining to human nature will be better informed and more discriminating as a consequence of this study. Additionally, some distinctions herein made also shed light on some assumptions made in contemporary debates in the philosophy of social science, especially those concerning the understanding of alien belief-systems.

I endeavour here to account for the nature and extent of Hume's belief in the constancy and uniformity of human nature and to explain the meaning of human nature as a concrete universal in Hegel. I make use of a concept of contextualisation to specify the nature of the difference between Hume's and Hegel's accounts of the relationship between human nature and society and, since these relationships are temporal as well as spatial, crucial to the difference between Hume and Hegel is their estimation and conception of history.

This is neither a work of analytical philosophy nor is it a work of the history of ideas strictly so termed but, rather, it is an exercise in intellectual history. This explains its tri-partite structure. The first Part sketches a general intellectual milieu into which the discussions of Hume and Hegel, in Parts II and III respectively, are placed. I am not here tracing the development or movement of ideas about human nature between Hume and Hegel: the lack of any sustained discussion of Rousseau would then have been inexcusable. Rather, I put forward a general interpretation of the theories of human nature held by Hume and Hegel and trace some of the consequences of their respective theories on the rest of their thought. Although in Part III there is some comparative discussion, the work is not intended as a systematic piece of comparison. The treatments are relatively discrete and can stand on their own, but they also comprise an overall picture. Parts II and III exhibit a similar formal thematic structure. Each is divided into four chapters of which the first is devoted to Hume's and Hegel's concept of human nature itself; the second to its impact on their notions of the character and constitution of society; the third to their explanation of social diversity and the fourth to their interpretation of the interaction between men and society. Additionally, there are a number of persistent themes, which coalesce around the issue of a change, which is sketched in Part I, that occurred in the understanding of, and conceptualisation of, human nature between the writings of Hume and Hegel.

I have utilised where available existing translations but supply a precise reference to the original. With respect to Hegel, the basic text is the Lasson edition, but this is supplemented by referring to the first edition of 1845 et seq. of Gans and his associates, as well as to the Jubilee edition of Glockner. Full details of the works cited in the Notes are given in the Bibliography.

I have incurred many debts. Portions of my own manuscript, at various stages in its career, have been read by colleagues and friends. At my own university I have benefited from the comments of, and discussions with, Harold Betteridge, Dudley Knowles, Michael Lessnoff, David Lloyd-Jones, Andrew Lockyer, Bill Mackenzie, Adrienne Redshaw and Eva Schaper. Outside Glasgow I am indebted to John Chapman, Jim Moore, Peter Nicholson and Stewart Sutherland. As is customarily proper they should be absolved from all responsibility for what follows.

This book was a long time in the writing and a long time has elapsed since it was written. Its appearance has been made possible by the generosity and persistence of the Publications Board of the University of Glasgow to whom I tender my grateful thanks. Gratitude is also owed to Elspeth Shaw, Jean Barclay, Celia Wallace and Barbara Cooper for shouldering the onerous task of typing and copying.

For the right to reproduce the odd paragraph and sentence scattered in the text I am grateful for the permission of @ Journal of the History of Ideas, Inc. for 'From Hume to Hegel: the Case of the Social Contract', Vol. 38, No. 4 (Oct. – Dec., 1977) pp. 691 – 704; of @ New York University 1980 for 'Property and Possession: Two replies to Locke – Hume and Hegel' in *Property (NOMOS XXII)*, edited by J. Roland Pennock and John W. Chapman; of @ Pergamon Press Ltd. for 'Hegel on the World-Historical' in *History of European Ideas*, Vol. 2, No. 2 (1981); of @ Wesleyan University for 'Hume on Rationality in History and Social Life' in *History and Theory*, Vol. 21 (1982, May).

In accord with prefatory tradition, the final word is familial: more than thanks to my parents, to whom I dedicate this work, to Christine and to Craig and Paul, whose arrivals put the whole enterprise into perspective.

INTRODUCTION

According to Stuart Hampshire, "it is possible to characterise philosophy itself as a search for 'a definition of man', and to interpret the great philosophers of the past as each producing a different account of the powers essential to man"[1] and according to Maurice Mandelbaum, "there arose significantly new forms of thought and standards for evaluation in the post-Enlightenment period and . . . these marked a radically new epoch in intellectual history".[2] These two eminent philosophers are here giving voice to two widely accepted views. This study is an examination of their conjunction in the persons of Hume and Hegel.

It is unquestionable that Hume and Hegel are major philosophers and though Hegel was born six years before Hume's death in 1776 they belong to the different epochs specified by Mandelbaum. How Hume and Hegel each defined man, or human nature, can thus, potentially, tell us much not only about their respective philosophies but also, given the arguable centrality of a theory of human nature to social, political, aesthetical, ethical and religious thought, can tell us much about these two epochs. Indeed, it is a guiding assumption (but one, it is hoped, that is vindicated) of this study that the decisive difference between these epochs can be seen to be exemplified in Hume's and Hegel's respective conceptualisations of man.

In Part I, two key factors are identified as making for this shift in conceptualisation. The first is philosophical, narrowly conceived. Philosophically, the Enlightenment's assumption that man was to all intents and purposes the passive recipient of sensory information was overturned by the Kantian 'revolution', which held man to be an active agent, who necessarily imposes a structure on what would otherwise be the mere incoherence of sensory input. Kant, in this way, is a decisive mediator between Hume and Hegel for it was Hume's 'hard-headed' empiricism that aroused Kant from his celebrated 'slumber' to appreciate that since Hume's argument was valid but his conclusions were unacceptable then his premises must be at fault. For all his criticisms of Kant, and his in-

1. *Thought and Action*, p. 232.
2. *History, Man and Reason*, p. 5.

debtedness to Aristotle and Spinoza, Hegel accepts the validity of Kant's critique of Hume.

The second factor accounting for the shift in conceptualisations is anthropological, loosely conceived. It was the common Enlightenment view that though man was a social creature this sociality was not constitutive so that, despite the differences between societies, human nature remained constant and uniform. This position, too, was overturned, and, though there is no one thinker to play a role equivalent to Kant on the philosophical front, it is here argued that the work of Herder is of particular significance. Again, for all his criticism of Romanticism and general disdain for Herder, Hegel nevertheless firmly adhered to the view that the individual's particular social setting was constitutive of that individual's 'human nature'. This view that sociality is specific and constitutive is here termed contextualist.

That human nature is in some manner and to some extent contextual is now something of a commonplace. If this observation is accepted, then, the shift in conceptualisations of man between Hume and Hegel is of considerable significance not only for its own intrinsic sake but also extrinsically for the illumination it sheds on subsequent thought, including our own − what is now a commonplace was not always so regarded. In addition, to see this shift in conceptualisations exemplified in the *difference* between the thought of Hume and Hegel runs counter to the view that the thought of these two philosophers, as the product of two bourgeois thinkers and thus ideologically supportive or derivative of a nascent capitalist society, is 'really' of *similar* import. To account for the emergence of contextualism by the conservative reaction to the radical ideas of the Enlightenment (and their partial implementation in the French Revolution) fails to account for the theory's persistence. Indeed, it is one of the more intriguing as well as problematic aspects of Marx's thought that he subscribes most assuredly and categorically to a far-reaching form of contextualism.

The nature of the relationship between human nature and social experience (the nub of contextualism) provides a background theme throughout the three Parts of the study. More precisely, is it possible to have an intelligible concept of human nature as such or is its contextual character such that the very variety and multiplicity of societal forms deprives the concept of any general non-specific intelligibility? Or more simply, is the concept of human nature culturally relative?

It has never been denied that really (as opposed to analytically) man ever existed apart from society, or that there are differences between societies, but the move from sociality, and diversity or plurality, to relativism hinges on the extent to which 'man' is culturally specific. The view that the Azande, or the Athenians at the time of Pericles, can be understood by the twentieth-century Briton as transparently as he understands his fellow Britons is scarcely supportable. Associated with this view is an increased sensitivity to the dangers of arrogant and ignorant parochialism (as found in much nineteenth-century anthropology) whereby an indigenous culture is appraised by criteria that are 'external' to it. What is not clear is how extensive a commitment to relativism these considerations involve. The relativist position is in turn frequently held to be logically inconsistent — is the truth of relativism itself relative?

Much of the debate can be, not unfairly, characterised as concerned with some form of compromise; in particular, with the location of some defensible constants. Due to the problems recognised in cross-cultural comprehension, such constants tend to be formal in character. Perhaps, the most frequently invoked (although there are attempts to utilise some form of biological substratum) is some notion of minimal rationality, which is to say, the application of certain constitutive or presuppositional features of social intercourse per se (for example, some distinction between the 'real' and the 'unreal') that will pertain equally to twentieth-century Britons, the Azande and Periclean Athenians.

We shall see that neither Hume nor Hegel is a relativist but that they arrive at this rejection from different assumptions and premises. Indeed, their positions provide a counterpart to much modern analysis. These inter-relations are distinguished, in the ensuing discussion, by the employment of certain stipulative terms. The view that the differences between societies are immaterial to a comprehension of human nature is termed a formal account of social life. The reverse of this that the differences between societies do make a material difference to the comprehension of human nature is termed a substantive account of social life. The view that it is only through the invocation of some non-material presuppositional features of social intercourse that cross-cultural comparison and comprehension is possible is termed a formal account of rationality. The reverse of this that cross-cultural comprehension, indeed cross-cultural appraisal, is possible in terms of some concrete material criteria is termed a substantive account of rationality. In these terms, the 'modern compromise' typically provides a substantive account of social life and a formal account of rationality, Hume provides a formal account of social life but a substantive account of rationality and Hegel provides a substantive account of both social life and rationality (tendentiously, Marx's theory could be similarly so designated).

It is, in conclusion, possible to make a more general point concerning the relationship between Hume and Hegel and modern thought. At a certain level, and from a particular perspective, Hume and Hegel do provide (for what it is worth) enduring 'relevance' as distinct poles in answer to the perennial question of life's meaning. Either the cosmos and man's place in it is contingent and bereft of intrinsic meaning or it has, and mankind has, some inherent significance. It is not surprising that modern thought has been depicted both as an amendment, development and reaction to Hume[3] and as an amendment, development and reaction to Hegel.[4]

3. John Chapman, for example, has written "I hold that the work of Hume is of significance in that he demolished certain ways of thinking and in that modern types of theory arose from the disintegration of his own position", 'Political Theory: Logical Structure and Enduring Types' in *L'Idée de Philosophie Politique* (1965) p. 65 also p. 71.

4. Merleau-Ponty, for example, has written "All the great philosophical ideas of the past century, the philosophies of Marx and Nietzsche, phenomenology, German existentialism and psychoanalysis find their beginnings in Hegel", quoted in C. Taylor *Hegel*, p. 538, and whilst Taylor demurs from a full subscription to this view, nevertheless himself adds that "the scope of Hegel's influence is beyond question".

I. THE INTELLECTUAL BACKCLOTH

INTRODUCTION

The aim of this opening Part is to provide the background for the discussions of Hume and Hegel in Parts II and III, respectively. This background will provide both a context and an element of continuity for the more or less discrete treatments in the following Parts.

Accordingly, this Part will consist of a *sketch* of some of the intellectual currents à propos man and society from the late seventeenth century to the early nineteenth century. More precisely, this sketch will be concerned with changes in the intellectual reaction to the recognition of the diversity of social practices and its concomitant effect on an understanding and evaluation of an adequate conceptualisation of human nature. It will be suggested in Chapter 1 that this reaction in the guise of the response made to relativism was in many ways a central preoccupation of the Enlightenment and that, in Chapter 2, the response of the Romantic movement is a response to the Enlightenment's resolution of this issue. This Chapter will concentrate on the work of Herder. In Chapter 3 the more narrowly philosophical issues will be briefly charted in the form of a discussion of Kant's thought.

1. THE ENLIGHTENMENT: A SITUATION

The validity of historical generalisations is a vexed issue. In many ways, they are unavoidable yet there is the ever-present danger that what starts out as a heuristic device ends up as a substantive entity so that, instead of it being used to explain phenomena, the reverse takes place with phenomena being understood and utilised only in so far as they fit the generalisation. The terms 'Enlightenment' and 'Romanticism' have been subject to such vicissitudes.[1] With these thoughts in mind the generalisations 'Enlightenment' and 'Romanticism' will be used but only (it is hoped) as aids.

Michael Oakeshott has written that to search for origins is to read the past backwards and has argued that this is the purview of the 'practical' man not the 'historian'.[2] For all Oakeshott's imagery about the past a start has to be made somewhere. Here I shall posit a construct — the Middle Ages[3] — out of which can be seen to emanate diverse 'events' and 'currents' which shaped the cognitive world of the Enlightenment (Oakeshott himself talks of the development out of the Middle Ages of two modes of theorising about politics).[4] Cardinal amongst these 'events' are the Renaissance, Reformation and the Scientific Revolution of the fifteenth and sixteenth centuries, and amongst the 'currents' are humanism, individualism, experimentalism together with such diverse though related phenomena as the 'spirit of capitalism', the 'discovery of the sea', and the

1. Cf., *inter alia*, P. Gay, *The Enlightenment: The Rise of Modern Paganism* and *The Enlightenment: The Science of Freedom*; I.O. Wade, *The Intellectual Origins of the French Enlightenment*; F.L. Ford, 'The Enlightenment: Towards a Useful Redefinition' in R.F. Brissenden (ed.), *Studies in the Eighteenth Century* pp. 17–29: A.O. Lovejoy, 'The Meaning of Romanticism for the Historian of Ideas', *JHI* (1941) 257–278; R. Wellek, 'The Concept of "Romanticism" in Literary History', *Comparative Literature* (1949) 1–23 & 147–172; M. Peckham, 'Toward a Theory of Romanticism Reconsiderations', *Studies in Romanticism* (1961) 1–8.

2. 'The Activity of being a Historian' in *Rationalism in Politics and other essays*, p. 160.

3. This locution is chosen to avoid falling foul of E. Curtius' magisterial judgment that "It is a fallacy to talk of the Middle Ages as if they were a uniform age", 'The Medieval Bases of Western Thought' appended to the *European Literature in the Latin Middle Ages*, p. 589.

4. Cf. 'On the Character of a Modern European State' in his *On Human Conduct*, pp. 185–326.

'decline' of both magic and hell. Out of this complex I wish here merely to highlight two strands.

The first of these is the discovery of the 'New World' and the gradual dissemination of information about its inhabitants. It is true that knowledge of the 'East' was available earlier (from Marco Polo for example) but the discovery of the 'unknown' tribes of the Americas was, if only by its very unexpectedness, a great object of both curiosity and speculation. From the beginning, journals were compiled recording the 'culture' (as we would now term it) of these tribes. Thus, to cite just one example, Amerigo Vespucci, writing in 1502 about the Guarani tribe in Brazil, remarked, amongst other things, that:

they have no laws or faith, and live according to nature. They do not recognise the immortality of the soul. . . They obey nobody, each is lord unto himself; no justice, no gratitude, which to them is unnecessary because it is not part of their code. They live in common in houses made like very large cabins. . . The meat which they eat commonly is human flesh. . . The men are accustomed to bore holes in their lips and cheeks and in these holes they place bones and stones. . . Their marriages are not with one woman but with as many as they like and without much ceremony. . . They are a very prolific people but have no heirs because they hold no property; when their children, that is the girls, reach the age of puberty, the first man to corrupt them must be the nearest relative except the father, after which they can be married.[5]

Though at first only a trickle, by the eighteenth century this literature had reached torrential proportions. A vast quantity of information about cultures – Asian, Polynesian as well as Amerindian – other than those of Western Europe was thus available (not that knowledge of Europe's own culture (its past) remained static for there was, in particular, intense activity and debate, aided by philological researches, in legal history). There can be no doubt that this information was avidly read. This reading had a number of consequences. There was, beside the production of bogus voyages, the writing of records and accounts especially for this readership dilating on issues which had proved of interest whether they be sexual customs, religious observances or linguistic competence. Finally, for our purposes, we can note the utilisation of the popularity of this literature for satirical purposes, either fantastical by Swift or less obliquely in, perhaps the two best known eighteenth century representatives of this genre, Montesquieu's *Lettres Persanes* (1721) and Diderot's *Supplément au voyage de Bougainville* (published 1796) and note, similarly, its utilisation in another related genre also much in vogue, namely, the drawing up of Utopias (indeed, the originator of this literature, Thomas More, portrayed his hypothetical narrator as having voyaged with Vespucci).

The second strand is more complex. It is the intellectual response, in what is now regarded as philosophy, to the disintegration of the medieval world. Obviously this is only a particular response but in this regard a pivotal role is played by Descartes. It is in the recognition of this role that the kernel of truth in the

5. Letter to Lorenzo di Pier Francesco de Medici (1502) in S.M. Morison, *The European Discovery of America: The Southern Voyages 1492–1616*, p. 285.

famous, not to say hackneyed, depiction of him as 'the father of modern philosophy' is to be found. Indeed, the making of modernity is very broadly the question here at issue.

Central to Descartes' programme is the quest for certainty. What can be taken as given? What can unquestionably provide a starting point? The very asking of these and similar questions, even aside from Descartes' answers, marks, to generalise, the recognition of an arena of dispute which is post-medieval. It is not necessary here to rehearse Descartes' position in any detail, however, two general points need to be made.

The first of these does concern Descartes' answers to these afore-mentioned questions. An unquestionable starting point can be located by a procedure of systematic or methodical doubt, since through its operation I am left with the one indubitable fact − I am doubting. Man is indubitably a thinking being − *cogito ergo sum*. By thought Descartes means that of which we are immediately conscious and it thus incorporates understanding, willing, imagining and perceiving. A consequence of this is that the thinking part (mind) is not only different from the corporeal part (body) but is precedent to it in that it possesses a higher degree of certitude as "there is nothing really existing apart from our thought".[6] From this indubitable foundation Descartes proceeds to deduce the necessary existence of God from which, in turn, it follows that all that is clearly and distinctly perceived is true − for God cannot deceive. The paradigm of what is clearly and distinctly perceived is mathematical truths.

This leads to the second point, namely, that everyone potentially is capable of appreciating truth. Whatever can be clearly and distinctly perceived can be so perceived by all. This is attributed to what Descartes variously calls natural light, common notions and innate ideas. What natural light shows to be true is indubitable and hence the *cogito* itself is an example of what is known in this manner. Common notions are discovered by the mind when it demonstrates indubitable propositions such as the properties of a triangle whereby the sum of the interior angles is equal to the sum of right-angles.[7] But chief among these notions in the mind is that of an omniscient, omnipotent, absolutely perfect being − God. This is an innate idea, that is to say, an idea implanted by God and derived from thought alone. The common notions cannot arise, by the very virtue of their commonality, from anything particular, that is, from any experiential source.

For all Descartes' rejection of Scholasticism (ivy on a tree) the essence of his position seemingly is that man, by definition, is a thinking being who possesses the capacity to apprehend objective truth. This capacity may not be fully utilised, since man is susceptible to prejudices and hence error, but its existence holds good irrespective of time and place. Indeed, one of the reasons why mathematics is so highly regarded by Descartes is that it possesses precisely this indifference to

6. *Principia Philosophia*(Everyman Library), p. 167: *Oeuvres Philosophiques* (Garnier, Paris, 1973), Vol. III, p. 95.

7. *Principia*, p. 170: *Oeuvres* III, 99.

location, that is, spatiality and temporality are hindrances to clarity and distinctness. This preference for mathematics is intimately linked with Descartes' high regard for reason when compared to the imagination or the senses.[8] Though, as we shall see, this regard became overturned, nevertheless the assumption that truths could be posited independent of time and place was to endure and remain crucial to the Enlightenment.

Descartes and his successors were, because of this emphasis placed upon and centrality allotted to reason, subsequently dubbed Rationalists. Such dubbing is however liable to mislead especially when it is juxtaposed to Empiricism, which is commonly depicted as developing in opposition to Rationalism: a confusion which is abetted when the Enlightenment is regarded at one and the same time as the Age of Reason and yet its members as philosophical epigoni of the leading Empirical philosopher – John Locke. Indeed, the confusion is all the more apparent when it is realised that Locke's own empiricism is far from unambiguous.[9]

Locke is an important figure and we shall discuss aspects of his philosophy in Part II but it is necessary here to pick out a few salient points from his thought, namely, his attitude to innate ideas or principles and, very briefly, his understanding of 'experience'.

While Locke is, indeed, critical of Cartesianism and devotes Book 1 of the *Essay concerning Human Understanding* (1690) to demonstrating that there are no innate principles in the mind, he is at pains, even within this first book, to forestall the applicability of some possible inferences from his position. Accordingly, he affirms that there are "natural tendencies imprinted on the minds of men" including desire for happiness and aversion to misery. These are innate practical principles, which he distinguishes from what he is attacking, namely 'innate characters' that is "principles of knowledge regulating our practice" (Essay Bk. 1; Chap. 3; Sect.3). But this attack itself should not be misconstrued. Locke is explicit that it does not follow that he is thereby denying natural law or that it is a consequence of his argument that only positive laws can be admitted. Rather he maintains, in an important passage,

There is a great deal of difference between an innate law, and a law of nature; between something imprinted on our minds in their very original and something that we being ignorant of, may attain to the knowledge of by the use and due application of our natural faculties. (Essay I; 3; 13)

This means that knowledge of the moral order can be attained in the same way that Locke allows any knowledge to be attained, namely, by an inward process of reasoning starting from sense experience.[10] This includes knowledge of a God.

8. *Discours de la Méthode* (Everyman Library), p. 32: *Oeuvres* I, 612.

9. For example, his conviction (seemingly 'rationalist' par excellence) that morality is as capable of demonstration as is mathematics – see *Essay concerning Human Understanding*, Bk. III, Chap. 11, Sect. 16 & IV, 3, 18. Cf. the short discussion of D. Odegaard 'Locke as an Empiricist', *Philosophy* (1965) 185–196.

10. Cf. his early (1660) *Essays on Law of Nature*, ed. W. Von Leyden, esp. Lecture IV. See H. Aarsleff, 'The State of Nature and the Nature of Man' in *John Locke: Problems and Perspectives*, ed. J.W. Yolton, pp. 99–136.

Moreover, it follows, as a strong presumption, that if such fundamental knowledge is not innate then no other knowledge (of consequently lesser import) will be innate (Essay I; 4; 17).

It is noteworthy that Locke frequently deploys as an argument against innateness (especially against universal consent as a demonstration of it) the evidence available as to differences in knowledge and judgment. For example, whilst he alludes to the immature condition of children and idiots he also draws attention variously to the behaviour of 'savages', illiterate people (Essay I; 2; 12, 27) and to the enormities to be found in social practices, which enable it to be said that whole nations reject some moral rules (Essay I; 3; 9, 11). In other words, the general relativity of beliefs and principles means that ". . . propositions how remote soever from reason are so sacred somewhere or other" (Essay I; 3; 21); indeed, the discoveries of 'navigation' have even brought to light whole nations amongst whom there was to be found no idea of God or religion (Essay I; 4; 8).

Having elucidated the status of innate principles, Locke (in Book 2) is able to turn to the ostensibly more positive part of his programme. To Locke all our ideas − all the materials of reason and knowledge − come from 'experience', prior to experience the mind may be supposed to be 'white paper' (Essay II; 1; 2) (or an 'empty cabinet' (Essay I; 2; 15)). We shall consider pertinent details of Locke's system in Part II but it is here more appropriate to take heed of the popularity and impact of Locke's position.

All general discussions of the Enlightenment draw attention to Locke's impact. With some possible reservations about Germany,[11] in England and, especially, in France, Locke's philosophy became adopted. To give just one example; in that manifesto of the Enlightenment − D'Alembert's *Discours Préliminaire* (1751) to the Encyclopedia − Locke is compared to Newton (the other great mentor of the age) "it can be said that he [Locke] created metaphysics almost as Newton had created physics":[12] knowledge has now been set on the right lines. This is not to say that Locke was swallowed without alteration; indeed, from his earliest reception in France his system was amended. This amendment, as we shall note in Part II, took the form of endeavouring to render Locke's notion of 'experience' less ambiguous. Nor should it be thought that the success of Locke means the complete eclipse of Descartes. The extent of Cartesianism in the Enlightenment is a contentious matter, and one to which we shall have to return, but it is important for current purposes to note that the belief in certain constants persisted.

11. Cf. K.P. Fischer, 'John Locke in the German Enlightenment', *JHI* (1975) 431−446. The persistence of Leibniz' influence (abetted by the publication of his *Nouveaux Essais* 1765) entails, as one consequence, that the argument here put forward to identify a focal problem for the Enlightenment must be qualified in the case of Germany. For the 'uniqueness' of the German Enlightenment see L.W. Beck *Early German Philosophy: Kant and his Predecessors*, p. 245ff., also Chap. 2 infra passim.

12. Ed. & tr. R. Schwab & W. Rex, p. 83: Ed. F. Picavet, p. 103.

I now want to draw together these two post-medieval strands. On the one hand, great knowledge has been accumulated about different societies and diverse social practices and, on the other, there is an acceptance that it is to experience, especially as understood in the sensationalist or modified Lockean sense, that one is to look for knowledge. When these two strands are interwoven it would seem to follow that men in different societies have different experiences. That as it stands is unexceptional. However, it is but a short step from there to the position that our experiences in Western Europe are likewise the product of our social circumstances and given different circumstances, as in Tahiti say, then knowledge and behaviour currently taken for granted (as 'natural') could be seen to be parochial. The seemingly inevitable question now is – is everything parochial? Are there any overarching standards? Relativism is thus confronted. This confrontation is a central pre-occupation of the Enlightenment.

This pre-occupation took the form of accounting for diversity. Diversity as such could not be assimilated. Though the different social practices (especially the religious and sexual) were highlighted to taunt the traditional theist, nevertheless, the conclusion that there were no standards applicable to all societies was not accepted. This is put most celebratedly by Montesquieu in the Preface, significantly, to his great work *De l'Esprit des Lois* (1748) (a work that has been claimed as the most influential in the eighteenth century)[13] – "I believed that this infinite diversity of laws and customs was not solely the product of whim (*uniquement conduits par leurs fantaisies*) (*Oeuvres Complètes* [Nagel Edition] Vol. 1, p. lix). There are, in other words, principles applying universally, under which this diversity is subsumable. This desire to account for diversity was not merely to explain it but in a real sense to explain it away; to make the similar override the different. Further, the methodological and conceptual practice of applying universal principles to explain the diversity simultaneously provided a standard.[14] That which was universal was accorded a normatively superior status; its very uniformity or constancy bore witness to its greater importance and significance. Hence, evaluation was still possible, judgment could still be passed, so that social practices could be labelled superstitious and barbarous or 'unnatural'.

Indeed, the term 'nature' was systematically ambiguous. At one and the same time it referred to what existed and also to what should exist. Though, of course, the Enlightenment has not been alone in exploiting this ambiguity, we can see a clear case of it in operation in Montesquieu's treatment of Despotism. In the *Esprit*, Despotism was one of the three types of government delineated by Montesquieu. Although as in Monarchies, and unlike in Republics (the other two types), in Despotisms rule is by one, this rule is distinctive because of its arbitrary, capricious, non-constitutional *'nature'*. This is brought out clearly

---

13. P. Gay, *The Enlightenment: Science of Freedom*, p. 325.

14. Cf. A. Lovejoy, who after having declared that 'uniformitarianism' was "the first and fundamental principle" of the pervasive philosophy of the Enlightenment, observes that "universality of appeal or of acceptance tends to be taken not only as an effect but as in itself a mark or criterion of truth", 'The Parallel of Deism and Classicism' in his *Essays in the History of Ideas*, p. 79, 80.

in the corresponding *'principe'* that Montesquieu allots to Despotism, namely, fear. The significance of the three-fold typology, together with the *nature/principe* distinction, is that Montesquieu is using them to order the diversity of social experience (Bk. III, Chap. 1: Nagel I, 25n). Each of the governments, and their institutions and laws, is conditioned by such factors as climate (see later), size and topography.

Though there is an undoubted polemical aspect to the *Esprit*, whereby Montesquieu champions constitutional monarchy and the *thèse nobiliaire*, nevertheless he provides an explanation of why, for example, Despotism holds sway in Asia. Despotisms thus exist and there are sound reasons for them doing so. However, Montesquieu goes on to declare that Despotism "is corrupt by nature" and that its structure is intrinsically flawed (*'vice intérieur'*) (VIII, 10: Nagel I, 158). Despite Montesquieu's use of *'nature'* in a quasi-technical sense, his meaning here revolves around the term's traditional ambiguity by referring, at one and the same time, to what exists and what should exist. It is clear that for Montesquieu Despotism is an unnatural form of government and, as such, it means that there is some non-empirical norm of naturalness (unlike mere existence) in operation. Of course, Montesquieu is adamant that there are such norms. In the opening chapter of the opening Book of the *Esprit* he had defined laws as "necessary relations deriving from the nature of things" (I, 1: Nagel I, 1), and, more dramatically, in his earlier *Lettres Persanes* justice is defined as a constant relation between two things and, decisively, it is "eternal, it does not depend on human conventions" (Nagel I, 170).[15] The point of this short discussion has been to point up a central ambiguity, in the thought of one of the most important of Enlightenment thinkers, between the recognition of diversity and the desire to locate the factors responsible for it and yet the wish to pass judgment on diverse social practices.

Before looking more closely at the Enlightenment's attitude to the explanation of diversity it should be acknowledged that seeing the problem of relativism as focal to the Enlightenment does not mean that it is a completely novel problem. The Greeks (as ever) are cited, with Herodotus, Heraclitus and Protagoras figuring most prominently.[16] But leaving aside these pieties, more immediately and pertinently, Descartes' own preoccupations with certitude are to be seen, at least in part, against the background of pyrrhonism, which received its most celebrated expression in the writings of Montaigne.[17] In his *Apologie pour R. Sebonde* (c.1576), for example, Montaigne had drawn attention to the variety in laws and customs — "there is nothing so extreme" whether it be infanticide,

15. For a pertinent discussion of Montesquieu see the recent study of Sheila M. Mason, *Montesquieu's Idea of Justice* who brings out not only Montesquieu's relationship to his predecessors but also his retention of "the classical notion of an unchanging human nature" within an appreciation of the relativistic and deterministic character of social milieu, p. 146 – 7.

16. Cf. E. Vivas, 'Reiterations and Second Thoughts on Cultural Relativism' in *Relativism and the Study of Man*, ed. H. Schoeck & J. Wiggins, p. 45: K. Popper, *The Open Society and its Enemies*, Vol. 1, p. 17.

17. Cf. R. Popkin, *The History of Scepticism from Erasmus to Descartes* (revised edition).

patricide or voluptuousness of whatever sort "that is not allowed by the customs of some nation".[18] If nothing else, the conservative moral that Montaigne drew from this relativism, that is, that since nothing can be known for certain then to obey the laws of one's own land is the most appropriate response, was far removed from the moral most men of the Enlightenment were endeavouring to promote. Thus it is, buttressed with a Lockean philosophy, which was read as destroying the foundation of Descartes' location of certitude in innateness (Descartes, as noted above, had downgraded the senses whilst Montaigne had declared them to be "the beginning and the end of human knowledge"),[19] and yet not willing to suspend judgment, that the Enlightenment found the question of social diversity and relativity one of such acute importance. To accept relativism would be in strictly logical terms to undermine their programme. But more than that it would sap its emotional strength. Why *écrasez* if *l'infâme* was perhaps suited to the circumstances? Hence the tension identified above in Montesquieu and, indeed, the contemporary criticism of Montesquieu for providing as much comfort as he did for upholders of the status quo.

We may proceed to look briefly at the accounts given to explain diversity in the Enlightenment. We shall examine the role played by theories of progress and theories of climate (and human physiology) to this end. Particular attention will be drawn to noting how an understanding of human nature is central to both these theories. Finally, in this chapter, we shall see, in more detail, how, as an instance of this understanding, it operated in the aesthetic thought of the period.

We shall have occasion to discuss climate and progress in Part II, but here we can see how they both operate as ordering principles, whereby intelligibility is introduced into the widespread evidence of diversity. Whilst progress was not, as is frequently alleged, the fully-fledged creed of the Enlightenment (the nineteenth century is more deserving of the epithet of the Age of Progress) it was evoked to establish some form of coherence. The idea of progress in many ways was the product of matching the knowledge of the ancient Greeks, Romans and Germans, drawn from such 'classical' authors as Thucydides, Herodotus, Livy and especially Tacitus, with the ethnographic information now available. If contemporary Amerindians parallel our own ancestors then time itself can be seen as a dimension of societies. Thus, writes Turgot:

the present state of the world, marked as it is by these infinite variations in inequality, spreads out before us at one and the same time all the gradations from barbarism to refinement, thereby revealing to us at a single glance, as it were, the records and remains of all the steps taken by the human mind [*esprit*], a reflection of all the stages through which it has passed, and the history of all ages.[20]

Quite what was measured along this dimension did differ. In addition to the 'economism' of the Scots, which will be discussed in Part II, the other chief can-

18. In *Essays of Montaigne*, tr. G.B. Ives, Vol. II, p. 373: ed. P. Porteau, p. 234.

19. Ives II, 382: Porteau, p. 245.

20. *Tableau philosophique des progrès de l'esprit humain* (1750), tr. R. Meek in *Turgot on Progress, Sociology and Economics*, p. 43: *Oeuvres*, ed. E. Daire & H. Dussard, Vol. II, p. 599.

didate, as seen in Condorcet, the subsequently most renowned of all eighteenth-century progress theorists, was the growth of knowledge. These, of course, are not mutually exclusive – Hume, as we shall see, upholds both.

Central to this understanding of time as a dimension was that, although knowledge was gained or the means of subsistence changed, men still remained the same. It was by virtue of this assumption of the constancy of human nature that it was not only possible to regard the ancient Germans as similar to the contemporary Amerindians but also to see ourselves, in Western Europe, as having progressed from their state. That men were superstitious or that they were hunters were incidental not constitutive characteristics of men. All men partake of a common constant human nature. Moreover, this assumption of a constant human nature enabled the Enlightenment historian to fill in any 'gaps': given evidence about the situation of men it was perfectly feasible for him to conjecture what the 'natural' response of Man would be in that situation (a procedure that we shall examine at length in Part II).

In many writers progress vied with climate, the second ordering principle mentioned above. The more primitive the society then the more climate was thought to hold sway; but, as men progress one of the marks of their progress is that they become increasingly independent of climatic determination. Climate was held to work in two related ways; physiologically and thence by derivation sociologically. The latter was often attacked and, as we shall see, Hume was one of the leaders in this assault, with his advocacy of moral, in contrast to physical, causes to explain national character.

Physiologically, climate was used, for example, by Buffon to explain the stature, physiognomy and pigmentation of men.[21] The sociological derivation stems from the consequences drawn from different physiological effects: consequences such as a differentiation, in line with differences in climate, in sexual mores, belligerence, economic endeavour, languages and pronunciation and aesthetic sensibility.[22] A variant of looking at man from a physiological perspective was the speculation about his relation to the other animals. What is important about using climate is that its operation can explain the different races, sizes and colour of man yet still leave the species homo sapiens basic.

This is the structure of the pervasive Enlightenment argument that there must be, amidst all the empirically attested variety, certain constants; that there are ordering principles which can provide an evaluative perspective. Such principles, in virtue of their function, were themselves set apart from that which they ordered or structured and thereby accorded a methodological, as well as in some cases an explicitly normative priority. This general programme is neatly set out by Ferguson:

21. *Natural History*, tr. W. Smellie, Vol. III, p. 302ff., 405, 437: *Oeuvres Complètes*, ed. M. Flourens, Vol. II, p. 137ff., 195, 215.

22. Cf. Montesquieu, *Esprit des Lois*, Bk. 14, Chap. 1 et seq.; R. Dubos, *Réflexions critiques sur la Poesie et la Peinture*, 6th edit., Vol. II, p. 500 et passim; C. Bullet, *Mémoires sur la Langue Celtique*, Vol. 1, p. 7.

If in human nature there are qualities by which it is distinguished from every other part of animal creation, men are themselves in different climates and in different ages greatly diversified. So far as we are able to account for this diversity on principles either moral or physical, we perform a task of great curiosity or signal utility. It appears necessary, however, that we attend to the universal qualities of our nature, before we regard its varieties, or attempt to explain differences consisting in the unequal possession or application of dispositions and powers that are in some measure common to all mankind.[23]

It is this aspect of the Enlightenment that is often picked up when its representatives are challenged with philosophical naiveté; in particular that their alleged empiricism was in fact held together by a priori definitions.[24] We shall return to this but must now look more closely at the basic postulation of Man or human nature that was held to constitute these constants. Enlightenment literature is replete with instances and we shall examine Hume's own stance in some detail in Part II. But to demonstrate that Hume is not here being egregious we shall briefly take note of the arguments of some of his contemporaries.

The precise location of this constancy in Man did differ but, to repeat, the reason for its postulation was shared; it functioned as a bulwark against an enervating relativism or quietistic Montaigne-like conservatism.[25]

This constancy could be found in the mere physiological identity that we noted above as an aspect of the climatic argument. Hubert, indeed, argued that in the last analysis the Encyclopedic theory of human nature rested on the identity between the species and the individual.[26] This, however, is in itself perhaps not the last analysis since underlying it is the conviction of the uniformity of Nature. This is a key presupposition in Hume's thought but was one widely shared; it is basic to the programme of the *Encyclopédie* as D'Alembert makes plain in his *Discours*,[27] to both Condorcet and Turgot it is an indispensable postulate of their theories of the progress of the human spirit[28] and to Voltaire it is a methodological principle in his investigation of a people's *moeurs*.[29] Again, it is vital to Volney whose declaration of the principle also brings out the connexion and significance of this belief to an understanding of man:

Man is governed, like the world of which he forms a part, by natural laws, regular in their operation, consequent in their effects, immutable in their essence; and these laws, the common source of good

23. A. Ferguson, *Essay on the History of Civil Society* (1767), ed. D. Forbes, p. 10.

24. Cf. R. Emerson, 'Peter Gay and the Heavenly City', *JHI* (1967) 383 – 402, esp. 386 – 8.

25. Rousseau provides a clear example of the dismissal of Montaigne's scepticism in the name of the "clear and universal agreement of all peoples", for there is "striking unanimity in the judgment of mankind", *Emile (Profession de Foi du Savoyard Vicaire)*, tr. B. Foxley, p. 252: *Oeuvres* (Pleiade), Vol. 4, p. 598.

26. *Les Sciences Sociales dans l'Encyclopédie*, p. 167.

27. Schwab & Rex, p. 61: Picavet, p. 76.

28. Condorcet, *Esquisse d'un Tableau Historique des Progrès de l'Esprit Humain* (1793), ed. O. Prior, p. 9: Turgot in Meek, p. 41; *Oeuvres* II, p. 597.

29. *Essai sur les Moeurs* (1756), Introd. tr. J.H. Brumfitt in *Voltaire: The Age of Louis XIV & Other selected writings*, p. 255: *Oeuvres Complètes*, Vol. XI, p. 15 – 6.

and evil, are neither written in the distant stars nor concealed in mysterious codes; inherent in the nature of all terrestrial beings, identified with their existence, they are at all times, and in all places, present to the human mind; they act upon the senses, inform the intellect, and annex to every action its punishment and its reward. Let man study these laws, let him understand the nature of the beings that surround him, and his own nature and he will know the springs of his destiny, the causes of his evils, and the remedies to be applied.[30]

Thus the invocation of Nature was no mere neutral device.[31] The uniformities of the law of Nature were not mere physical regularities but also moral imperatives. Again, we can cite Volney, the title of one of whose works, makes this clear – *The Law of Nature or Principles of Morality: Deduced from the Physical Constitution of Mankind and the Universe* (1793). In the work itself he draws a tenfold characterisation of the Law of nature, which moves from being anterior to all other laws, and consequently uniform and invariable, to being reasonable, just and, of itself, sufficient to render men happier and better.[32] Here, for all Volney's possibly unrepresentative simplicity, is a frequent feature of much Enlightenment thought. All men are the same because of universal drives. These drives will operate independently of any location.

Chief among these drives was that toward self-preservation – Holbach, for instance, stipulates:

we shall call *nature* in man the collection of properties and qualities which constitute him what he is, which are inherent to his species, which distinguish him from other animal species or which he has in common with them. . .every man feels, thinks, acts and seeks his well-being at all times; these are the qualities and properties that constitute human nature. . . .[33]

Inextricably linked with this drive was the acknowledgement of Locke's two natural tendencies – pleasure and pain. These of course became the basis of Utilitarianism (the moral theory that Hegel identified with the Enlightenment). Helvétius, who exercised great influence on Bentham, whilst allowing that there was an *esprit* which was localised and dependent on particular factors, nevertheless maintained that there was another *esprit*, being:

the eternal utility, unalterable and independent of the customs and varieties of governments, applying to the very nature of man and consequently always invariable, and which can be regarded as the true *esprit*, that is, the most desirable.[34]

30. *Les Ruines* (1791), tr. (slightly amended) introd. C. Bradlaugh, p. 14 – 15: *Oeuvres Complètes*, Vol. I, p. 26 – 7.

31. Cf. J.A. Leith, 'Peter Gay's Enlightenment', *Eighteenth Century Studies* (1971), 157 – 171, esp. p. 162. Leith also points out the limitations to the relativism of the *philosophes*.

32. *Oeuvres*, Vol. 1, p. 255 et seq.

33. *La Morale Universelle ou les devoirs de l'homme fondés sur sa Nature* (1776), Vol. I, p. 4 – 5, tr. (slightly amended) and quoted in L.G. Crocker, *An Age of Crisis: Man and World in Eighteenth Century French Thought*, p. 190.

34. *De l'Esprit* (1758), ed. P. Christian, p. 125.

Bentham himself, who, though he is generally omitted from the standard exposi-
tions of the Enlightenment, is very much of their world, provides a good illustration of the interplay between constancy and variety. Having declared in the opening sentence of his *Principles of Morals and Legislation* (1789) that "Nature has
placed mankind under the governance of two sovereign masters, *pain* and
pleasure"[35] he later, in his essay *Of the Influence of Time and Place in Matters of
Legislation*,[36] devoted some attention to the application of this declaration in different societies. Yet from the outset this is merely a technical problem. This is so
because Bentham affirms that the end of every good law is the prevention of
mischief, which, in turn, is reducible to pain or its calculably equivalent loss of
pleasure. Since human nature is everywhere the same then different countries do
not have different catalogues of pleasure and pain. Thus the differences are to be
located in the circumstances affecting sensibility. Hence, whilst there is little
modification in laws regarding simple corporeal injuries (save that a wound
might be more dangerous in hot climates than in cold) when it comes to offences
against property or reputation there is almost infinite diversity according to the
state of opinions and manners. But once information as to local circumstances
has been gleaned then the legislator, knowing that human nature is ever the same,
can reform the laws and even transplant them from one society to another.

Here the Enlightenment programme and its attitude to diversity is encapsulated. The law must be reformed, indeed, for Bentham, legislation must be
made a science, and although there are differing social circumstances these do
not mean that the would-be reformer must acquiesce in them, because there are
constants which enable evaluation and thence reform to take place. It is worth
noting in passing that one of the outgrowths of Romanticism and change in approach to human nature that we are here charting was the Historical School of
Law. This School saw the law as firmly rooted in the life of a people and that it
was, as a result, culturally or societally specific. Moreover, it was held to follow
that it was mere 'rationalism' (in Oakeshott's pejorative sense of the word)[37] to
judge such a 'fit' between the law and its cultural context by a universal and thus
meaninglessly abstract yardstick. Yet, it is indicative of Hegel's general 'situation' that whilst he acknowledges the specificity of law he, like Bentham, urges
its rationalisation and codification.

As is well known the argument of Helvétius, and to a lesser extent Holbach,
did not meet with universal approval.[38] Though the location of this constancy in
human nature in self-love might be correct it was both insufficient to its task and
too restrictive. The 'passions' more generally were held to be constant. This is, as
we shall see, close to Hume's own position. It is noteworthy that not only did the
vastly influential Montesquieu enunciate this principle but also that he did so

35. Ed. W. Harrison, p. 125.

36. *Works*, ed. J. Bowring, Vol. I, pp. 171 – 194. This essay was first published in French by Du-
mont in 1802.

37. *Rationalism in Politics*, pp. 1 – 36.

38. Cf. D.W. Smith, *Helvétius: A Study in Persecution*.

with almost unparalleled clarity in his introduction to his most explicitly historical work, *Considérations sur les Causes de la Grandeur des Romains et de leur Décadence* (1734).

for, as men have had at all times the same passions, the occasions that produce great changes are different, but the causes are always the same.[39]

Hume, too, most unequivocally enunciates his view of human nature in his characterisation of the function and premises of historical knowledge. As a further illustration, we can cite perhaps the most renowned author of the time — Voltaire — who, significantly, uses this argument from the passions to extinguish the case for the relativity of moral standards:

It is said that there are savages who eat men, and believe they do well. I say those savages have the same idea of right and wrong as ourselves. As we do, they make war from anger and passion: the same crimes are committed everywhere: to eat your enemies is an extra ceremonial. The wrong does not consist in roasting, but in killing them.[40]

However, perhaps the chief challenge to Helvétius' argument was that it omitted reason; an omission for which Diderot, for example, took him to task in his analysis of Helvétius' posthumous work, *De l'Homme* (1772).[41] Though Diderot did not dissent from the importance of pleasure and pain in determining actions he went on to remark that this is too narrow since such determination applies equally well to animals (indeed there were other writers such as LaMettrie who rigorously pursued this line). Such an argument was widespread (though also absent from Hume) and we may note here just two instances. In Buffon's elaborate classification he is adamant that man's nature is infinitely removed from that of animals, because "man is a reasoning being".[42] Secondly, Voltaire, in one passage, announces unambiguously that:

God has given us a principle of universal reason just as he has given feathers to birds and fur to bears; and this principle is so constant that it continues to exist despite all the passions that fight against it, despite the tyrants who would like to drown it in blood, and despite the impostors who want to annihilate it in superstition.[43]

It is perhaps in this connexion with reason that the normative conception of

---

39. Nagel, Vol. I, p. 354.

40. Letter to Frederick, Royal Prince of Prussia, October 1737 in *Candide and other writings*, ed. H.M. Block, p. 502: *Correspondence*, ed. T. Bestermann, Vol. IV (1969), p. 383.

41. *Réfutation. . .suivie de l'ouvrage d'Helvétius* in *Oeuvres Philosophiques*, ed. P. Vernière, p. 576ff. For the wider context of Diderot's criticisms see D.G. Creighton, 'Man and Mind in Diderot and Helvétius', *PMLA* (1956) 705 – 724; D.W. Smith, *Helvétius*, Chaps. 14 and 15.

42. Smellie, Vol. III, p. 108: Flourens, Vol. II, p. 9.

43. *Essai sur les Moeurs*, p. 263: *Oeuvres*, Vol. XI, p. 23.

human nature as used in the Enlightenment[44] is seen at its most explicit. This conception is truly pervasive. Human nature was itself a standard, a norm removed from the flux of contingency. It is this feature of Enlightenment thought that has caused many commentators to see within it a strong current of Cartesianism despite all the overt remarks critical of Descartes himself.[45] This, in its turn, is usually closely associated with the limitations of the Enlightenment's socio-historical thought; it has indeed been called their "most striking error".[46]

It is part of the intention of this study to look at why this position is so frequently seen as erroneous. The answer in essence is that the understanding of what *history* means – that it is impossible to abstract meaningfully from its ordering principles – only came about at the end of the eighteenth century and early nineteenth century. Before passing on to look at this new understanding and its attendant reconceptualisation of human nature it will be useful, in conclusion to this chapter, briefly to examine the aesthetic thought of the Enlightenment. This will be useful for two reasons: one, it provides a more extensive and sustained illustration of the above argument concerning the Enlightenment's response to relativism and two, it was, as the next chapter will demonstrate, from a reaction to this aesthetic theory that the first notions which burgeoned into Romanticism were expressed and it is as part and parcel of this burgeoning that the new understanding of history and man took place.

The same concern which prompted attention to the problem of relativity in morals was also felt in the aesthetic sphere. The same broad movement of ideas sketched above was responsible for the problematic nature of discussions on beauty etc., but, due to a well-established body of critical literature going back to Aristotle, and fortified in France by the achievement of Racine and Corneille, the problem was apparent and unavoidable. Indeed, almost without exception, the leading writers of the Enlightenment discussed aesthetics at some time. In certain ways, of course, the relativity of aesthetic standards is easier to comprehend (and accept) than that of moral diversity with its theological overtones. After all the Sermon on the Mount did not lay down the distinguishing principles between epic and lyrical poetry and, in addition, the classical tag *de gustibus non disputandum est*, which was quoted by many writers, had established a precedent.

Yet, though perhaps easier to understand and accept, this acceptance was within very exacting limits; despite declarations which seemingly represent a wholehearted commitment to relativism. Voltaire, for example, in his entry under *Beau*, in his *Dictionnaire Philosophique* (1764), remarked:

44. Cf. R.V. Sampson, *Progress in the Age of Reason*, Chap. IV; S. Goyard-Fabre *La Philosophie des Lumières en France, Chap. IV, esp. p. 199.*

45. Cf. esp. A. Vartanian, *Diderot and Descartes: A Study of scientific naturalism in the Enlightenment*; also, *inter alia*, C. Frankel, 'The Faith of Reason', Chaps. 2, 6 & Conclusion; I.F. Knight, *The Geometric Spirit: Abbé Condillac and the French Enlightenment*, esp. Epilogue; Emerson, *JHI* (1967); L.G. Crocker, *Nature and Culture: Ethical Thought in the French Enlightenment, Chap. 3.*

46. R.N. Stromberg, *'History in the Eighteenth Century'*, *JHI* (1951) 295 – 304 (p. 301).

Ask a toad what beauty is, absolute beauty, the *to kalon*. He will answer that it is his female, with two large round eyes sticking out of her little head, a large and flat snout, a yellow belly, a brown back. Question a Negro from Guinea; for him beauty is black oily skin, sunken eyes, a flat nose[47]

and he concludes by making a philosopher, as a purveyor of grandiloquent nonsense, announce that beauty is decidedly relative. But, as we shall see, this is not (arguably) consistently Voltaire's own considered view.

To appreciate not only Voltaire's own stance but also that of his contemporaries a brief recapitulation will be profitable. The aim of classical aesthetics, latterly embodied in Boileau, had been to make aesthetics an exact science. Its central presupposition was that beauty was objective, that is, beauty existed independently of the observer. There were, accordingly, precise rules which laid down the criteria of what was beautiful. But the acceptance of a Lockean inspired epistemology in the eighteenth century led in aesthetics toward subjectivism. Beauty was now held to be an experience – it was 'something' felt by the individual – and was not an inherent quality of the object being observed. The logical outcome of this empiricism was that just as every person is unique (has different experiences) so every person will have a different idea of what is beautiful.

However, just as we have illustrated above in the case of relativism generally, the rigorous reduction of aesthetics to personal preference was unpalatable. A situation where beauty was seemingly indistinguishable from individual whim was regarded as unacceptable. It is in this context that the evocation of the Standard of Taste is to be understood. By such a Standard it was believed that objectivity could be retained whilst still being able to maintain that beauty was an experience. Underlying this standard is, yet again, the belief in an immutable human nature.

We shall discuss Hume's *Essay on Taste* in Part II but here we may examine by way of example the principle of Taste in operation in the writings of some of his contemporaries. Lord Kames' *Elements of Criticism* (1761) provides a clear example not only of the tie in between moral and aesthetic speculation (especially prevalent in Scotland through the impact of Hutcheson's theory of moral sense – and behind him the work of Shaftesbury) but also the role played by a theory of human nature:

Taste in the fine arts goes hand in hand with the moral sense, to which indeed it is nearly allied: both of them discover what is right and what is wrong: fashion, temper and education, have an influence to vitiate both, or to preserve them pure and untainted: neither of them are arbitrary nor local; being rooted in human nature and governed by principles common to all men.[48]

In his chapter devoted to the Standard of Taste, Kames endeavours to locate the common standard in nature and reiterates the uniformity and immutability of

---

47. Ed. & Tr. T. Bestermann, p. 63: *Oeuvres*, Vol. XVII, p. 557.

48. Sixth Edit. with author's last corrections and additions (1785), p. 6. Cf. H.W. Randall, *Critical Theory of Lord Kames*.

human nature despite differences in culture and manners. Moreover, it is the very conviction that this common standard exists that provides the evaluative yardstick that constitutes Taste, since all deviations from it impress us as imperfect, irregular and painful.[49] But, to Kames, it does not follow that every person may thus be consulted since:

Those who depend for food on bodily labour are totally devoid of taste; of such taste at least as can be of use in the fine arts. This consideration bars the greater part of mankind; and of the remaining part, many by a corrupted taste are unqualified for voting. The common sense of mankind must then be confined to the few that fall not under these exceptions.[50]

Montesquieu, in an essay on Taste published posthumously in Diderot's *Encyclopédie* (1757), clearly stated that the different pleasures of the mind constitute the proper objects of taste, that is, that taste is an internal sense.[51] As such it is bound up with the constitution of our nature so that had our constitution been different then all our feelings and perceptions (including those of taste) would also have been different. But, this, in fact, now only emphasises the possibility of an aesthetic standard by rooting it in the human mind. Taste is thus a property of man and this constitutes 'natural taste'; but, there is also, Montesquieu acknowledges, 'acquired taste'.[52] This distinction appears, in various guises, in most writers. As we saw in Kames, though Taste is rooted in human nature and is thus able to transcend caprice this does not mean that everyone is a 'Man of Taste'. Alexander Gerard, whose *Essay on Taste* won the gold medal awarded by the Edinburgh Society in 1755 for deliberations upon the subject, whilst he saw in human nature the locus of *variety* in taste nevertheless declares there is still a Standard. This is so because he distinguishes between Taste as a species of sensation and as a species of discernment. With respect to the former there can be no Standard, since it is different due to the experience of different sensations but, with respect to the latter, since it is capable of being assisted by proper culture then "men who are affected differently may not withstanding judge alike".[53] The conditions making for such judgment (and here he follows Kames) being confined to certain sections of the community.

Finally we can return to Voltaire. In his early essay on *Epic Poetry* (first written in English in 1727 though revised for the 1733 French version) whilst he drew attention to the relativism that we noted above in his *Dictionnaire* he also enunciated certain rules of epic poetry which "nature dictates to all the nations that cultivate the written word".[54] Again, in his short essay on Taste he distinguishes

---

49. *Elements*, p. 491.
50. *Elements*, p. 499.
51. Nagel, Vol. I, p. 611. Cf. C.J. Beyer, 'Montesquieu et le relativisme esthetique', *VS* (1963) 171 – 182, who remarks (179) "L'esthetique de Montesquieu, comme tout le reste de sa pensée. . . [lies] dans son effort de concilier l'absolu et le relatif".
52. Nagel, Vol. I, p. 613.
53. Third Edition (1780) p. 219. Cf. M. Grene, 'Gerard's Essay on Taste', *MP* (1943) 45 – 58.
54. In Block, p. 210: *Oeuvres*, Vol. VIII, p. 309.

between sensual taste, about which there truly can be no dispute, and intellectual taste, which, because it relates to the arts where real beauties (*beautés réeles*) pertain, then:

there is in reality a good taste which discerns them, and a bad one which does not, and a defective character (*défaut d'esprit*) responsible for a faulty taste is correctible.[55]

But this good taste occurs only under certain favourable circumstances and has in fact been confined to certain countries and periods in Europe. This reflects the well-known pronouncement in his Introduction to his *de l'Histoire de l'Age de Louis XIV* (1751) where the Man of Taste (that rare specimen) is said to number just four ages when the arts were brought to perfection. These ages (classical Greece, Rome, the Italy of the Medici and Leo X and the age of Louis XIV), marking an era of greatness of the human mind, provide a true example. Here Voltaire animadverts to the chief characteristic of neoclassic criticism – imitation – to which we shall return in the next chapter. Indeed, finally, Voltaire, in a letter to Walpole (July 15, 1768), criticises Britons for not observing the three classic unities of time, place and action and for not submitting themselves to the rulings of Boileau, the leading French theorist of neoclassicism.[56]

This brief sortie into eighteenth-century aesthetics has endeavoured to demonstrate more precisely the general interpretation here given of the intellectual context or situation of the Enlightenment. Though the thinkers of the Enlightenment were aware of differences in aesthetic sensibility, the conclusion they drew was not that therefore one man's judgment was as good as another's, or that what one society commended as beautiful depended on local circumstances, so that those experiencing different circumstances lacked the resources to comment evaluatively on this commendation, but, rather, the conclusion was that owing to the immutable uniformity of human nature standards were possible.

55. *Oeuvres*, Vol. XIX, p. 272.
56. Block, p. 539–40: *Correspondence*, Vol. XXXIII (1974), p. 449.

The following abbreviations are inserted in parentheses in the text throughout.

SW   – *Sämmtliche Werke*, ed. B. Suphan.

US   – *Ursprung der Sprache*, in F. Barnard, *Herder on Social and Political Culture*.

APG   – *Auch eine Philosophie der Geschichte*, in Barnard.

IdB   – *Ideen zur Philosophie der Geschichte der Menschheit*, in Barnard.

IdM   – *Ideen*, etc., tr. J. Churchill, ed. F. Manuel as *Reflections in the Philosophy of the History of Mankind*.

RDN   – Fichte, *Reden an die deutsche Nation*, tr. R. Jones & C. Turnbull with additions by G.A. Kelly: *Sämmtliche Werke*, ed. I. H. Fichte, Vol. VII in appended parentheses.

2. HUMAN NATURE IN CONTEXT: HERDER'S CONTRIBUTION

The object of this Chapter is to trace the movement of ideas about human nature that came to change the understanding of it. This movement can be subsumed under that notoriously elusive term Romanticism, though, perhaps, equally appropriate to our concerns is the new attitude to history (the 'historicist revolution'). In a nutshell, the Enlightenment's conviction that human nature was comprehensible, and could be used as a source of standards, removed or apart from the differing circumstances of social life, was rejected, because human nature was now seen to be inseparable and unintelligible apart from these differences. There is an organic union between a man and his own society: that is, no longer did it seem meaningful to talk of Man independent of any particular society. Thus the Enlightenment's understanding of human nature as uniform and constant gave way to a concrete specific understanding: an understanding here termed contextualist.[1]

There were, of course, many factors at work to bring about this new understanding. Nevertheless, although, as we shall shortly see, this did not happen all at once but rather emerged, the work of Herder can be seen to have been a decisive formative force. Accordingly, the bulk of this chapter will be given over to a discussion of the pertinent aspects of his thought; however, it should be emphasised that these are only aspects, so that no thorough-going treatment of either his thought or personality will be presented.

We can commence by illustrating the gradual 'emergence' of this new understanding. This illustration will be afforded by looking at the career of a group of related ideas, namely, genius, originality and imagination. The choice of these ideas has historical justification for (as we shall see), they lead to the concerns of the German Storm and Stress movement and to Herder in particular.

It was mentioned at the end of the previous Chapter that the notion of imitation was central to neo-classic aesthetics. The object of imitation was to be Nature or, more strictly, *la belle Nature* or, again as Anglicised by Pope, 'Nature

---

1. Though its use and elaboration are mine the term itself is appropriated from J.G. Gunnell, *Political Philosophy and Time*, p. 255.

104,988

LIBRARY
College of St. Francis
JOLIET, ILL.

methodiz'd'. This imitation or copying was governed by rules such as proportionality, regularity and harmony. The imitation of Nature was differentiated from the imitation of authors or painters. In this Edward Young and Sir Joshua Reynolds concurred but Young called the imitations of Nature 'originals' and confined the term 'imitation' to that of authors etc. . . .[2] Crucially, Young elaborated upon this distinction:

An Original may be said to be of a vegetable nature; it rises spontaneously from the vital root of Genius; it grows, it is not made: Imitations are often a sort of Manufacture wrought up by these Mechanics, Art and Labour, out of pre-existent materials not their own.[3]

What is important here is not only the organic imagery, which was to become a focal point in later thought, but the connexion between originality and genius.

Genius is "from Heaven" and Shakespeare was thus "inspired". Shakespeare was a problem for neo-classical theory. To Voltaire, for example,

He is precisely to my mind like Lope de Vega, the Spaniard, and like Calderon. He is a fine but barbarous nature: he has neither regularity, nor propriety, nor art: in the midst of his sublimity he sometimes descends to grossness, and in the most impressive scenes, to buffoonery: his tragedy is chaos, illuminated by a hundred rays of light. . .

indeed, had Shakespeare been a contemporary of Addison his genius would have been augmented with elegance and purity.[4] Again, to Blair, the admiration of Shakespeare was explicable since although he truly transgressed some rules yet he obeyed others –

They [Shakespeare's plays] possess other beauties which are conformable to just rules; and the force of these beauties has been so great as to overpower all censure, and to give the public a degree of satisfaction superior to the disgust arising from their blemishes. Shakespeare pleases, not by his bringing the transaction of many years into one play; not by his grotesque mixtures of tragedy and comedy in one piece, nor by the strained thoughts, and affected witticisms, which he sometimes employs. These we consider as blemishes, and impute them to the grossness of the age in which he lived. But he pleases by his animated and masterly representations of characters, by the liveliness of his descriptions, the force of his sentiments, and his possessing, beyond all writers, the natural language of passion: beauties which true criticism no less teaches us to feel.[5]

Shakespeare achieves this transcendence because, to Blair also, he is a genius.

But in the neo-classic canon genius is correctible. Reynolds went so far as to declare that genius is really the "child of imitation". In other words, although Reynolds subscribes to the common eighteenth-century view that "invention is one of the marks of genius", he, nevertheless, believes that we learn to invent, so

2. *Conjectures on Original Composition* (1759), p. 9.
3. *Conjectures*, p. 12.
4. Letter to Horace Walpole, July 15, 1768 in *Candide and other writings*, ed.
5. *Lectures on Rhetoric and Belles-Lettres* (1838), p. 26.

that works of genius must have rules;[6] a judgment indeed echoed by Hume, who declared that works of genius must have some plan or object since, without such, a production "would resemble more the ravings of a madman than the sober efforts of genius and learning".[7] To Condillac, we do not, properly speaking, create ideas but combine them, and invention consists in making new combinations. Condillac, however, distinguishes *talent* from *genie*. *Talent* deals with ideas already known, whilst *genie* adds creatively to this and thus invents new arts or new styles in existing arts. As such the genius is inimitable, he is an original.[8] A broadly similar approach is to be found in one of the chief British critics in the Associationist 'School' – Alexander Gerard. In his *Essay on Genius* (1774), Gerard, whilst declaring that "genius is properly the faculty of invention" regards invention as "assembling ideas" which is, in turn, the work of the imagination.[9] Accordingly, "genius of every kind derives its immediate origin from the imagination", but, as we shall see similarly in Part II, in Hume's case, the operation of the imagination is not capricious but "for the most part observes general and observed rules".[10]

If we now return to Young we can see and appreciate a difference. To him these associative processes are *mechanisms*, the 'manufacture' of 'pre-existing materials'. As such this cannot fit genius properly understood as spontaneous originality – "Shakespeare mingled no water with his wine, lower'd his Genius by no vapid Imitation".[11] Rules are crutches for the lame and, in fact, hindrances to the strength of genius.[12] Before seeing how these ideas were taken up, and ultimately transformed, in Germany, there is another aspect to these same ideas that we may fruitfully explore. This further aspect is the particular notion of 'original genius'. This notion was formulated, above all, in the elucidation of the (supposed) Scottish primitive bard – Ossian.

This elucidation can be seen in William Duff's *Essay on Original Genius* (1767). To Duff (following Blackwell's treatment of Homer) original poetic genius will only display its vigour in "early and uncultivated periods of society".[13] This is put down variously to the antiquity of the period and consequent appearance of novelty in objects, to simplicity of manners, to the leisure and tranquility of uncultivated life and to exemption from the rules of criticism; all of which Ossian exhibits and thus his poetry is no fabrication. Much the same argument is to be found in Blair.

---

6. *Discourses*, ed. E. Goss, No. 6, p. 88, 90.

7. *Enquiry concerning the Human Understanding*, ed. G. Hendel, p. 33. Hume, too, applies this to Shakespeare who though "a great and fertile genius" his work is disfigured by "great irregularities and even sometimes, absurdities", thus proving how genius alone is unable to attain "excellence in the finer arts", *History of Great Britain*, ed. D. Forbes, p. 248.

8. *Essai sur les connoissances humaines*, Pt. I, Sect. 2., Chap. 9: *Oeuvres* (1792), Vol. I, p. 106.

9. Gerard, p. 27.

10. *Genius*, p. 39. The similarity to Hume is of course not incidental – see Part II infra for Hume's associationist criticism.

11. *Conjectures*, p. 78.

12. *Conjectures*, p. 28.

13. Duff, p. 260.

But again what is important is the assimilation of the argument to current conventions. Thus Ossian's poems are authentic; there is no recourse to general ideas (a later development) but rather Ossian's imagery "is without exception, copied from the face of nature which he saw before his eyes".[14] His language is properly metaphorical. There was, indeed, considerable speculation on the origin of metaphors. However, what is important for our purpose is not that Herder was taken in by Ossian but that in taking up the idea of genius from, amongst others, Young (whose work was translated into German in 1760 and in Abrams' words "became a primary document in the canon of storm and stress")[15] and in elaborating upon the characteristics of Ossian's primitive expressions he came to forge a new synthesis.

Though there is much justification in Cassirer's judgment that Herder is the "Copernicus of history"[16] his historical thinking, as Gillies pointed out,[17] was the offshoot of his literary concerns. We can commence our analysis of Herder's thought by pursuing the question of metaphors as broached in the last paragraph. Eighteenth-century speculation on metaphors focused on the character of early or primitive speech.[18] One popular explanation of the presence of metaphors was that such speech was passionate. A persistent theme in explaining the passionate nature of early speech was its actual tonal quality. The basis of this view was the conviction that language arose from 'natural cries' and so early language still shared many attributes of such cries (as still seen in interjections). Blackwell's *Enquiry into the Life and Times of Homer* (1735) is an important source here (and one well known to Herder). To Blackwell, the speech of 'original' man was "expressive commonly of the highest passions" (which made

---

14. *A Critical Dissertation on the Poems of Ossian* (1763), appended to *Poems of Ossian*, ed. A. Stewart, p. 133.

15. *The Mirror and the Lamp: Romantic Theory and the Critical Tradition*, p. 202.

16. *The Problem of Knowledge*, p. 218. Similarly, F. Meinecke sees Herder as "perhaps" like Columbus in that he did not fully realise (despite an awareness of things to come) that he had discovered a new world, to wit, *Historismus: Die Entstehung des Historismus*, 2nd Edit., p. 466 and Dilthey closes his examination of the historical world of the eighteenth-century with a discussion of Herder's thought, which is held to transcend the limits of the century and lead directly to the Romantics and Hegel *Das Achtzehnte Jahrhundert und die Geschichtliche Welt* in *Gesammelte Schriften*, Vol. III, p. 268. But cf. P.H. Reill, *The German Enlightenment and the rise of Historicism*, who argues that the historians and theologians of the Aufklärung are to be regarded as the originators of historicism. Though the German Enlightenment is clearly to be differentiated from its contemporary counterparts (see Chap. 1, n. 11 supra) nevertheless much of the writing that Reill discusses has echoes elsewhere (especially in Scotland – both were university and Protestant based). Additionally, however, the linking of historical experience with human nature (see infra) is not to be found in these writers, for, as Reill himself brings out, their thought is riven between acceptance of relativism and the employment of ahistorical normative analysis (p. 125, 192 et passim). Of course, Herder himself exhibits these same tensions and his thought did not come out of a vacuum – also see infra.

17. *Herder*, p. 57.

18. Cf. C.J. Berry, 'Eighteenth-century approaches to the Origin of Metaphor', *Neuphilologische Mitteilungen* (1973), 690–713.

it metaphoric) and it follows that men at first "uttered these [rude, accidental] sounds in a much higher note than we do our Words now" so much so that "they would seem to sing".[19] This became a popular eighteenth-century view and one to which Herder subscribed. To Herder song (*tönende Sprache*) was natural to man and it was from such 'song' that poetry originated (SW V, 58).

This was how Herder received and understood Ossian — "Ossian's poems are songs, folk-songs, songs of an uncultured (*ungebildeten*), emotional people, which have sung their way down the ages on the lips of native tradition". (SW V, 160)[20] Herder's terminology here gives a clue to his later preoccupations. The vitality of the Ossianic epic was what was attractive. It was not the work of a mere imitator of 'dead reason' but the work of genius. Just as Blackwell had accounted for the quality of Homer's work by his 'manners' or social circumstances so Herder saw seminally that literature was the product of a people. The untutored spontaneous products of a people — their folk-songs — are not to be disparaged as being in bad taste but are to be viewed as exhibiting *Kraft der Sprache*,[21] and as the emanations of what he later called *Volksgeist*. Similarly, though Herder, like Vico, rejects the historical personality of Homer, nevertheless 'his' works compose a unity as *Volkspoesie*. Again, it is in this context that Herder's interpretation and celebration of Shakespeare is to be placed. Shakespeare was the continuator (and creator anew) of popular literature, of its ballads and folk-songs; his work, like Sophocles', grew from a native literary soil.[22]

The consequences of this general insight are far-reaching. Since, as we have seen, imitation was basic to rules it means that such vital literature is truly original; it cannot be imitated. From here Herder went to the root of neoclassicism. The Greeks themselves cannot be imitated. Thus, as early as 1778, in his commentary on Winckelmann, Herder saw the pointlessness of that German subjection to the Greek ideal; the Greeks had had their day:[23] a pronouncement that Hegel (and Schiller) would come to echo and which, moreover, became central to Hegel's whole vision. For Herder, instead of pursuing the chimera of trying to recapture the unique sweetness of Greece, the richness of the German

19. Blackwell, p. 40, 37.

20. Trans. in Gillies *Herder*, p. 44n.

21. Cf. R.T. Clark Jr., 'Herder's Concept of *Kraft*', PMLA (1942) 737 – 752, esp. 747. For an exhaustive examination of the different uses and contexts of *Kraft* in Herder's thought see H.B. Nisbet, *Herder and Scientific Thought*.

22. Cf. A. Gillies, 'Herder's Essay on Shakespeare': *Das Herz der Untersuchung*', *Modern Language Review* (1937) 262 – 280, wherein Herder's debt to Percy's *Reliques* is emphasised as the key to his interpretation of Shakespeare. For the Sophocles comparison (as brothers) see e.g. SW V, 225.

23. Cf. IdM, 178 (slightly amended): SW XIV, 105 "If then we cannot be Greeks ourselves, let us at least rejoice that there once were Greeks and that like other flowers of human thought (*Denkart*) this also found a time and a place to put forth its loveliest growth". Also cf. E.M. Butler, "'Imitate the Greeks' commanded Winckelmann and Lessing. 'Impossible to do so' came Herder's mournful reply" *The Tyranny of Greece over Germany*, p. 77.

language should be cherished and utilised; it has a tradition and a vitality of its own (which Herder tried to demonstrate through his collection of folk-songs). Here Herder participates in, indeed plays a leading role in, the Storm and Stress movement with its abjuration of French models and influence.

The upshot of Herder's critique of the prevailing aesthetic norms, in terms of promoting the perceived alternative of a vital literature tied to the emotional roots of a people, was a wider based attack on Enlightenment preconceptions in his essay *Auch Eine Philosophie der Geschichte* (1774) and a more positive presentation of his approach in his essay *Ursprung der Sprache* (1772). It is in these two essays that Herder moves decisively beyond the Enlightenment's approach to relativism, diversity and human nature.

The thinkers of the Enlightenment, as we saw in the previous Chapter, wished to maintain standards so that judgment could be passed. It was crucial to their campaign, especially of course in France, but also, as will be argued in Part II, it is an important ingredient in Hume's thought, that institutions and practices could be attacked as superstitious or barbaric and that the clergy, in particular, were hindrances to enlightenment and that they obtained their position of influence in earlier, more primitive barbaric, days when men were ignorant and credulous. Further, contemporary 'savages' were seen still to partake of these attributes as manifest, for example, in the widespread practice of deforming their bodies.

It was Herder's great insight that the equation of the primitive with the barbaric was the mere imposition of a self-appointed West European superiority. For Herder, on the contrary, the primitive was something different and not something inferior. Each culture (an important word and one which, perhaps significantly, only achieved currency in English in the latter part of the nineteenth century) should be treated on its own merits and not judged by some faulty perspective, such as *la belle nature*, which was revered by the eighteenth-century aesthete. What we can find in Herder is a positive response to the diversity of social experience.[24] He accepts diversity, he does not try to explain it away as a mere contingent aspect of an underlying, and thereby more significant, uniformity. In his early writings, at least, Herder may be said to embrace relativism, as we understood it above.

Thus, in the *Auch eine Philosophie*, he writes "each nation (*Nation*) has its centre of happiness within itself just as every sphere has its centre of gravity" (APG, 186: SW V, 509). This explains how Herder gives a qualitative meaning to 'primitive' (in contrast to the quantitative chronological understanding that equates it with barbarism) and this means, in turn, that the Enlightenment's plan of unilinear progress, latterly embodied in Iselin,[25] is an imposition of unity

24. Cf. A.O. Lovejoy, "The substitution of what may be called diversitarianism for uniformitarianism" was the common factor in Romanticism and constituted a "profound and momentous change" in standards of value, *The Great Chain of Being*, Chap. 8.

25. Author of *Über die Geschichte der Menschheit* (1764). In an addition to the Introduction in 1774 Iselin declares that the leading idea in the work is "the progress of mankind from external

where there is in fact diversity. The unity must be imposed because it is simply the perspective of the philosopher-historian who judges all ages by *his* ideals. The more a society approximates his understanding of happiness then the more that society can be adjudged to have progressed. Whereas, for Herder, the very diversity of social experience was witness to the value of individuality. Each different experience is of value of itself and is moreover, as such, to be valued. As we shall see, this not only reflects Herder's own theological views but also his conviction that a true history would start from the recognition of the value of this diversity – "everything is both a means and an end simultaneously" (APG, 194: SW V, 527). Now if each culture (the criterion of which we shall discuss below) is individual it means that all comparison is unprofitable.

We have already seen one consequence that Herder draws from this, namely, the pointlessness of trying to recreate the Greek ideal, but its full significance is to be seen when its consequences on the role of the individual man, or human nature, are perceived. That is, the very emphasis upon the diversity of cultures, which makes comparison fruitless, has a further repercussion for the proper understanding of the individual member of that culture. This is the threshhold of a decisive re-orientation in conceptions of human nature. If cultures are indeed unique then if, further, human nature can no longer stand removed from, or above, its cultural context but must be understood in terms of, or as an integral part of, its particular context, then the members of that culture do also *differ* from members of another culture. As we shall proceed to demonstrate, when human nature is understood contextually in this manner then to use it, as the Enlightenment had done, as a point of comparison is meaningless. Such a view of human nature is at the heart of the 'historicist revolution' and Herder (and here is the justification for Cassirer's dictum quoted above) is the vanguard of this revolution.

For Herder, human nature is "not an independent deity" but has itself to "learn everything", that is, it is part and parcel of its culture. Human nature is embodied in culture; it is an intrinsic, integral part of it.[26] This constitutes the contextualist theory of human nature (this theory will be used as an interpretative perspective in Parts II and III). Once human nature is seen as unintelligible apart from its particular cultural context then the Enlightenment's (including Hume's as we shall see) use and understanding of the term is undermined. Herder roundly declares that

human nature is not the vessel of an absolute, unchanging and independent happiness, as defined by the philosopher; everywhere it attracts that measure of happiness of which it is capable; it is a pliant clay which assumes a different shape under different needs and circumstances. (APG, 185: SW V, 509)

simplicity to an ever higher level of light and prosperity" (5th Edit., 1786, p. xxxv). Herder's reference to happiness in the quotation just given is an allusion to Iselin.

26. This aspect of Herder's thought is termed 'expressivism' by C. Taylor (*Hegel*, p. 15) who, as he acknowledges, follows I. Berlin, 'J.G. Herder' in *Encounter*, July 1965, 29 – 48 and August 1965, 42 – 51 (reprinted with some additions in *Vico and Herder: Two studies in the History of Ideas.*).

Of course, Herder allows that men are similar, indeed, it is a presupposition of cultural transmission which was to figure so prominently in the later *Ideen zu einer Philosophie der Geschichte der Menschheit* (1784/91), but that does not mean that anything can be deduced from 'man' independent of his cultural context.

Herder's dismissal of the Enlightenment's conception of human nature as static, acultural and ahistorical rests on a more substantial footing that the above might suggest. This point can be substantiated by an examination of Herder's writings on language. It is language which provides the key to what makes a culture what it is; it is through language that human nature can be seen to be *specifically* embodied in culture. Since language has such a pivotal role not only in Herder but in later thought also we shall examine this topic in some detail. In Parts II and III we will discuss Hume's and Hegel's treatment of the subject but here, in line with the general rationale of this Part, we shall outline the general intellectual backcloth to these discussions.

Many writers in the eighteenth century discussed the question of language, within these discussions a number of issues were taken up. There were explanations of the origin of language; the relationship of language to society; the order of the development of the parts of speech and various projects to reform language. All of these discussions share two broad characteristics. These theorists were unaware of the 'family' of languages; they wrote by and large before the 'discovery' of Sanskrit. Secondly, instead, the theorists' approach to language in general was still 'prescriptive' and underlying this was the comprehension of language in terms of Latin grammar or the Aristotelean categories.[27]

An insight into a general feature of Enlightenment speculation on this subject may be gleaned from a brief examination of their schemes to reform language. To achieve the reform of language had been a prominent project of seventeenth-century thought. Their desire for reform can be seen in Bacon's depiction of the 'Idols of the Market'. Idols in general are a "corrupt predisposition. . .which distorts and infects all the anticipations of the understanding" and those, more particularly, of the Market concern the way in which words contribute to that end.[28] The remedy for this distortion and infection lies in definition and terms of art. In similar vein, it was an important part of the programme of the Royal Society (established 1654) to facilitate scientific progress by deliberately purging language of ambiguity. Indeed, a committee was set up 'to improve the English tongue, particularly for philosophical purposes'; a number of the Society's members, most notably John Wilkins, worked at producing a philosophical language.[29] Later Locke (himself a member of the Royal Society) devoted three

27. Cf. C. Berry, 'Adam Smith's *Considerations* on Language', *JHI* (1974) 130–8.

28. The Dignity and Advancement of Learning' in *Physical and Metaphysical Works of Lord Bacon*, ed. J. Devey, p. 207.

29. Wilkins' *An Essay towards a Real Character and a Philosophical Language (1668)* was designed to devise "a real universal character that should not signify words, but things and notions and

chapters of Book III of the *Essay* to the imperfection and abuse of words and to the remedy thereof.

The desire to reform language was a central part of the Enlightenment programme. Priests, for example, are able to hold the sway that they do because they are able to take refuge behind meaningless phrases and to promote obfuscation to further their own ends. Thus, to cite just a few examples, Helvétius closes the first Discourse in his book *De L'Esprit* (1759) with a discussion of the abuses of words and a commendation of Leibniz' philosophic language, where each word has a precise meaning.[30] Condorcet looks forward, in the future tenth stage of human progress, to a scientific language that will end equivocation. Finally, Bentham was insistent that the law should be clearly promulgated and much of his original work was achieved in working up a theory of fictions.[31]

A prominent feature of these reforms is the frequent reference to mathematics. Condillac, who devoted much time to speculation on language, for example, saw in algebra the perfect language.[32] What is important is the indication such aspirations give as to the understanding of language. That is, what is required is a perfect fit between words and that to which they refer. This leads to the central dilemma, as identified by Rousseau, in eighteenth-century speculation on language —

if men need speech to learn to think, they must have stood in much greater need of the art of thinking, to be able to invent that of speaking.[33]

Rousseau was here referring particularly to the attempt made by Condillac to circumvent this problem by a speculative explanation of the acquisition of language from natural cries whereby the development of reason or understanding was pari passu with that of language.[34] It is in this context that Monboddo's seemingly perverse account is to be understood since he, at least, was clear that thought was anterior to speech as speech itself was not necessary to man.[35]

Herder's treatment of language has been recognised as epochal.[36] He transform-

consequently might be legible by any Nation in their own tongue" quoted in W.S. Howell, *Eighteenth Century British Logic and Rhetoric*, p. 463. Cf. Barbara J. Shapiro, *John Wilkins 1614 – 1672: An Intellectual Biography*, esp. p. 203ff.

30. Helvétius, pp. 18 – 25.

31. See his *Theory of Fictions*, ed. C.K. Ogden. Bentham also wrote an 'Essay on Language' and 'Fragments on a Universal Grammar' both in *Works*, ed. J. Bowring, Vol. 8.

32. La Langue des Calculs (1798) in *Oeuvres Philosophiques*, ed. G. Leroy (1947), Vol. 2, p. 420. Cf. Isabel F. Knight, *The Geometric Spirit: The Abbé de Condillac and the French Enlightenment*, Chap. 6.

33. *Discours. . .de l'Inegalité parmi les Hommes* (Everyman Library), p. 175: *Oeuvres (Pléiade)*, Vol. III, p. 147.

34. *Essai sur les connoissances humaines*, Pt. 2, Sect. 1, Chap. 1. Cf. H. Aarsleff, 'The Tradition of Condillac' in D. Hymes (ed.), *Studies in the History of Linguistics*, pp. 93 – 156, esp. p. 110.

35. *Origin and Progress of Language* (1773 – 9), Vol. 1, Bk. 1, Chap. 1 et passim; also see his *Antient Metaphysics* (1779 – 99), Vol. III, Bk. 2, Chap. 1 et passim.

36. Cf. *inter alia* E. Sapir, 'Herder's *Ursprung der Sprache*', MP (1907) 109 – 42; R.H. Robins, *A Short History of Linguistics*, pp. 151 – 3; E. Cassirer, *The Philosophy of Symbolic Forms*, Vol. 1, p. 152 – 3.

ed the whole debate. This transformation can be seen in his prize-winning essay on language, referred to above. It is true that there are several arguments in the essay where Herder is in accord with 'mainstream' thought such as, as we have seen, his view of the poetic, musical and metaphoric character of early speech. Or, again, he is not averse to participating in the debate on the order of the development of parts of speech by declaring that verbs were the primitive parts of speech (a view shared by Adam Smith and contrary to the positions of, for example, Condillac, Priestley and Vico).[37] Nevertheless despite these comments the thrust of Herder's argument is that the basic question as to the relative priority of thought or speech is misconceived.

Language is not some contingent attribute of man which he can be conceived to be without; rather, it is a defining generic characteristic. Although such a position is traditionally Aristotelean, Herder's account significantly goes beyond the received wisdom. In accord with his approach, Herder rejects all the existing explanations of the origin of language whether orthodoxly Biblical or Theological (or unorthodoxly in his friend Hamann's case).[38] Rationalistic or Organic.[39] With respect to the last of these (the most popular Enlightenment variant), Herder discusses Condillac's speculative account and points out, as Rousseau had done, how this whole approach is faced with the dilemma of attributing priority to either thought or speech. But, whereas Rousseau still persisted with the Organic approach, Herder took it as proof that a 'gap' between thought and language is not conceptually possible.

This is announced in the very first sentence of the Essay — "Even as an animal man has a language" (US, 117: SV W, 5). Man is not just a creature who happens to speak, he is a speech-being so that although there are animalistic elements in speech these are not to be understood as the 'roots' of language so much as the 'sap', which accounts for its primitive vitality. In other words, these elements

37. Cf. Berry, *J.H.I.* (1974).

38. Hamann held that the world is God's word "Every phenomenon of nature was a word, the sign, image and pledge of a new, mysterious, inexpressible, but for that reason all the more inward union, communication and community of divine energies and ideas. Everything that man in the beginning heard, saw, gazed upon, and touched, was a living word" (tr. in R.G. Smith, *J.G. Hamann 1730–88: A Study in Christian Existence*, p. 73: 'Des Ritters von Rosenkreuz letzte Willenseinung' *Sämmtliche Werke*, ed. J. Nadler, Vol. III, p. 32). From this perspective it was held to follow that "since the instruments of language at least are a present from the *alma mater* Nature. . .and since, in accordance with the highest philosophical probability, the Creator of these artificial (*künstlichen*) instruments desired and had to establish the use of them as well, then certainly the origin of human language is divine" (Smith, p. 247: *Werke* III, p. 27). Though Herder rejected this theory his writings (generally and on language in particular) owe much to Hamann's preoccupations. Despite this debt in general philosophical orientation, together with close personal ties, Herder did not subscribe to Hamann's mystical irrationalism. Cf. R.T. Clark Jr., *Herder: His Life and Thought* who rejects (p. 3) the argument of Haym than Hamann was the chief influence on Herder, *Herder: nach seinem Leben und seinen Werken* (Vol. 1, p. 53). Similarly Berlin (July, p. 37 – 8) and L.W. Beck, *Early German Philosophy*, p. 389.

39. Cf. Berry, *JHI* (1974).

embody or express primitive man and as such they are bearers of meaning to him and for him. They are not, as Condillac and the others would have it, simply the automatic meaningless response to external stimuli out of which eventually developed meaningful discourse. Language, thus, from the start differentiated men from animals and, as such, there was no time when man was without language. Hence Rousseau's dilemma dissolves — thought and language are one. Indeed, Herder believes this indivisibility is expressed in a number of languages where "word and reason, concept and word, language and origin have one designation" — the recognition of a thing and naming it are not two actions but one (SW V, 47). This indivisibility was an aspect of Herder's poetic theory which had considerable impact on both Schiller and Goethe.[40] The poet had to express the inner continuum of feeling and sensation in an integrally appropriate form and if the outer form can be separated from its vital source then the poet has failed. Or, as Schiller himself put it when depicting the style of a genius as a "mode of expression in which the sign disappears completely in the thing signified and in which the language, whilst giving expression to a thought yet leaves it exposed".[41]

Herder draws an important and far-reaching conclusion from this unity between thought and language, for, if this is so, and language differentiates man, then his distinguishing mark is also to be found in this unity. In the essay on Language, to express this unity Herder uses stipulatively the term *Besonnenheit* by which he means reflective mind or consciousness which is co-terminous with man's distinctively *human* nature (US, 132: SW V, 30).[42] The fact that *Besonnenheit* is a unity means that Herder explicitly overthrows faculty-psychology — the understanding of the human mind in terms of certain elements or components like reason, will, judgment, passion; an understanding that has been pervasive in Western thought since Plato and in which both Hume and Kant partake as we shall see. However, to Herder "all individual faculties (*Kräfte*) of our mind or of that of the animal are nothing but metaphysical abstractions" (US, 131: SW V, 29). To speak of reason as a separate disconnected part of the mind is philosophical nonsense since "everywhere the total undivided mind is at work"(SW V, 30):[43] another conviction that is central to Hegel.

This view of the defining quality of man radically disengages him from

40. Cf. E.M. Wilkinson, 'The inexpressible and the unspeakable: Some Romantic Attitudes to Art and Language', GLL (1962/3) 308–320, esp. p. 316.

41. *Über Naive und Sentimentalische Dichtung*, tr. J. Ellias, p. 98: *Werke* (Nationalausgabe), Vol. 20, p. 426.

42. For discussion of *Besonnenheit* see F.M. Barnard, *Herder's Social and Political Thought*, p. 42f and Clark, *Life and Thought*, p. 134.

43. Cf. his *Vom Erkennen und Empfinden der Menschlichen Seele* (final draft 1778) (in SW VIII) where Herder attacks abstract intellectualism and emphasises the physiological base of psychology, that thought is inseparable from feelings. *Kraft* once again plays a key mediating role. M.H. Abrams (*Mirror and Lamp*, p. 204) has termed this work "a turning point in the history of ideas" since it "heralds the age of biologism" so that man is an organic unity of thought, feeling and will. Cf. also Herder's later explicit attack on Kant (*Metakritik* 1799) where the 'faculties' are juxtaposed to the living diversity of the soul, *SW* XXI, 19.

animality. It is an important characteristic of Romantic (but one which both Kant and Hegel share) thought that it broke completely from the Enlightenment's tendency to assimilate man to the brutes; a tendency that derived from their 'objective' or materialist/sensationalist approach in contrast to the 'Romantic' emphasis on internality and mind. It is true that Herder does take seriously man's relationship to the Orang Outang (here influenced by Monboddo and Camper) but despite the physiological similarities, and for Herder the important dissimilarities in terms of brain structure and upright gait, nevertheless it is speech, and with that reason and freedom, that differentiates man. Man can choose, man is king.[44] (SW XII, 146).

More immediately important for our purposes is that this view of man's distinctiveness ties in with Herder's view discussed above on the connexion between human nature and culture. If the language that is spoken is the essential expression of man then different languages mean different men. This is the thrust behind the concept of a *Volk*. Those who speak the same language have an internal link one with the other. What makes *these* men what they *are* serves to distinguish them radically from other men. Again the consequence is that there is no such thing as human nature simpliciter: it only subsists in, and can only be comprehended within, a context; it is a radically cultural concept. This contextualist view of human nature can be seen implied in what is perhaps for our purposes the focal sentence (as far as there can be such for a writer of Herder's mercurial talents and interests) in Herder's corpus – "For each people as a people has its own National culture as it has its language" (SW XIII, 257 – 8).

A culture and a language are as one so that as languages differ from another so too do cultures and so too, it follows, does human nature. These differences open up the problem of transcultural communication and comprehension. For example, Herder points to the difficulties that missionaries experience in communicating Christian ideas to aboriginals. It is not that these ideas are abstruse but that they express a different world-view. To the same end Herder cites the case of the chief dialect of Peru where:

the two sexes are indicated in so peculiar a manner that the word 'sister' referring to the sister of the brother, and the sister of the sister, the child of the father, and the child of the mother are termed differently; yet this same language has no proper plural! Each of these synonyms is closely connected with the customs, the character and the origin of a people; and everywhere it reveals the inventive spirit of the man. (APG, 150: SW V, 78)

More generally, this is why folk-songs and the like are important. They are cultural documents. The culture is the embodiment of a people's way of life; its way of making its sense of the world. Here we get Herder's qualitative primitivism; his affirmation of the worth of primitive experience as something generically different (as we shall see in Chapter 7 Hume does not possess this con-

---

44. Cf. P. Salmon, 'Herder's Essay on the Origin of Language and the place of Man in the Animal Kingdom', *GLL* (1968/9) 59 – 70.

cept of the primitive).[45] An instance of this recognition is a positive evaluation of mythology. No longer is it regarded as an imperfect state exhibiting confusion and equivocation but "the mythology of every people is an expression of their own distinctive way of viewing nature" (IdB, 300: SW XIII, 307), it is "a philosophical essay of the human mind". That primitive rituals and beliefs might seem to be meaningless mumbo-jumbo to the civilised eighteenth-century mind is no warrant to dismiss them because they do have meaning to and for the primitive.

Herder's view of the integrity of primitive experience involves a re-thinking of the assumptions of historical writing. What is increasingly seen to be a necessary requirement is the taking of the past at its own evaluation and not as it now seems from hindsight. History should study the past for its own sake and seek to tell it how it was in all its specificity. Although such a view strictly adopted leads to the abjuration of all super-historical categories such as progress and, although, also, such a view has its foundations in Herder's insights, the view itself cannot be attributed, in all its later rigour, to Herder himself. We saw in the last chapter how progress or development functioned as an ordering principle and it would seem, indeed, that Herder's cultural relativism precluded this. Yet Herder throughout his writings did profess a belief in progress and in the *Ideen* he made a conscious effort to synthesise this belief with a recognition of the intrinsic worth of each culture. Though it should be said that this synthesis was always implicitly present, even in the polemical *Auch eine Philosophie*.

A key to this synthesis is Herder's notion of Humanity (*Humanität*). However, lying behind this is a broader metaphysical view. The lynch-pin of this view is that the Cosmos is a living unity. A consequence of this is that its 'contents', as it were, are dynamically inter-related. This further entails that although men are different from Nature (as manifested in brutes) they are nevertheless still in harmony with it. Similarly, though *Völker* differ from each other yet they are still in harmony. There is unity in difference. Herder is here invoking the venerable Platonic vision, though his more immediate referents were Spinoza, Shaftesbury and Leibniz.

Theologically Herder came close to an immanental pantheism. God was everywhere in the world; He was the fundamental all-pervading force (*die Urkraft aller Kräfte*) (*Gott* [1787] SW XVI, 452). The Cosmos, as a whole, exhibits a living organic force (SW XIII, 274). Importantly, for our particular perspective, the same necessarily holds for the individual. As we have seen, Herder rejects faculty psychology in favour of an interpretation of the mind as a unity and the mind, so understood, itself exhibits this same organic force or *Kraft*. The individual is not merely part of a larger whole (his culture), rather his very identity is bound up with it. What a man is, what constitutes his self, is evidenced or embodied in his culture. Moreover, a man knows who he is by his

---

45. For a comparison of Herder and Hume see F. Manuel, *The Eighteenth-Century Confronts the Gods*, esp. p. 301, though he does not employ the term 'qualitative primitivism'. Herder paraphrased Hume's *Natural History of Religion*, SW XXXII, 195 – 197.

awareness of his culture. The language he speaks, for example and crucially, not only distinguishes him from those with a different tongue but also furnishes him with an understanding of the world and of his place in it. This conceptualisation of self-knowledge put Herder at odds with Kant as we shall see in the next chapter. Indeed, these ideas of the Cosmos and of the mind or self as an organism, as a living telos, were to become a central tenet of Romanticism and, suitably 'transcended' (*aufgehoben*) and systematised, of Hegel's thought also.

It is against this background that we can turn our attention back to Herder's notion of *Humanität* and its bearing on historical understanding. Herder still maintains that cultures are to be judged in their own terms but "if there is a God in nature, there is in history too" (IdM, 82: SW XIV, 207). The varieties and diversities of social experience are thus an expression of divine purpose in both the richness of their content as well as in the sheer multiplicity of their forms. Man's destiny on earth, as seen in this richness, which as such embodies God's immanental purpose, is *Humanität*: man "has had nothing in view and could aim at nothing else but Humanity" (IdM, 83: SW XIV, 208).

This aim has expressed itself in a multitude of forms "the muse of Time, History, herself sings with a hundred voices, speaks with a hundred tongues" (IdM, 107: SW XIV, 237). Though each people (Herder still affirms) bears "in itself the standard of its perfection, totally independent of all comparison with that of others" yet "one century instructs another" (IdM, 107: SW XIV, 237) so that through it all "the whole history of peoples is to us a school for instructing us in the course of which we are to attain the beautiful prize of humanity and worth" (IdM, 86 – 7 amended: SW XIV, 212 – 3). Reason has been inherited and mankind has progressed "whatever good appears in history to have been accomplished humanity was the gainer" (IdM, 83: SW XIV, 208) because "the history of mankind is necessarily a whole" (IdB, 312: SW XIV, 345). Through this history makes a difference. If history is the history of cultures and given that man is a cultural being then man, human nature, itself is part of the historical process. The primitive mind for such there now can be, is fundamentally different from that of ourselves, just as indeed the Greeks are. There is no meaningful common substratum since "the progress of time has influenced the mode of thinking (*Denkart*) of the human species" (IdM, 106: SW XIV, 237).

It should be easily appreciated from the above (alone) just how much Herder's thought broke new ground and laid the basis for future thought. In terms of the history of ideas the latter is, perhaps the more significant since a reasoned case can be established for Vico's philosophy incorporating a recognition of the historical dimension to human nature.[46] Furthermore, Herder is not, of course,

---

46. The lynch-pin of Vico's *New Science* (3rd edit. 1744) is that the world of civil society has been made by men and can thus be understood by men (within the modifications of their own minds) unlike Nature which God alone knows since He alone created it (para. 331). The Science will reveal the Universal and eternal principles on which all nations are founded (para. 332) and this describes "an ideal eternal history traversed in time by the history of every nation" (para. 349); a history which, as evidenced by philology, envelops the history of man himself through poetic, heroic and

alone in his preoccupations and outlook.

Lessing, for example, in his *Erziehung des Menschengeschlechts* (1780) had adopted a historical approach to Christianity, whereby the 'truths' of the Old Testament were regarded as those appropriate for the Israelites at that stage of their development (para. 27). This 'elementary' book was, in due course, replaced by the second great step in Man's education, namely, Christ's teaching in the New Testament (paras. 53, 54). Now we are approaching the third age, when reason can reign by itself and right will be done because it is right and not because of any arbitrary rewards attached to it (para. 85). Yet the relativism here suggested by Lessing is not unrelated to Herder's endeavours.[47]

Rousseau, to take another pertinent example, is perhaps more problematic. It has been maintained that it was "a basic feature of his social thought. . .that the nature of man did indeed change with the passing of time, and change very radically at that".[48] But, despite the argument of the Second Discourse, in particular, outlining man's (largely disastrous) social development this development does not destroy beyond redemption man's ability to live a properly moral life. *Le Mal* is produced by social interaction (it generates *amour-propre*) but unaffected underneath is man's natural (that is, societally indifferent) innocence and goodness.[49] It is thus possible, as Rousseau aims to demonstrate in *du Contrat Social*, for man so to arrange society (where *la volonté générale* is sovereign) so that man can therein be free and moral. The past can be undone or by-passed. Rousseau wishes to revivify the (supposed) integral harmony of the Greek polis, hence his rejection of representation and, hence too, Hegel's judgment that Rousseau has failed to come to terms with the 'bourgeois' character of the 'modern' world. For all his charting of the development of economies (and luxury), in the Discourses, this development, for Rousseau, as for other eighteenth-century expositors of 'economism', has not changed man in any radical sense.

---

human phases (para. 34). Erich Auerbach concludes his examination of Vico's aesthetic historicism by commenting that "Vico created and passionately maintained the concept of the historical nature of man. He identified human history and human nature, he conceived human nature as a function of history", 'Vico and Aesthetic Historism', *J. Aesthetics and Art Criticism* (1949), p. 118. For a painstaking analysis of Vico's understanding of human nature see L. Pompa, *Vico: A Study of the 'New Science'*, esp. Chaps. 3, 11, 12. The question of Vico's 'influence' and penetration is the subject of much speculation. For example, cases have been made for this impact on the Scottish Enlightenment, Montesquieu and with more certainty on Herder himself. But even if these cases hold (and in the first two cases this is very unlikely) little of import is thereby established.

47. Lewis S. Spitz remarks that Lessing received the inspiration for the *Erziehung* from suggestions in Herder's *Auch eine Philosophie* 'Natural Law and the Theory of History in Herder', *JHI* (1955), p. 473n. However, the importance of the 'new' Leibniz to both philosophers is crucial; see I. Stamm, 'Herder and Aufklärung: a Leibnizian Context', *Germanic Review* (1963) 197 – 208, who sees a parallel, from this perspective, between Herder and Lessing's essay. Lessing's debt to Leibniz in the *Erziehung* is brought out by H.E. Allison, *Lessing and the Enlightenment*, pp. 147 – 161.

48. D.M. Cameron, *The Social Thought of Rousseau and Burke*, p. 87. But Rousseau is not regarded as a precursor of nineteenth-century historicism, p. 92.

49. Cf. J. Starobinski, *Rousseau: La Transparence et l'Obstacle*, p. 33.

Human nature is not historicised.

Though Herder, like all his generation (and beyond), was influenced by Rousseau, he has intimated a new understanding of human nature. From the above sketch, the parallels between Herder and Hegel are evident and the debt that Romanticism owed to Herder is cogently summarised by Robert Clark Jr.:

Romanticism in Germany was largely based on Herder's own ideas – the importance of folk songs, a new attitude toward the Middle Ages, rejection of formalism in art, emphasis on religion as the carrier of all cultural values, the conception of language as the most important determinant in artistic consciousness, and the (Hamannian) idea of history and nature as the twin commentaries on the divine Logos. Without Herder's energetic defence of Spinoza, the Romanticists would hardly have blended pantheism into their philosophy of religion and nature.[50]

Although aspects of Herder's work were taken up into both political Romanticism (the emphasis on cultural specificity) and literary Romanticism (the emphasis on creative individuality) Herder was not a Romantic. Nor despite his conceptualisation of a *Volk* is he a Nationalist.

However, what is important for the purposes of this study is that as part of that general reorientation in thought, which is encapsulated in the term Romanticism, the conception of human nature changed. Abetted by the epochal work in language, in which Friedrich Schlegel – not coincidentally, a leader of the Romantic movement – played a prominent role, and by taking 'culture' seriously, the hitherto societally indifferent universalist uniformitarian notion of human nature, as conceived by Hume and others in Enlightenment, gave way to a contextualist notion; a notion which Hegel was to incorporate and systematise. Indeed, as we shall see in Part III, this systematisation was part and parcel of a broad historical (Herderian) vision going beyond the narrower preoccupations of the Romantics, as manifest most palpably in their nostalgia for the Middle Ages.

We shall here give just one instance of this aspect of this reorientation in operation – in Fichte's *Reden an die deutsche Nation* (1808). We can commence by once again citing Herder. A distinction is often drawn between cultural and political nationalism.[51] The basis of the former is to be found in cultural affinity and, following Herder, this affinity is expressed in the notion of a *Volk*. Herder himself had declared that Providence

has separated peoples not only by forests and mountains, seas and deserts, rivers and climates, but also, and more significantly, by languages, propensities and characters. (IdB, 311: SW XIII, 341)

50. *Life and Thought*, p. 417. Similarly far-reaching claims are made by Gillies (*Herder*, p. 116) "it is not too much to say that the whole of the Romantic movement in Germany is Herder's intellectual legacy" and Beck (*Early German Philosophy*, p. 367) "the influence of Herder cannot be overestimated. . .Eighteenth-century thought was fed into the nineteenth century through two channels: Kant and Herder".

51. Cf. F. Meinecke, *Cosmopolitanism and the National State*, Chap. 1.

In line with Herder's general impact these sentiments were echoed by many writers and though developed furthest in Germany, in the writings of F. Schlegel, Arndt as well as Fichte, similar sentiments can be found in the French Reaction.[52]

We shall not here enter into the various debates concerning the relationship of Fichte's *Reden* to later German Nationalism, nor indeed the extent to which Fichte's position is prefigured in his earlier writings, nor, again, the extent to which Fichte can be rightly called a Nationalist in the first place. The current purpose is to see the repercussions of his preoccupations on a theory of human nature. To Fichte "men are formed by language far more than language is formed by man" (RDN, 48 (314)). Like Herder he subscribes to the view that man is inseparable from language and, again like Herder, he sees that though there is but a single language, as the organ of social man, it never existed as such but always in the form of a *Volk*. A *Volk* is the living carrier of the same language. The consequence is that in the language is found

in complete unity the sum total of the sensuous and mental life of the nation deposited in the language, for the purpose of designating an idea that likewise is not arbitrary but necessarily proceeds from the whole previous life of the nation. (RDN, 58 (325))

The *Volk* then is the

totality of men continuing to live in society with each other and continually creating themselves naturally and spiritually out of themselves. (RDN, 115 (381))

The upshot is that the boundaries between states are 'internal' −

those who speak the same language are joined to each other by a multitude of invisible bonds by nature herself, long before any human art begins; they understand each other and have the power of continuing to make themselves understood more and more clearly; they belong together and are by nature one and an inseparable whole. (RDN, 190 (459))

The converse, of course, holds, namely, that those not partaking of these 'invisible bonds' can never fully participate with those that do. Man as such does not exist; what does exist are men. Men who, as specifically cultural beings, are radically different from those who are not similarly specified. Human nature is only intelligible when seen in context.

52. Cf. J. de Maistre, *Works*, ed. & tr. J. Lively, p. 99.

42

The following abbreviations are inserted in parentheses in the text throughout.

W   *Werke* (Prussian Academy edition).

RV   *Kritik der Reinen Vernunft* (1781), tr. N.K. Smith.

UK   *Kritik der Urteilskraft* (1788), tr. J.H. Bernard.

PKM   *Prolegomena zu einer jeden künftigen Metaphysik* (1783), tr. C.J. Friedrich in *The Philosophy of Kant.*

RGV   *Religion innerhalb der Grenzen der blossen Vernunft* (1793), tr. H.H. Hudson & T.M. Greene in Friedrich.

IGW   *Idee zu einer allgemeinen Geschichte in weltbürgerlicher Absicht* (1784), tr. L.W. Beck in *Kant on History.*

MAM   *Mutmasslicher Anfang der Menschengeschichte* (1786), tr. E. Fackenheim in Beck.

AP   *Anthropologie in pragmatischer Hinsicht* (1798), tr. M. Gregor.

3. THE KANTIAN REVOLUTION

In the period under consideration Kant's thought is clearly pivotal. In terms of academic philosophy he provides the bridge between Hume and Hegel. It is not here intended to detail this bridging: indeed, within the confines of the present work it would be a gross oversimplification, a travesty even, so to do. Nevertheless, some recognition has to be accorded to his role. Additionally, however, Kant is of moment to the more particular theme of this work — the relationship between theories of human nature and society — and this will be discussed. In this discussion Kant's own views on history and society, together with his connected concerns in aesthetics, will be broached. This discussion will also, in passing, take in Kant's disputes with Herder.

Kant was not alone in Germany in responding to Hume. Hamann, indeed, believed that he saw in Hume a vindication of faith since he had demonstrated the impotence of reason. That this attitude persisted even after Kant's response can be seen from Hamann's oft-quoted letter to Herder where he remarks "Hume is always my man, because he at least honours the principle of belief and has taken it up into his system. Our countryman [Kant] keeps on chewing the cud of Hume's fury against causality, without taking this matter of belief into account".[1] Nevertheless, Kant believed that his *Kritik der reinen Vernunft* (1781) had solved "Hume's problem" (PKM, 46: W IV, 260). This 'problem' concerned the inability of reason to discover necessity; there is no experiential basis for the attribution of necessity to the relationship between a cause and its effect. Accordingly, 'necessity' is 'subjective'; the product of habit (PKM, 43, cf. RV, 44: W IV, 258, III, 29). The perceived consequence of this position was, to Kant, that metaphysics was not possible since the concept of cause (and others) could not be thought of a priori by reason. Kant's solution was thus also simultaneously a

---

1. *Briefwechsel*, ed. A. Henkel, Vol. 4, p. 295 (10 May 1781). Translation as in R.G. Smith, *J.G. Hamann 1730–1788: A Study in Christian Existence*, p. 244. On Hamann's interpretation of Hume see C.W. Swain, 'Hamann and the philosophy of David Hume', *JHP* (1967) 343–51; I. Berlin, 'Hume and the Sources of German Anti-Rationalism', in *Hume: Bicentenary Papers*, ed. G.P. Morice, pp. 93–116; W.M. Alexander, *J.G. Hamann Philosophy and Faith*, Chap. 2.

vindication of metaphysics: but a 'critical' vindication within which all future metaphysics must be constrained.

The nub of this solution is the 'Copernican Revolution' whereby, to give Kant's own bald depiction, instead of proceeding on the assumption, as in empiricism, that all our knowledge must conform to objects, it is supposed that objects must conform to our knowledge (RV, 22: W III, 12). Kant does not doubt that all our knowledge begins with experience but, crucially, he goes on to remark that it does not thereby follow that all knowledge arises out of experience (RV, 41: W III, 27). Kant purports to demonstrate that there is in addition to empirical or a posteriori knowledge also a priori knowledge, which he defines as knowledge absolutely independent of experience (RV, 43: W III, 28). This a priori knowledge consists of concepts originating in the pure intellect. These concepts structure or categorise empirical knowledge — "they serve, as it were, to 'spell out'' phenomena so that these may be 'read' as experience" (PKM, 84: W IV, 312). It is the presence of these concepts that makes experience possible and it is in this presuppositional sense that objects must conform to knowledge. The systematisation of these concepts is the proper, and indispensable work, of metaphysics.

In this way Kant thinks he has established the validity of objective necessity. A consequence of this, for Kant, is that he has preserved 'natural science'. Hume had reduced the propositions of natural science to mere empirical regularity but Kant, by demonstrating that there are synthetic a priori principles which structure all experience, had retained the intellectual validity of general laws of nature. It was, in other words, no mere accident (the product of contingently repeated associations) that men agree on what constitutes the laws of nature (PKM, 71; RV, 237: W IV, 298, III, 184).

The repercussions of this for an understanding of human nature are evident. Kant achieves his vindication of objective necessity through a demonstration that the intellect necessarily prescribes a structure of experience: accordingly —

what experience teaches me under certain circumstances it must teach me, and every other person as well, at all times; its validity is not limited to the subject or to the state of such a subject at a particular time. All such judgments are stated as objectively valid. (PKM, 72–3: W IV, 299)

Kant here has gone far beyond the Enlightenment's understanding of the universality of human nature. If indeed this is so then the relationship of his thought to Herder's critique of the Enlightenment merits further a attention. A comparative analysis of Herder and Kant will reveal not only the extent, if any, of Kant's divergence from the Enlightenment but can also be seen to have considerable bearing on the relationship of Hegel to them both.

As we saw in the last Chapter, Herder criticised the Enlightenment's understanding of human nature on two different grounds. Firstly, they had used their own cultural perspective and preoccupations, with its understanding of what constitutes human nature, to evaluate different cultures or social practices. To Herder, by contrast, since all cultural phenomena were a unique expression of the worth of that culture then distortion was the only result of comparison. Secondly, the conceptualisation of the human mind into separate faculties was rejected for the notion of the mind as an organic unity. With respect to the second of these two criticisms Kant retains the language of faculty psychology. Indeed, it constitutes the indispensable framework for the whole 'critical' philosophy. For example, in the introduction to the *Kritik der Urteilskraft* (1788), Kant spells out a tri-partite division of the mind into faculties (*Vermögen*) of desire, feelings of pleasure and pain (*Unlust*) and cognition (UK, 41: W V, 198). As we also saw in the last Chapter and will develop in Part III, Hegel rejects faculty psychology and adopts the Herderian position of the mind's unity. But with respect to the first of Herder's criticisms, matters are more complex and an examination of Kant's attitudes to man, culture and history is required.

Before these attitudes can be fully appreciated two broader aspects of Kant's philosophy must be noted: one, his radical disjunction between Nature and morality or culture and, two, his understanding of purposiveness. To take the first of these: it follows from Kant's preservation of metaphysics that it is confined to possible experience or empirical intuition (RV, 259: W III, 298). Such possible experience (things as known) refers to the phenomenal world. But in addition to the phenomenal world which consists of appearances there is the "real per se" (*wirklich an sich*) (RV, 24: W III, 13). This is the thing-in-itself or noumenon (RV, 27: W III, 16), which, by definition, cannot be *known* but it can be *thought* (RV, 27, cf. 161: W III, 16, 116). However, for such thought to be a real possibility, to have objective validity, depends on its principles being 'practical'. This practicality is found in human action, that is, in morality or "the practical legislation of Reason in accordance with the concept of Freedom" (UK, 7: W V, 171).

A number of pertinent consequences can now be seen to ensue. Natural science is an analysis of the phenomenal world within which the principle of universal causation operates. Man is part of the natural world and, in that sense (Hume's sense), his actions are determined and not free. But, there is no contradiction in saying, with respect to the human soul (Kant's own example) that it is free as a thing-in-itself, as a participant in the noumenal world. Of course, such freedom cannot be known but it can be thought and Kant maintains that this is sufficient for morality. What Kant has endeavoured to do, therefore, by his subscription of man to membership of both the phenomenal and noumenal worlds, is to uphold freedom (the necessary presupposition of morality) within a determinate world of Nature.

A further consequence is that this analysis of the two realms applies to Kant's theory of the 'self' (an issue notoriously problematic for Hume). To Kant, it is an objective condition of all knowledge that there must be a unity of consciousness or apperception. This is necessary because only by virtue of this unity does an 'intuition' (a representation prior to all thought) become an "object for me" (RV, 156: W III, 112). It follows, for Kant, that this pure apperception (the self as 'I think') is not itself an item of experience but that which precedes and belongs to every experience (RV, 378: W III, 276). It is, as such, an instance of what Kant calls transcendental knowledge. By this he means "such knowledge as concerns the a priori possibility of knowledge or its a priori employment" (RV, 96: W III, 78). Accordingly, this pure apperception of self is presupposed in the 'empirical self' or unity of consciousness (derivable from association) which can only possess subjective validity. Now if I am conscious of myself only that I am (RV, 168, 381: W III, 123, 279) then it is illicit to proceed to maintain that this self-consciousness yields any *knowledge* of myself. The 'I' belongs to thought in general (RV, 378n: W III, 276n) and no knowledge of self — as a thing-in-itself, as noumenon — is possible. This is so, to Kant, because I know myself as I appear to myself but this self-consciousness is a series of temporally conditioned 'states', which means that it pertains to the phenomenal world (RV, 169, 440: W III, 124, 339).

This denial of any distinction between (privileged) knowledge of myself and knowledge of others or Nature, as a consequence of the maintenance of the thing-in-itself, was to prove unacceptable to Kant's German contemporaries and successors. It is symptomatic of this reception that Herder's most explicit attack on Kant's system, in his *Metakritik* of 1799, had the widest circulation of all his works.[2] Herder's vision of an all-prevading organicism was radically at odds with Kant's phenomenal/noumenal distinction and was, as we saw in the last chapter, a seminal influence on the Romantic movement. More specifically (and here is the justification for this discussion of the place of 'self' in Kant's philosophy) to Herder, by virtue of his notion of *Kraft*, the self is in interaction with its surroundings and can be known in this interaction. Indeed, as we would expect from our earlier discussion of Herder, the *Metakritik* opens with a discussion of language, but even in the earlier *Ideen* (Part II, 1785) Herder had remarked that the notion of pure reason without language was utopian.[3] It is this recognition that self-knowledge is to be gained from the responses of others, that we know ourselves in and through others, that Hegel exploits.

We can now turn to the second of the two broader aspects noted above — purposiveness. Though Kant thus sets up two realms — phenomenal or sensible (Nature) and noumenal or supersensible (freedom) — the latter is nevertheless meant to have influence upon the former. The transition between the two realms is outlined in the Third Critique[4] (Judgment). Judgment in general is designated by Kant as "the faculty of thinking the particular as contained under the Universal" (UK, 16: W V, 179). The significance of this is that within the operation of a priori principles of understanding (the natural realm) there are an infinite variety of empirical laws (UK, 23: W V, 184). Now although these laws may be *contingent* with respect to *our* understanding, nevertheless since, in accord with the concept of Nature, they must be law-like and systematic, they must be regarded as *necessary* and as comprising a unity. This unity is the transcendental principle of the faculty of Judgment. The form this principle takes is pur-

2. A. Gillies, *Herder*, p. 111.

3. *SW*, Vol. XIII, p. 357. The *Metakritik* is in Volume XXI.

4. P. Gay in *The Enlightenment: The Science of Freedom* calls the Third Critique "a typical product of the Enlightenment", p. 312.

posiveness — "conformity of the contingent to law is called purposiveness" (UK, 318: W V, 404). This means that the particular empirical laws are considered by this faculty as possessing a unity *as if* they did fall in with the universal laws of nature. This it is important to note is not an identification of purpose within Nature but an Idea, by which we can reflect on the connexion of phenomena in all their variety (UK, 18 – 9: W V, 181). Since this point is crucial to Kant's understanding of history, in particular, but also to his aesthetic thought a lengthy quotation here will assist the subsequent discussion —

The Judgment does not cognise this a priori in nature, but assumes it on behalf of a natural order cognisable by our Understanding in the division which it makes of the universal laws of nature when it wishes to subordinate to these the variety of particular laws. If then we say that nature specifies its universal laws according to the principles of purposiveness for our cognitive faculty, i.e. in accordance with the necessary business of the human Understanding of finding the universal for the particular which perception offers it, and again of finding connection for the diverse (which however is a universal for each species) in the unity of a principle — we thus neither prescribe to nature a law, nor we do learn from it by observation (although such a principle may be confirmed by this means). For it is not a principle of the determinant but merely of the reflective Judgment. (UK, 25 – 6: W V, 186)

Kant proceeds to distinguish subjective purposiveness — the realm of aesthetic judgment — from objective purposiveness — the realm of teleology. Before turning to a brief discussion of Kant's aesthetics and then a more extensive analysis of the place of teleology in his thought we can now note how, in Kant's eyes, this Third Critique provides the bridge between the phenomenal and noumenal worlds —

It makes possible the transition from the conformity to law in accordance with the former [concept of nature] to the final purpose in accordance with the latter [concept of freedom], and this by the concept of purposiveness in nature. For thus is cognised the possibility of the final purpose which alone can be actualised in nature in harmony with its laws. (UK, 39: W V, 196)

Kant's aesthetics is of particular interest as a clear illustration of his subscription to the ideas and conventions of the Enlightenment whilst formulating his revolution of their philosophical premises. Kant recognised that the classical ideal was untenable since aesthetical judgment is inescapably subjective. However, such subjectivity does not preclude judgment and, to make this judgment, Kant appropriates the term 'taste', which, as we saw in Chapter 1, was the device employed by the Enlightenment to retain aesthetic standards once classical objectivity had been rejected.

Kant distinguished the Pleasant or Agreeable, which, as a subjective sensation or feeling, arouses an interest or inclination in the subject, from the Beautiful, about which the subject is disinterested. This disinterest permits aesthetic judgment. Taste is the faculty of judging an object as it partakes of this disinterestedness, as it qualifies as Beautiful. The decisive fact about disinterestedness that enables it to permit judgment is that it "implies a ground of satisfaction for all men" and consequently the judgment of taste, accompanied with the consciousness of separation from all interest, must claim validity for every man, without this universality depending on Objects. That is, there must be bound up with it a title to subjective universality. (UK, 56: W V, 212)

It is the universality of this subjectivity that distinguishes the Beautiful from the Agreeable, but that it is subjective which distinguishes the Beautiful from the Good, which partakes of objective universality.

Though taste functions for Kant in a typical Enlightenment fashion its justification is radically far-removed from those current. To Kant, for the judgment of taste to be valid

there must lie at its basis some a priori principle. . .to which we can never attain by seeking out the empirical laws of mental changes. For these only enable us to know how we judge, but do not prescribe to us how we ought to judge.(UK, 149: W V, 278)

The empirical alternative is 'Hume's problem' in aesthetic guise. All claim to necessary universal agreement is groundless so that taste can only be held to be correct through the accidental fact that many people agree, which itself is only derivable from the "contingent similar organisation of the different subjects" (UK, 241: W V, 345–6) – that is, the Humean assumption of a passionately uniform human nature (see Part II). Despite Kant's enunciation of an a priori principle of taste he is committed, by virtue of his distinction between the Beautiful and the Good, to the position that this principle does not postulate universal agreement but rather only *imputes* it (UK, 62: W V, 216). The universality of the aesthetic judgment is only an Idea. It is regulative not constitutive:

the pleasure that we feel is, in a judgment of taste, necessarily imputed to every one else; as if, when we call a thing beautiful, it is to be regarded as a characteristic of the object which is determined in it according to concepts. (UK, 65: W V, 218)

We shall see, as stated above, that this notion of a regulative idea (the presence of which is indicated by the phrase 'as if') has a vital role to play in Kant's historical thought.

But before turning to Kant's view of history we should note some further instances of Kant's affinity to the Enlightenment and, by contrast, his distance from Romanticism and the Storm and Stress movement. For example, whilst "beautiful art cannot itself devise the rule according to which it can bring about its product" nevertheless "every art presupposes rules by means of which in the first instance a product, if it is to be called artistic, is represented as possible" (UK, 189: W V, 307). Although this only means that art is designed, what is significant is that for Kant it must not appear to be so – "beautiful art must *look* like nature" (UK, 188: W V, 307). This ability to be artistic, to give rules without seeming so to do, is the prerogative of genius. From this Kant proceeds to enumerate the familiar eighteenth-century depictions of the characteristics of genius. It possesses originality ("*everyone is agreed* that genius is entirely opposed to the spirit of imitation" (UK, 190: W V, 308, my emphasis)); it serves as a standard and, as a natural gift, the genius does not know how his 'art' came about and cannot reproduce it at will. All of which results in Kant's replication of the standard assessment, which Lessing's *Laokoon* (1776) had latterly striven to clarify, that poetry is the most worthy of all the arts (it sets the imagination free) and owes its "origin almost entirely to genius" (UK, 215: W V, 326). Kant's revindication of rules, in connection with genius, was hailed by Goethe as re-establishing the propriety of the term 'genius' against its trivialisation, since it had, through indiscriminate usage, come to warrant the abandonment of any constraint.[5]

To turn now to Kant's discussion of teleology, which is central to an appreciation of his view of history: Kant's analysis of teleology focuses on what can be broadly termed organisation − on the relationship of parts to a whole − "an organised product of nature is one in which every part is reciprocally end (*Zweck*) and means" (UK, 280: W V, 376). Kant distinguishes between Nature understood teleologically and understood mechanically. Though we should always endeavour to pursue mechanical explanation (efficient causation) as far as possible it is impossible to eliminate teleological explanation (final causation or explanation by means of purposes) even for something as 'simple' as a blade of grass. It is accordingly necessary as a fact of human nature (the constitution of the human cognitive faculties) to "seek the supreme ground of these purposive combinations in an original Understanding as the cause of the world" (UK, 326: W V, 410), wherein the unity of the teleological and mechanical principles are located in a supersensible substrate. But, it is again important to stress that this is a maxim of the reflective judgment and thus only subjectively valid. It is regulative and not constitutive since

we do not, properly speaking *observe* the purposes in nature as designed, but only in our reflection upon its products *think* this concept as a guiding thread for our Judgment. (UK, 312: W V, 399)

This same process is of course applicable to man. In terms of reflective judgment man is not merely an organised being but is also the ultimate purpose of nature on earth if nature is regarded as a teleological system (UK, 354: W V, 431). This ultimacy is derivable from man's unique property of being able to form a concept of purposes which he can systematise (UK, 349: W V, 427). This ultimacy thus rests in what man can do for himself and this aptitude Kant denominates 'culture'. This now is where Kant's theory of history (and politics) enters the scene since, as he puts it elsewhere, culture is the "genuine education (*Erziehung*) of man as man and citizen" (MAM, 62: W VIII, 116) or again, "it is man's predisposition to become civilised by culture" (AP, 185: W VII, 323).

In our treatment of Kant's understanding of history we shall confine ourselves to comments that pertain to our broad interests. The first comment concerns the

5. *Dichtung und Wahrheit*, Pt. 4, Bk. 19, tr. J. Oxenford, Vol. 2, p. 142. Cf. E. Cassirer, *Rousseau Kant and Goethe*, p. 87−8.

nature of Kant's interpretation of history. Here two features can be noted. One, history for Kant is teleological, it is purposive, but, two, this character, is only an attribution, it is a regulative Idea. This is made clear in the title of perhaps the best known of his historical essays – *Idea for a Universal History from a Cosmopolitan Point of View* (1785).

A second comment to be made follows on from this since it concerns the telos itself. For Kant the telos, the goal of history, is a cosmopolitan society existing in a state of perpetual peace. Such a condition is the only one that is consonant with man as a moral agent, as an end in himself. The chief attribution of man's moral agency is self-legislation. Accordingly, the State must be republican since only it is in conformity with man's freedom as a human being, with his equality with others as a subject and with his independence as a citizen.[6] The connexion between this telos and the teleological principle as a regulative Idea is that not only is it an interpretative perspective but also it is a depiction of man's destiny (as noumenon) which he should endeavour to realise. Our final two comments take up, firstly, this idea of an interpretative perspective and then, in conclusion, the question of the 'subject' of the realisation.

Kant's interpretative perspective, as the product of a regulative Idea, means that he is offering a reading of history *as if* the teleological principle was operative. There are two important aspects of this reading. Firstly, with regard to man it is transformist. Just as Kant's political thought owes much to Rousseau so his theory of history as exhibiting the transformation of man is greatly indebted (with open acknowledgment) to the Genevan. Man is held to undergo a change in the historical perspective. This for Kant is explicitly developmental (MAM, 59: W VIII, 115). The development consists in man's emergence from the 'womb of nature' to be a moral agent. Man's history can be read as a

transition from an uncultured, merely animal condition to the state of humanity, from bondage to instinct to rational control – in a word, from the tutelage of nature to the state of freedom. (MAM, 60: W VIII, 115)

Yet this is not a smooth road and this introduces the second aspect of Kant's reading of history, namely, the notion of Providence or unintended consequences. This notion, as we shall see, plays a significant role in both Hume and Hegel. Kant's most famous utilisation of this notion is in his *Idea for a Universal History*. There man is seen as activated by discord. Although

he wishes to live comfortably and pleasantly: Nature wills that he should be plunged from sloth and passive contentment into labour and trouble, in order that he may find means of extricating himself from them. The natural urges to this, the sources of unsociableness (*Ungeselligkeit*) and mutual opposition from which so many evils arise, drive men to new exertions of their forces and thus to the manifold development of their capacities. (IGW, 16: W VIII, 21)

---

6. *Über den Gemeinspruch: Das mag in der Theorie richtig sein, taugt aber nicht für die Praxis* (1793), tr. H. Nisbet in H. Reiss, *Kant's Political Writings*, p. 74 (W VIII, 290).

Similarly, although war is undesigned yet it is

perhaps a deep-ridden and designed enterprise of supreme Wisdom for preparing, if not establishing, conformity to law amid the freedom of states, and with this a unity of a morally grounded system of those states. (UK, 357, cf. AP, 183, "perhaps" is an addition in the Second Edition 1793: W V, 433, VII, 322)

There is then an important disjunction between what man intends and what he achieves. Though the achievements of men are thus unintentional when they are read within the teleological perspective of man's growth to culture a point or purpose can be discerned. A purpose that Kant attributes to Nature. Incidentally, Kant's use of conflict as the chief example of this disjunction between intention and achievement echoes the earlier argument of Adam Ferguson (and other Scots) which had so impressed Lessing.[7]

This view now leads to the concluding comment, that is, the 'subject' of the realisation of history. This notion of unintended consequences, working through conflict, entails that though man as an individual is disputatious, when considered as a species his development can be seen. Kant devoted considerable attention to both these propositions. In the *Idea for Universal History* he calls man a crooked piece of wood (*krummes Holz*) (IGW, 17: W VIII, 23) and in his essay *Religion innerhalb der Grenzen der blossen Vernunft* (1793) he devotes the opening book to a treatment of the problem of radical evil in human nature. This is a corollary of man's participation in both the phenomenal world of nature and the noumenal world of freedom. As a member of the former man is subject to the demands of his animal nature, to passions and inclinations, and in so far as man pays heed to these demands and not those of the moral law then he is corrupt or perverse (RGV, 377: W VI, 30). Thus that man is evil can mean only that he is conscious of the moral law and thus free but nevertheless in his conduct occasionally deviates therefrom (RGV, 379: W VI, 32). Yet, though the individual is inevitably prey to these tensions, the species, spurred by the offspring of these same tensions in the guise of conflict, as a species of rational beings, strives in "constant progress toward the good" (AP, 193: W VII, 333).

We can close our examination of Kant by returning to the relationship between Kant and Herder, this time in the context of their understanding of history. Kant reviewed in generally unfavourable terms the first two Parts of Herder's *Ideen*.[8] The general thrust of this criticism was that Herder was a dogmatist. More particularly, Herder's leitmotif, the notion of *Kraft* (organic force), could at best be only an 'Idea' (and then it would be unproductive), but Herder treats it unwarrantedly as constitutive and thus goes beyond experience. It will be recalled that Herder's notion of *Kraft* as an organic cosmic force was central not only to his

7. Cf. E. Flajole, 'Lessing's Retrieval of Lost Truths', *PMLA* (1959) 52–66; J.K. Riches, 'Lessing's Change of Mind', *J. of Theological Studies* (1978) 121–136.

8. A critique of Herder can also be seen in Kant's later essays MAM and RGV. Cf. H. Saner, *Kant's Political Thought*, p. 169.

theory of self and the human mind but also to his idea of *Humanität*, whereby each individual and cultural expression was worthy in its own right. Herder rejected Kant's idea of species as put forward in the *Idea for a Universal History*, because of its repudiation of this notion of intrinsic worth, and hence in Part II of the *Ideen*, he criticised Kant to this effect.

There is one passage in this debate upon which it will be profitable to dilate because of the wider issues that can be drawn from it. Kant in his rebuttal of Herder's argument that each man has his own measure of happiness cites the case of Tahitians —

Does the author [Herder] mean that, if the happy inhabitants of Tahiti, never visited by more civilised nations, were destined to live in their quiet indolence for thousands of centuries, one could give a satisfactory answer to the question why they bothered to exist at all, and whether it would not have been just as well that this island should have been occupied by happy sheep and cattle as by happy men engaged in mere pleasure.[9]

Here Kant's teleological conception with its utilisation of the perspective of the species to 'place' or evaluate the Tahitians and their 'uncivilised' order, is reminiscent of the Enlightenment's view (criticised by Herder) where history is seen in terms of the growth of reason, with ourselves as rational compared to the superstitious credulity of savages. Although, of course, Kant's criticism of the Tahitians for their happy indolence reflects his conviction that such a condition is a barrier to their achievement of freedom and rationality; an achievement only attainable, as we have seen, through 'labour', 'trouble' and 'exertion'. Accordingly, the Tahitian way of life cannot be universalised for this would mean that the species would not develop.[10]

In conclusion, we can see how this point pertains to Hegel. Although Hegel adopts an openly teleological view, which employs a universal perspective (*Geist*) to evaluate cultures, his idea of culture and its relationship to the contextualisation of human nature is, as we have already seen, indebted directly or indirectly to Herder. This debt expresses itself in Hegel's rejection of Kant's ethical theory as empty formalism. Thus whilst for Hegel all philosophers before Kant are inadequate (hence the exiguous treatment of Hume), because Kant truly was a Copernicus, nevertheless Kant himself is inadequate. He lacks the concrete historical dimension. Kant, as indeed he prided himself on being, is an *Aufklärer*. The man with whom he operates is ahistorical. This holds despite Kant's transformism. To repeat, this transformation is a regulative Idea. The anthropologist or historian must, as Kant himself did, start from the conceptualisa-

9. Tr. from Jenaische Litteraturzeitung (1785) in Beck, *Kant on History*, p. 50–1 (W VIII, 65). In his comments upon the literature spawned by the discovery of Tahiti Kant noted "The world would not lose anything if Otaheite perished", quoted in Saner, p. 236.

10. Cf. Grundlegung zur Metaphysik der Sitten (1785) (W IV, 423), tr. as *The Moral Law* by H.J. Paton, p. 90, where Kant refers to South Sea Islanders as an instance where talents go to rust in a life devoted to idle enjoyment.

tion of knowledge as adumbrated in the First Critique.[11] Each individual irrespective of time and place must cognise experience as experience in one way. This further entails, for Kant, a necessary separation of man, qua noumenon, from nature (society) and a complementary transcendental theory of the self. The only way then in the face of his rejection of these entailments that Hegel can still regard Kant's philosophy as epochal is if the grounds of knowledge, the categories themselves, are historical. The historicisation of human nature which Herder saw needs to be preserved within the philosophical revolution inaugurated by Kant.

11. Cf. Gregor, *AP*, Introd., p. x.

II. HUMAN NATURE AND SOCIETY IN HUME

INTRODUCTION

Against the background outlined in Part I, Hume's own thought will now be examined. This examination will be selective since it will focus on what Hume understands by human nature and how this understanding relates to his accounts of the make-up of society and of the differences that exist between societies. Within this focus special attention will be paid to the role that habit or custom plays in his thought; it provides a 'bridge' between his epistemology and his social philosophy and this application by Hume of his philosophical reasoning to society constitutes one of the dominant motifs in his endeavour to establish a 'science of man'.

What character Hume attributes to human nature – that above all it is constant and uniform – and what he holds to be constitutive of it, together with a sketch of the reasons why Hume should have upheld the view that he did, is discussed in Chapter 4. The consequences of his maintenance of this view is then considered in terms of what can be broadly called his conception of social cohesiveness, including as it does, inter alia, both his theory of justice and sympathy (Chapter 5). The extent to which Hume sees societies differing whilst abjuring relativism in any significant sense is discussed in Chapter 6. A concluding Chapter will draw together and develop the broad theme of the preceding Chapters by analysing in some detail particular passages to demonstrate that Hume does not subscribe to a contextualist theory of human nature.

Finally a stylistic point; due to the specificity of the focus the argument has an interwoven character. This require the introduction of issues at one point and their postponement until they can be considered at length in their own right.

56

The following abbreviations are inserted in parentheses in the text throughout this Part.

T   *A Treatise of Human Nature* (1739/40), ed. L.A. Selby-Bigge.
U   *An Enquiry concerning Human Understanding* (1748), ed. C.W. Hendel.
A   *An Abstract of a Treatise of Human Nature* (1740), in U.
M   *An Enquiry concerning the Principles of Morals* (1751), ed. C.W. Hendel.
P   *A Dissertation on the Passions* (1757), in *Works*, Vol. IV (1854).
N   *The Natural History of Religion* (1757), in *Hume on Religion*, ed. R. Wollheim.
D   *Dialogues concerning Natural Religion* (publ. 1779), in Wollheim.
H   *The History of Great Britain: The Reigns of James I & Charles I* (1754), ed. D. Forbes.
HE   *The History of England from the invasion of Caesar to the Revolution in 1688*, in one volume (1824).
L   *Letters*, 2 Volumes, ed. J.Y.T. Greig.
E   *Essays: Moral, Political and Literary* Individual Essays are abbreviated as follows:

    BGMR   *Whether the British Government inclines more to Absolute Monarchy or to a Republic* (1741).
    LP   *Of the Liberty of the Press* (1741).
    PS   *That Politics might be reduced to a Science* (1741).
    FPG   *Of the First Principles of Government* (1741).
    SH   *Of the Study of History* (1741).
    IP   *Of the Independency of Parliament* (1741).
    PG   *Of Parties in General* (1741).
    PGB   *Of the Parties of Great Britain* (1741).
    SE   *Of Superstition and Enthusiasm* (1741).
    DMHN   *Of the Dignity or Meanness of Human Nature* (1741).
    CL   *Of Civil Liberty* (1741 – original title, Of Liberty and Despotism).
    PD   *Of Polygamy and Divorces* (1742).
    Sc   *The Sceptic* (1742).
    El   *Of Eloquence* (1742).
    RPAS   *Of the Rise and Progress of the Arts and Sciences* (1742).
    NC   *Of National Characters* (1748).
    OC   *Of the Original Contract* (1748).
    PAN   *Of the Populousness of Ancient Nations* (1752).
    RC   *Of Some Remarkable Customs* (1752).
    BP   *Of the Balance of Power* (1752).
    IPC   *Idea of a Perfect Commonwealth* (1752).
    PrS   *Of the Protestant Succession* (1752).
    Int   *Of Interest* (1752).
    Mon   *Of Money* (1752).
    RA   *Of Refinement in Arts* (1752 – original title, Of Luxury).
    Com   *Of Commerce* (1752).
    ST   *Of the Standard of Taste* (1757).
    OG   *Of the Origin of Government* (1774 – published 1777).
    Sui   *Of Suicide* (publ. 1777).
    MOL   *My Own Life* (publ. 1777).

4. THE CONSTITUTION OF HUMAN NATURE

In his anonymous review of his own *Treatise of Human Nature*, Hume states that the author "purposes to anatomise human nature" (A, 183; cf. T, 263; T, 620; L I, 32) and in the important introduction to the *Treatise* itself Hume declares, in a striking military metaphor, that the aim of the work is "instead of taking now and then a castle or village on the frontier to march up directly to the capital, or centre of these sciences [logic, morals, criticism, politics] to human nature itself" (T, xx). This is to be accomplished, as the subtitle of the work notifies, by the experimental method, which means "that we are unable to go beyond experience" and "must therefore glean up our experiments in this science [of man] from a cautious observation of human life" (T, xxiii).

Thus human nature is (and remains) central to Hume's concern but what does this term mean for him? This question can best be answered by focusing upon what is, given Hume's programme as outlined above, its most important characteristic – its constancy (constructions from his writings that seem to belie this character will be examined in Chapter 7). This all important character plays a vital role in many aspects of Hume's thought but it may be illustrated by his conception of history.

Hume wrote a short essay – *Of the Study of History* – wherein his design was to recommend history to "my female readers", although the advantages he proceeds to outline that flow from its study are "suited to everyone" (E (SH) 558). These advantages are three-fold – "as it amuses the fancy, as it improves the understanding and as it strengthens virtue" (Ib., 560). Though, Hume was later to declare that this essay was "too frivolous" (L I, 168), and he did omit it from later editions of his *Essays*, nevertheless he here reflects a general eighteenth-century understanding of history.

History was a branch of literature and thus matters of 'interest' were at a premium. As Kames put it "the perfection of historical composition. . .is a relation of interesting facts connected with their motives and consequences"[1] and

---

1. *Sketches on the History of Man* (1774, 3rd Edit.), Vol. 1, p. 148. Cf. similarly Voltaire's opening comments to his *Essai sur les Moeurs* (1756).

58

Hume, himself, admitted of the first volume of his own *History* that he had therein entered "into no Detail of minute, uninteresting Facts" but rather had adopted his customary "philosophical Spirit" (L I, 193).[2] A corollary of this was the derogative dismissal of annalists or chroniclers because of their preoccupation with facts. Bolingbroke, whose delineation of history was contemporaneously influential, put this point graphically — "it is the business. . .of others to separate the pure ore from the dross, to stamp it into coin, and to enrich and not encumber mankind. When there are none sufficient to this task, there may be antiquaries, and there may be journalists or annalists but there are no historians".[3] Such comments have been seized upon by detractors of the eighteenth-century's sense of history from contemporaries onwards (recall Herder from Chapter 2). But, perhaps above its literary pretensions, history was seen to be an important vehicle for, in Hume's words, 'strengthening virtue'. This 'humanist' perspective (neatly encapsulated in perhaps the best known of Bolingbroke's remarks — "history is philosophy teaching by examples"[4]) is the real thrust behind the deprecation of antiquarians. To study the past for its own sake is an inferior and less worthwhile pursuit than its utilisation à propos contemporary concerns.

Though Hume's remarks on the scope and function of history — "the great mistress of wisdom" (H, 687) — are scattered through his *History*, his most famous or notorious pronouncements are those of interest here, since it is in these that the assumption (see later) of a constant human nature is exposed. These pronouncements are to be found in the Chapter on Liberty and Necessity in the *First Enquiry* (though the corresponding Chapter in the *Treatise* contains the same argument). In this Chapter Hume avers "it is universally acknowledged that there is a great uniformity among the actions of men, in all nations and ages, and that human nature remains still the same in its principles and operations" (U, 92) so it now follows

mankind are so much the same in all times and places, that history informs us of nothing new or strange in this particular. Its chief use is only to discover the constant and universal principles of human nature by showing men in all varieties of circumstances and situations and furnishing us with materials from which we may form our observations and become acquainted with the regular springs of human action and behaviour. (U, 93; cf. U, 34)[5]

2 Cf. from the *History* itself, "History also being a collection of facts which are multiplying without end, is obliged to adopt such arts of abridgement, to retain the more material events, and to drop all the minute circumstances which are only interesting during the time or to the persons engaged in the transaction. . .What mortal could have the patience to write or read a long detail of such frivolous events as those with which it is filled, or attend to a tedious narrative which would follow through a series of 56 years, the caprices of so mean a prince as Henry II" (HE, 143).

3. *Letters on the Study and Use of History* (1735), p. 37.

4. Bolingbroke, p. 18. Cf. H. Blair, "The general idea of History is a record of truth for the instruction of mankind", *Lectures on Rhetoric and Belles-Lettres* (1783), p. 482 or Hume himself "The object of. . .history is to instruct" (E (ST) 246).

5. As C.N. Stockton has noted Hume's practice conformed to this principle ('Economics and the

Whilst Flew is correct to draw attention to the 'classical' reference in this passage as a whole,[6] the important point about these pronouncements is the general understanding of history and human nature thereby implied. In the *Second Enquiry*, Hume gives an analogy which can be seen to be expressive of this understanding – "men in different times and places frame their houses differently" but because the purposes which they serve are "everywhere exactly similar" then "all houses have a roof and walls, windows and chimneys" (M, 33). This is an analogy (to the ubiquity of property laws) which permits a distinction between constants (roofs etc.) and the contingencies of time and place of (say here) the size, shape and fabric of houses. This distinction is vital. There is no attempt to avoid the evidence of the variety of fabrics etc., but within all this variety, there are roofs. The fabric only constitutes a house, and can only be understood as such, because it is put to constant uses. The roofs are constant because they pertain to universals (exactly similar purposes). Similarly, without these constant universals – "were there no uniformity in human actions" (U, 95) – then "it were impossible to collect any general observations concerning mankind"; more particularly, "what would become of history had we not a dependence on the veracity of historians according to the experience we have had of mankind" (U, 99; cf. A, 187; A, 197; M, 50; U, 121). Crucially, 'we' are able to have this experience because the principles of human nature are, as such, common to all and operate in a constant and uniform manner, so that the 'pastness' of what these historians relate is no obstacle to its comprehension. Human nature is not historically defined.

The uniform presence of these principles and the constancy of their operation means there is 'necessity' in human action, it is causally explicable by reference to these principles. No matter what variety of 'circumstances and situations' history reveals there still exists in human institutions and behaviour, by virtue of their being human, certain constitutive constancies, which render them explicable. These constancies are revealed in the experience of everyday life. As we will develop at length, these constancies within experience take the basic form of habitual expectations. It is from this experience that historical knowledge is made possible. Since we are able to understand what writers about, and in, the past tell

---

Mechanism of Progress' in D. Livingston and J. King, *Hume: a re-evaluation*, p. 297). For example: "This crisis [the Reformation] was now visibly approaching in Scotland; and whoever considers merely the transactions resulting from it, will be inclined to throw the blame equally on both parties; whoever enlarges his view and reflects on the situation will remark the *necessary* progress of human affairs and the operation of those principles which are inherent in human nature" (HE, 440, my emphasis). Cf. Paul H. Mayer who holds that Hume's practice in the *History* reflects a change, indeed "we have some reason for surmising that in the course of his historical investigations he had considerably modified his earlier belief in the uniformity of human nature and we find indications of a historical relativism", 'Voltaire and Hume as Historians' in *PLMA* (1958), p. 55. But even allowing for the tentativeness of this remark, the relativism that can be seen in Hume is present in his early work (see infra) and thus provides little evidence for modification. In addition, the *History* itself, as the quotation here demonstrates, can provide material for many interpretations.

6. *Hume's Philosophy of Belief*, p. 145 – 6.

us (history tells us 'nothing new or strange' about human nature – it does not upset our continually reinforced habitual expectations) history can be used to confirm our scientific conclusions. This is explicit. Hume remarks that the study of history "confirms the reasonings of true philosophy [the science of man]" when it shows the "original qualities of human nature", to wit here, that political controversies are subordinate to the interests of peace and liberty (T, 562). In a similar vein, in the key passage in the *First Enquiry*, Hume remarks that the historical record provides "experiments" that enable the "politician or moral philosopher" to fix the "principles of his science" (U, 93). There is accordingly nothing 'special' about history and this helps to explain the somewhat dismissive tone of Hume's comments about its 'chief use' (it is perhaps this tone as much as anything else that has given these remarks their notoriety).

It is necessary now to examine this universal constant more closely. What for Hume constitutes this constant?

There are a considerable number of references in Hume's writings where 'human nature' is synonymous with the human race, mankind or, explicitly in one place, "man in general" (T, 481). It is seemingly in such a sense that statements like the "Roman Emperors were the most frightful tyrants that ever disgraced human nature" (E (LP) 10) or that "enormous monarchies are probably destructive of human nature in their progress" (E (BP) 347) are to be interpreted. But, such usages do not, by any means, exhaust Hume's employment of the phrase.

Indeed, allowing some latitude by including the phrase 'human mind' (Hume in his discussion is clearly not simply dealing with physiological factors[7]) Hume uses the following terms in this connexion – Faculty, Property, Principle, Quality, Disposition, Propensity, Inclination, Structure and Capacity. Though some of these terms are technical,[8] it is improbable, in the face of such an array, that Hume was using them stipulatively. Nevertheless, some observations can be made. As just noted, Hume does subscribe to a faculty psychology or 'mental geography' – to an 'obvious' division of the mind into imagination, will, understanding and passions (U, 22–23), which has the consequence that "the faculties of the mind are supposed to be naturally alike in every individual" (U, 90).[9] True to his anatomical intent Hume does, in the *Treatise*, break down the passions into direct and indirect. This distinction when further analysed (T, 276–7) produces the following – desire, aversion, grief, hope, joy, fear, despair, security and pride, humility, ambition, vanity, love, hatred, envy, pity,

7. Cf. R.F. Anderson, *Hume's First Principles*, who takes 'human nature' to be the same as the human mind or the 'self' (p. 23) & T.E. Jessop, 'Some Misunderstandings of Hume' in *Hume*, ed. V.C. Chappell who takes 'human nature' to be "beliefs, emotions and reactions and the introspectively evident processes" (p. 42).

8. Cf. N.K. Smith, *The Philosophy of David Hume*, that Hume used the term 'principle' 'frequently' in the Newtonian sense of an ultimate (p. 55).

9. This is despite his criticism of 'ancient philosophy' for having recourse to faculties and occult qualities (see T, 224). Cf. P.S. Ardal, *Passion and Value in Hume's Treatise*, p. 81–3.

malice and generosity. All men are supposed to be susceptible to these feelings and, as such, they are constant constituents of human nature. This can be substantiated by noting what Hume has to say about just two of these — "can we imagine it possible that while human nature remains the same, men will ever become entirely indifferent to their power, riches, beauty or personal merit and their pride and vanity will not be affected by these advantages?" (T, 281).

Since this pertains to human nature as such it means that it holds good independent of specific societal context. Indeed, this independence is so marked that a traveller's report which did describe men as bereft of avarice and ambition would immediately be detected a 'falsehood' (U, 94; cf. U, 140). Of course, there are differences between men (and societies) but, significantly, Hume immediately follows this last quotation from the *Treatise* with the remark that any variation "proceeds from nothing but a difference in the tempers and complexions of men and is, besides very inconsiderable". He repeats the point later, "there are also characters peculiar to different nations and particular persons, as well as common to mankind. The knowledge of these characters is founded on the observation of an uniformity in the actions that flow from them" (T, 403). Thus, and this is an important point, the comprehension of these peculiar or variable 'characters' is still founded on knowledge of constant uniformity. This is the 'essence' of the necessity inherent in human behaviour. All human behaviour, even if it has a peculiar or local character, is comprehensible and explicable because, as human behaviour, it is constituted by 'regular springs' and 'constant and universal principles' which have uniform effects. It is here in accounting for these variable characters that the principle of habituation plays a crucial role — "are the manners of men different in different ages and countries? We learn thence the great force of custom and education which mould the human mind from its infancy and form it into a fixed and established character" (U, 95). The different manners of men in different ages and places (variables) are accordingly the habituation (constant principle) of particular contingencies. Uniformity is presupposed in variety. This point will be explored later.

We must now, however, return to our question, because we have not exhausted our examination of what according to Hume is a constant constituent of human nature. A reading produces the following universal attributions — sympathy and fellow-feeling (T, 318; T, 577; T, 618; M, 47; M, 51 etc.); fortification through unanimity (E (PG) 59); an assumption of resemblance between the experienced and non-experienced (U, 124); dissatisfaction with a short-falling from a standard (T, 372); benevolence and resentment, love of life and kindness to children (T, 417, cf. N, 31); arrogance and presumptuousness (E (RPAS) 127); a delight in liberty yet a submission to necessity (E (PD) 193); a craving for employment (E (Int) 309); credulity (T, 112); a seeking for society (T, 363; T, 402); personification (T, 224; N, 41); a diminution of aversion through familiarisation (T, 355); a despising of that to which one is accustomed (T, 291); stimulation in the face of mild opposition (T, 433); curiosity (T, 453); unpleasantness of too sudden a change (T, 453); a preference for the contiguous over the remote (T, 535); an addiction to general rules (T, 551); blaming the present and admiring the past

(E (PAN)451; H, 238); selfishness (T, 583; M, 46); principles of taste (E (ST) 249); a sense of morals (T, 619); a disapproval of barbarity and treachery (M, 111); a tenacity of memory (U, 119); an inclination to truth (T, 448; U, 119); shame in the detection of committing a falsehood (U, 119); imitativeness (E (NC) 207); a propensity to the marvellous (U, 127), to self-overvaluation (M, 86), to adulation (N, 86), to fame (M, 118), to divide into factions (E (PG) 56), to believe what is to the disadvantage rather than to the advantage of government (E (LP) 11) and to believe in an intelligent and invisible power (N, 97); and, finally and importantly for our purposes, the contraction of habits (U, 57; U, 160; T, 133; T, 179; T, 422 – 3; E (OG) 37).

This list is not exhaustive, since there are also a number of mental processes that Hume invokes, especially in the *Treatise*, nevertheless it gives an indication of what Hume regards as constituents as human nature, which, though distinguishable from 'original instinct[s]' are yet "general attendant[s] of human nature" (N, 97) and, as inseparable, can be justifiably regarded as 'natural' (cf. T, 484). Thus, whilst habitual action is not instinctive, human nature is such that men form habits so that this propensity is truly a constant, universal constituent.[10]

From these constant, universal and necessary principles it is possible to come to far-reaching conclusions, for example,

The different stations of life influence the whole fabric, external and internal; and these stations arise necessarily, because uniformly, from the necessary and uniform principles of human nature. Men cannot live without society and cannot be associated without government. Government makes a distinction of property and establishes the different ranks of men. This produces industry, traffic, manufactures, law-suits, war, leagues, alliances, voyages, travels, cities, fleets, ports and all those other actions and objects which cause such a diversity and at the same time maintain such an uniformity in human life. (T, 402; we shall have occasion to return to some of the points in this statement; the last phrase in particular is crucial)

Hence, Hume's conception of human nature is that it possesses certain constant and universal principles, 'regular springs', the operation of which are, as such, unaffected by history or, more generally for here space and time are co-relative, by different socio-cultural contexts. These contexts do provide evidence of diversity and variety but, decisively, they are not constitutive or definitive of human nature.

Although Hume is far from indifferent to the impact of these contingencies of time and place, he does not regard them as relevant to an adequate comprehension of human nature, for, despite these variations, "mankind are so much the same in all times and places". Here is a point of cardinal importance. Hume has a non-

10. Cf. T. Reid who whilst distinguishing habit from instinct (the former being 'acquired' rather than natural') nevertheless remarks "I conceive it [habit] to be part of our constitution, that what we have been accustomed to do, we acquire not only a facility but a proneness to do on like occasions", *Essays on the Active Powers of the Human Mind* (1788), Essay III, pt. 3 in *Works*, ed. W. Hamilton, p. 550. Before Hume, Bishop Butler (whose opinion of the *Treatise* the young Hume was eager to solicit) had stressed the capacity in human nature to 'finish' itself through acquiring habits *Analogy of Religion* (1736), Bk. 1, Chap. 5, paras. 15 – 16.

contextualist theory of human nature; man as the fit subject for science is not a local phenomenon only to be comprehended parochially but is a universal exhibiting necessary uniformities and constancies. It would be contrary to the Newtonian canon of economy (Rule 1) if these variations were not explicable by a few simple causes (cf. T, xxi; T, 282; A, 183) but had to be accounted for in their own various and specific non-subsumable constitutive terms (as is upheld by those contemporary philosophers who reject the adequacy or appropriateness of the 'covering-law' method of explanation in history). The fact that Hume's theory of human nature does not regard the diverse forms of social life as constitutive entails that this universality is, in Hegelian terms, abstract.

This point should not be misunderstood. To anticipate future argument (and as intimated in the Introduction), we can distinguish analytically three different (stipulated) positions with regard to social life and rationality (human nature); that of Hume which consists of a formal account of social life with a substantive theory of rationality; that of many modern analysts, which consists of a substantive account of social life with a formal theory of rationality, and that of Hegel, which consists of a substantive account of both social life and rationality. The formality of Hume's account of social life stems from its non-constitutive character with respect to human nature. The behaviour of men, though it takes place in diverse settings, can be understood and explained independently of these settings, because it instantiates universals. But, this very independence means that human nature is not historically or societally defined. Though man cannot be understood outside society, he can be understood without reference to the specific society in which he is found. Such specificity is irrelevant to the science of man. It is this relationship between human nature and society that makes the account of social life that Hume proffers formal.

There is, however, a further dimension. Though these principles, operations and springs (the passions (cf. U, 93)) in human nature are abstract, in the sense of pertaining regardless of specific context, this does not mean that what Hume, in fact, regards as constant is devoid of content. Rather, as the list just supplied indicates, Hume's delineation of the content, of what is constant in human nature, is extensive and reveals that human nature for him is no mere residual cipher, although such an ascription is implied by those recent commentators who wish to correct the common interpretation of Hume's theory of human nature as naively uniformitarian.[11]

---

11. Thus S.K. Wertz, 'Hume, History and Human Nature', *JHI* (1975), pp. 481–96, maintains (correctly) that constancy of human nature for Hume is a "methodological principle" and he criticises J.B. Black (*The Art of History* 1926) for not distinguishing between methodological and substantial uniformity and similarly D. Forbes (*Hume's Philosophical Politics*) maintains (also correctly) that the universal principles of human nature for Hume are abstractions from concrete variety (p. 119). Nevertheless, Hume did operate with a normatively loaded view of human nature and cannot be entirely excused from parochiality (but see infra). J. Burke also sees Hume as a relativist and not a uniformitarian but bases this on his emphasis on accidents in his actual narrative 'Hume's History of England', in *Studies in C18th Culture*, Vol. 7, pp. 225–250.

Again, due caution should be exercised. Though Hume's examples are often those of an eighteenth-century gentleman, and although, further, these often read as universal propositions (for example, "our forefathers being regarded as our nearest relations everyone naturally effects to be of a good family and to be descended from a long succession of rich and honourable ancestors" (P, 204)) it is important to note that they are only examples. Hume is concerned to explain individual and social behaviour by universal properties of human nature (in the above example by the operation of the principles of association) and, as such, in line with the formality of his account of social life, these properties could, in principle, equally well illustrate Amerindian customs (the implications of this indeed being the case will be examined later). Furthermore, it is a plausible conjecture, given the contemporary lack of awareness that there was any 'problem' to be associated with the comprehension of 'exotica' (also see later), that the suasiveness of Hume's argument would be enhanced by making the familiar (to his readers) conform to his system.

Hume's awareness of diversity (see Chapter 6) is too acute for him directly to universalise the prejudices of the eighteenth century. Yet, as the inclusion, in the list of constants, of 'taste', 'craving for employment', 'arrogance' etc. suggests human nature, for Hume, is no mere neutral residuum. This is not simply his parochiality coming through (though it is undeniably present) because it is a basic ingredient of his thought that human nature functions as a benchmark or normative principle (it is here, if anywhere, that Hume himself derives an 'ought' from an 'is'). It is because the specificity of societal location is irrelevant to the comprehension of human nature, or to the 'findings' of the science of man, that Hume is able to evaluate social practices, so that they can, for example and in particular, be legitimately condemned as superstitious. This is Hume's substantive theory of rationality – some social practices are more rational, or more 'in tune' with human nature, than others.

Before concluding this Chapter it is perhaps worthwhile to heed the meaning of certain passages in which Hume draws attention to the *in*constancy of human nature. The most notable of these passages is when he remarks – "human nature is too inconstant to admit of any such regularity [confining itself to one passion]. Changeableness is essential to it", (T, 283; cf. U, 97). This remark occurs in Hume's treatment of certain properties of human nature. But, we have already seen, that human nature is a complex of passions, qualities, propensities etc. and the inconstancy here referred to is *between* these elements. What changes and what differentiates individuals (or indeed a single individual at one time from another) is the precise combination of these elements. Changeableness is essential therefore as other constituents are essential, it is a common fact, illustrative once more of basic uniformity.[12]

12. Cf. Wertz, *JHI*, p. 492–3 who after citing some passages from the *History* (H, 508, 533) fails to see how Hume's discussion of inconstancy here parallels the discussion in the *Treatise* and is in fact part of human nature's constancy so that it does *not* thus "fall outside the uniformity which Newtonian science and philosophy demand". This is seen by O. Brunet, *Philosophie et Esthétique chez D. Hume*, p. 131.

Now, in conclusion to this Chapter, we can, at the risk of being over-schematic, briefly inquire as to why Hume should have upheld this belief in the constancy of human nature. This inquiry can utilise a number of approaches. First, Hume's text can be studied and his argument on this issue analysed. From this perspective Hume seems to regard constancy as a fact of nature. A fact derivable (observable from the experience of 'human life') from the uniformity and steadiness of the operation of the human mind. Though these observations ('experiments') reveal variation this, as we have seen, still bears witness to the necessity implicit in human behaviour. This does mean that any evidence, howsoever bizarre, that presents itself to Hume can be labelled as a 'variable' or, indeed, as we noted above, can be dismissed outright as a falsehood and in no way, accordingly, can the status of his attribution of constancy to human nature be assailed.

If this is so it is possible to move to a second approach and ask why should Hume have upheld this non-contextualist view of the relationship between human nature and society. One way of answering this in principle is to demonstrate that no alternative was conceptualised. As we argued in Part I much of Herder's importance stems from his being one of the first to cast serious doubt on this understanding of human nature (of course Vico had done so earlier but he remained an isolated phenomenon). It is not strictly possible, therefore, to hold that Hume *could* not have arrived at a understanding of human nature which did not perceive it in constant/non-contextual terms. But, this approach does still have an explanatory force. By paying attention to the issues to which Hume was addressing himself, to the arguments he was trying to refute, to the resources that were actually available to him it is possible to recreate in a large measure his own perspective.[13]

Within that perspective it is possible to indicate that this understanding of human nature was taken for granted. Thus, for example, Hume's development of Locke and Hutcheson, and his critiques of the Cartesians, that is, his general philosophical milieu was one that regarded history indifferently.[14] Indeed, any epistemology which seriously believed that its findings were culture-bound, and did not pertain to Man, would have seemed self-defeating. It is, of course, a nodal point of Hegel's endeavour to incorporate a dynamic so that the human mind itself truly has a history; man has not always apprehended the world in the

13. For the elaboration of this approach see several writings by Q. Skinner, in particular 'Meaning and Understanding in the History of Ideas', *HT* (1969) 3 – 53; also J. Dunn, 'The Identity of the History of Ideas', *Philosophy* (1968) 85 – 116 and J. Pocock, 'Languages and their Implications' in his *Politics, Language and Time*, pp. 3 – 41.

14. For Descartes' attitude to history see his *Discourse de La Méthode* (1637), Pt. 1 and for Locke's doubts as to its reliability see *Essay concerning Human Understanding* (1690), Bk. 4, Chap. 16, Sect. 11. It is true that in the eighteenth century there did develop a counter-offensive to restore some degree of certitude to history's findings. See R. Mercier, *La Réhabilitation de la Nature Humaine 1700 – 50*, esp. p. 171ff. on Buffier; also see G. Pflug, 'The Development of Historical Method in the Eighteenth-Century', *HT* (Beiheft 11, 1971) 1 – 23. Hume himself discussed the probabilistic nature of historical knowledge in his examination of miracles (U, 117 – 141).

same way. A further example is Hume's own stress on the utility of history, with his downgrading of 'mere facts', because such a stress is evidence that he shares the assumptions of a prevalent disposition or approach to history. Fundamental to such assumptions was the constancy of human nature.[15] Aside from the persistence of the general 'humanist' or homiletic approach to the past mentioned above, the maintenance of this assumption was greatly aided by the fact that much of the history that was written was characterised by its polemical or political nature. Thus, the preoccupation by English historians of the seventeenth and early-eighteenth century with the Ancient Constitution and extent of the Norman Conquest is explicable by its perceived bearing on contemporary political practice and policy or, again, the dispute in France, ostensibly over the Frankish kings, between the supporters of the *thèse nobiliaire* and the *thèse royale* is to be accounted for by its relevance to the contemporary debate as to the proper relationship between the crown and the members of the 'robe and sword'. The upshot of all this was to take for granted that 'pastness' made no difference to the explanation and comprehension of human action. What men now consider to be rational (that, for example, government must be based on a contract) will always have been so considered (thus there was an original contract).[16]

If Hume merely reflected a commonplace when he characterised human nature as constant "in all nations and ages" then this now regresses into a second way of answering the question, namely, why was it a commonplace? Why did Hume's referents make the same assumptions as he did? This answer is obviously a study in its own right. Meinecke's explanation is that Hume's 'reason' was bound within the Natural Law tradition. In this respect Hume always remained within the Enlightenment, since, Meinecke believes, in the Enlightenment itself it was the dominance of *naturrechtliche Denkweise* which imprinted this conviction as to the stability of human nature and human reason.[17] In other words, Hume and his contemporaries were operating within a 'tradition' which postulated a constant human nature. There are two aspects to this explanation – one methodological, the other substantive.

Methodologically what is involved is an understanding of a tradition as constituting a 'paradigm' *within* which discourse takes place, and, the further claim, that *all* thought is in this way paradigmatic.[18] The paradigm within which Hume,

15. Cf. Bolingbroke, *Letter* III. To Blair knowledge of human nature is necessary to fulfil the end of history in order to "account for the conduct of individuals and to give just views of their character", *Lectures*, p. 483.

16. Cf. M.P. Thompson, 'A note on "Reason" and "History" in late seventeenth-century Political Thought", *Political Theory* (1976) 491 – 504. Hume himself is not exempt – "the maxim of preserving the balance of power is founded so much on common sense and obvious reasoning that it is impossible it could altogether have escaped antiquity" (E (BP) 344).

17. *Die Entstehung des Historismus*, 2nd Edit., pp. 199, 3.

18. For a discussion of the uses of paradigms in the history of thought see Pocock, 'Languages and their Implications'. I have examined (and employed) the notion in a different context, see C.J. Berry, 'On the Meaning of Progress and Providence in the Fourth Century AD', *Heythrop Journal* (1977) 257 – 70.

and his referents, thought of human nature, the questions they asked and the assumptions they made, held it to be constant. This was not an issue to be addressed but an assumption more or less unconsciously made. This understanding of Hume's thought on this matter permits a number of consequences to be drawn. In particular, it serves to bring out its historical specificity. Hence, the possible objections that Hume's use of the term 'human nature' was guileless and unthinking, and thus that little of import hinges upon the point, or that it is a mere contingent accident of only minor significance to the comprehension of Hume's thought that he wrote before this topic became problematic, ignore the weight that such an assumption about human nature bears. The fact that Hume's understanding of human nature was contemporaneously orthodox is significant because this is evidence of his acceptance of a particular view of human nature. This acceptance is an important fact about *Hume's* thought, which can only be dismissed at the cost of dismissing Hume as a *historical* actor.[19]

Substantively, in broad terms, Meinecke's argument, though unacceptable in much detail, is here persuasive. Of course, in this he is not alone since the argument is also found in Dilthey and Cassirer amongst others. By Natural Law in the Enlightenment is meant not, as Becker would have it,[20] the Thomistic theistic variant but rather the Ciceronic deistic variety, according to which there is "one law, eternal and unchangeable binding at all times upon all peoples".[21] Again, we can make two brief points about this.

One, Cicero was one of the Enlightenment's most popular authorities. Aside from the far from insignificant fact that Cicero's writings were a staple part of the intellectual diet of the education of the period, his appeal derives partly from the exemplary force of his career[22] and partly because he represented what Peter Gay has called 'pagan humanism', through asserting "man's importance as a cultivated being, in control of his moral universe".[23] With respect to Hume himself, the content of Cicero's thought is not unimportant. There is a well-known letter from Hume to Hutcheson, written when the *Treatise* was nearing completion, wherein he reveals that he had Cicero's *Offices* "in my Eye in all my Reasonings" (L I, 34). Certainly, the distinction between a common nature shared by all men and more particular individual variations is enunciated therein by Cicero (Book 1, Chap. xxx).

Two, it is the case that Natural Law theorising did receive a reformulation in the seventeenth century, the thrust of which was to make man's reason the

19. Many interpretations of Hume fail to attend to the historically specific situation of his thought. It is defensible to use Hume's ideas as part of the author's *own* argument but it is a mistake to attribute *that* argument to Hume. H.H. Price is at least clear as to what he is doing (regardless of how the tenor of his comments are taken) "My remarks are addressed to those who write about him as philosophers, not as mere historians of philosophical literature" and Hume's argument is explicitly to be used as a means to help us understand the world, *Hume's Theory of the External World*, pp. 3, 4.

20. *The Heavenly City of the Eighteenth-Century Philosophers.*

21. *De Republica*, III, xxii, tr. G. Sabine & S. Smith, p. 216. Cf. *De Officiis*, I, xxx; III, v – vi.

22. Cf. G. Gawlick, 'Cicero and the Enlightenment', *VS* (1963) 657 – 682.

23. *The Enlightenment: The Rise of Modern Paganism*, p. 107.

touchstone of rectitude. If, after the Reformation, God was no longer a neutral 'umpire', to whom appeal could be made, then another source of appeal had to be established. Reason was held to possess the requisite universality. The work of Grotius is often interpreted in this manner and regardless of the accuracy of this interpretation[24] his work (and that of his successors) did provide a back-drop to the thought of the Enlightenment. As a generalisation, as we saw in Part I, the Enlightenment persisted with this need for a criterion by which to 'order' different circumstances. Though the Natural Law tradition was clearly not homogeneous, it is defensible to maintain that the constancy of human nature remained a postulate and that European thought operated with this postulate. This holds even for Hobbes, who whilst rejecting reason as the seat of constancy replaced it with a 'scientific' theory of the passions, which was held to hold as such for all men as particles of matter in motion.

Although Hume is often interpreted as having destroyed the epistemological basis of Natural Law[25] nevertheless, as we have seen, he still subscribes to an interpretation of human nature as constant. He is in this precise sense working within this ultimately Stoic tradition; a tradition that was strong in Scotland due to its transmission through Scots Law.[26] But, the language of Natural Law contains many idioms. The fact that Hume's thought has for one of its assumptions a Natural Law commonplace tells little substantively about the uses to which it will be put or the propriety of labelling him a Natural Law theorist. It remains, nonetheless, an important 'prop' of this study that Hume's belief that human nature is constant and uniform informs his thought as a whole.

This brings us back to our starting point, namely, that Hume believed that the evidence supplied warranted this interpretation of human nature as comprising constant 'principles and operations' and 'regular springs' (the passions). To ask further the 'reason' for these constants Hume regards as illicit, since they are in the Newtonian sense an ultimate. This means that in his own eyes his theory of human nature can be used to explain but cannot itself be explained.

24. For Grotius as founder of the modern theory of Natural Law see A.P. D'Entreves, *Natural Law*, Chap. III. But see for an interpretation of Grotius as a late medievalist C. Edwards, 'The Law of Nature in the Thought of Hugo Grotius', *JP* (1970) 784 – 807. Grotius, Pufendorf et al. were more than sincere believers, since for all their emphasis on man's reason their systems themselves depended for their cogency on God's existence; see L. Krieger, *The Politics of Discretion: Pufendorf and the acceptance of Natural Law.*

25. Cf. T.R. Hanley's comment affixed to H. Rommen, *The Natural Law*, "Hume's psychological analysis of causation flatly constitutes an affront to and mutilation of the human intellect", p. 114n.

26. Cf. A.L. Macfie, 'The Scottish tradition in Economic Thought', repr. in his *The Individual in Society*, pp. 19 – 41. Also D. Forbes, *Hume's Philosophical Politics*, p. 17f.

5. SOCIAL COHESIVENESS

Thus far we have seen that Hume allots to a human nature a number of properties and processes and, since these apply uniformly, because necessarily, their application is independent of their specific social location. However, they clearly do not apply independent of society because, from the list of 'constants', it is apparent that they do relate to other men. We have now to consider Hume's treatment of inter-human relationships, of society. Our theme shall be the factors that Hume sees as responsible for social cohesiveness and how this is related to his understanding of human nature. More precisely, we are seeking the answer to the question: to what view of society does Hume subscribe given his view of human nature as constant and uniform?

This answer will require a somewhat lengthy introduction. The preliminary task is to identify the link between this theme and human nature. It is here that an examination of the role that custom or habit plays in Hume's thought is instructive. First, the propensity to contract habits is a constant property of human nature. In essence, upon the observation of a series of constant conjunctions human nature is such that it is able to form habits of association.[1] This ability is an ultimate with which we must remain content.[2] It is just 'there' in human nature. The presence of this ability or propensity to contract habits is of crucial importance in Hume's entire thought.[3] This we shall illustrate with brief reference to his account of causation. But, first Hume's associationism needs to be explained.

1. Cf. J. Beattie to whom custom or habit is one of the principles of association (others are resemblance, contrariety, contiguity and cause) *Elements of Moral Science*, 3rd Edit. (1817), Vol. 1, pp. 79 – 82. He repeats the point in his *Dissertations Moral, Critical and Literary* (1783), pp. 78 – 96; as does his colleague A. Gerard, *Essay on Genius* (1774), Pt. 2, Sect. 2.

2. Cf. A. Leroy, *La Critique et la Réligion chez David Hume*, p. 219.

3. Hume's stress on habit has led to comparisons with Pascal – J. Laird, *Hume's Philosophy of Human Nature*, p. 41; R.W. Church, *Hume's Theory of the Understanding*, p. 47. Whilst Pascal casts doubt on an easy distinction between nature and custom (see *Pensées*, esp. 93 on Brunchswicg's numeration) Hume, as Laird points out, sees habitual association as applying to all mental connextions. This means that it is a constituent of human nature; an "instinct" as Hume on occasion refers to it (U, 68; U, 167).

Locke, having rejected innate ideas (see Chapter 1), declared that experience was the source of knowledge (*Essay concerning Human Understanding*, 1690, Book II, Chapter 1, Section 2). Experience was gained in two ways — through sensation and reflection; the latter being the ideas the mind obtains by reflecting on its own principles within itself (*Essay* II; 2; 4). Both sensation and reflection are sources of 'simple ideas' and in both instances the mind is passive. However, with these simple ideas the mind has the power to form them into 'complex ideas', which are, Locke admits, infinite, though reducible to modes, substances and relations (*Essay* II; 12; 3). Much eighteenth-century philosophy took upon itself the task of smoothing out the apparent ambiguities in Locke's account, especially the role assigned to the mind's activity; a task that in France led to theories of education and progress, especially in the work of Helvétius and his successors. Hume, himself, belongs in this post-Lockean tradition and he explicitly says that he is trying to rescue the term 'idea' from Locke's misleading usage (T, 2n).

The relationship between simple and complex ideas was to provide the focus for associationism. Locke, himself, added a chapter to Book II of the fourth edition of the *Essay* entitled 'Of the Association of Ideas'. The subject of this chapter is an explanation of the occurrence of error. Locke maintains that amongst our ideas there is a "natural correspondence or connexion" but that there is also a connexion "wholly owing to chance or custom" or, indeed, education (*Essay* II; 33; 5). These latter factors are responsible for giving "sense to jargon, demonstration to absurdities and consistency to nonsense, and is the foundation of the greatest, I almost said of all, the errors in the world" (*Essay* II; 33; 18).

It should be noted, however, that in his *Some Thoughts concerning Education* (1693) Locke put forward a much more positive view of custom in the guise of education; habits should be woven "into the very Principles of his [the child's] Nature" (Section 41). Indeed, the principles of association are decisive to this end — "by repeating the same action, till it be grown habitual in them, the Performance will not depend on Memory, or Reflection the Concomitant of Prudence and Age, and not of Childhood, but will be natural in them" (Section 62). Though the link between Helvétius is here evident it must be observed, firstly, that Locke retains "native Propensions" (Section 97) so that education is responsible for "Nine parts out of Ten" of what men are (Section 1) and, secondly, that the influence of this pamphlet on this score (as opposed to its detailed prescriptions on child-rearing) was limited.[4]

The subsequent history of associationism in eighteenth-century thought is beyond our purview but the endeavour of Hume to unite associationism with a

---

4. For this (and generally, though he does not discuss Locke's treatment of custom as between the *Essay* and the pamphlet) see J.A. Passmore, 'The Malleability of Man in Eighteenth-Century Thought' in E.R. Wassermann, ed., *Aspects of the Eighteenth-Century*, pp. 21–46. Also M. Mandelbaum, *History, Man and Reason*, pp. 150–1.

Newtonian methodology (economy of causes) was not his prerogative alone,[5] and we might also add that a number of Locke's successors accepted the *Essay's* view that custom was a source of error.[6] As we have stated Hume connects custom and association but he is concerned to demonstrate that there can be no knowable 'natural' source of connexion. The full importance of this will become apparent but clearly 'custom' now has a wider scope; it cannot simply be confined to explaining the occurrence of error.

To Hume, given that the principle of innate ideas is false (T, 160), the data of the human mind are comprised of 'perceptions', which he divides into 'ideas' and 'impressions' (T, 1). These differ solely as to their degree of vivacity with simple impressions always taking precedence over their correspondent ideas, so that all our simple ideas proceed from impressions (T, 5). These simple ideas can be separated and reunified by the faculty of imagination. However, this faculty is not capricious in its operations, since it is guided by "some universal principles which render it, in some measure, uniform with itself in all times and places". There is in fact a "gentle force, which commonly prevails", to wit, "an associating quality" whereby simple ideas regularly fall into complex ones (T, 10). An example Hume supplies of this phenomenon is the familiar one of the similarity of languages.[7] Hume proceeds to give three principles of association – resemblance, contiguity of time and place and cause and effect (T, 11). The last of these is especially important in Hume's own argument and we shall now, as promised above, examine this argument briefly.

We can commence by returning to our starting point, to custom as a principle of human nature. In, perhaps, his most explicit avowal of this point, Hume declares that habit or custom is a principle of human nature "universally acknowledged and which is well known by its effects" (U, 57). The 'effects' cited here are the customary transition of the mind in expecting heat from flame or the future to be like the past (and, elsewhere, importantly, linking certain motives with certain human actions and characters (T, 404)). The presence of this ability since it is the basis of reasoning (T, 149), judgment (T, 147) and belief (T, 114) is of crucial importance in Hume's philosophy of mind and, indeed, more generally, custom is declared to be the "great guide of human life" (U, 58; cf. A, 189).

What is important at this juncture are the links in Hume's thought between custom, cause and uniformity. If our knowledge is derived from perceptions, which are discrete particulars, then it follows that what is not perceived cannot be known. Thus, of course, Hume's corrosion of much of the hitherto solid subject-matter of philosophy – natural causation and power, self, substance, rational moral distinctions. For Hume strictly a priori "anything may be the cause or effect of anything" (T, 249), yet the world appears in experience as orderly and not

---

5. D. Hartley's *Observations on Man* (1749) is perhaps the most notable – see Chapter 1 for the statement of his intention and the enunciation of his methodology.

6. See F. Hutcheson, *Essay on the Nature and Conduct of the Passions and Affections* (1728), esp. p. 127 but passim. For further references see Laird, *Hume's Philosophy*, p. 40.

7. Cf. Hutcheson, *Essay*, p. 10 – 11.

capricious; it exhibits regularity. Accordingly, it is to experience that this regularity must be traced. It will be seen that the effective basis of such order is customary expectation or belief that indeed the future will be like the past, that "like objects placed in like circumstances will always produce like effects" (T, 105), which is to say that "nature will continue uniformly the same" (A, 188). This must be the product of custom (it is "deriv'd entirely from habit" (T, 134)) for Hume has shown that such uniformity can emanate neither from demonstrative reasoning nor probability (T, 89 – 90).

It is, crucially, this expectation that nature will behave uniformly that underlies the belief in causation, which alone can take the mind "beyond experience" (T, 74) –

All those objects, of which we call the one *cause* and the other *effect* consider'd in themselves, are as distinct and separate from each other as any two things in nature, nor can we ever, by the most accurate survey of them, infer the existence of one from that of the other. 'Tis only from the experience and observation of their constant union, that we are able to form this inference; and even after all, the inference is nothing but the effects of custom on the imagination. (T, 405; cf. T, 103)

The regularity apparent in experience, due to the habitual character of the connexions, enables reality to be distinguished from fiction. In addition to the operation of memory, whereby "we form a kind of system" consisting of what is remembered, together with "present impressions", the mind –

finding with this system of perceptions, there is another connected by custom, or if you will, by the relation of cause and effect, it proceeds to the consideration of their ideas; and as it feels that 'tis in a manner necessarily determin'd to view these particular ideas, and that the custom or relation, by which it is determin'd, admits not of the least change, it forms them into a new system, which it likewise dignifies with the title of realities. (T, 108)

Though such are indeed "nothing but ideas" yet by virtue of their "force and settled order, arising from custom and the relation of cause and effect, they distinguish themselves from other ideas, which are merely the offspring of imagination" (T, 108).[8]

8. Clearly Hume's references to 'imagination' are ambiguous (cf. N.K. Smith, *The Philosophy of David Hume*, p. 459ff. H.H. Price, *Hume's Theory of the External World*, p. 15 – 16). In the one case, imagination is the basis of all inference (including causal) but, in the other, it is the source of 'mere ideas' which are to be contrasted with those arising causally. However, Hume does make the distinction explicit: "I must distinguish in the imagination betwixt the principles which are permanent, irresistable and universal; such as the customary transition from causes to effects, and from effects to causes; And the principles which are changeable, weak and irregular. . .The former are the foundation of all our thoughts and actions so that upon their removal human nature must immediately perish and go to ruin. The latter are neither unavoidable to mankind, nor necessary or so much as useful in the conduct of life" (T, 225). The latter sense is apparently elsewhere denominated 'fancy', the 'trivial suggestions' of which are contrasted with the "understanding, that is to the more general and more establish'd properties of the imagination" (T, 267), though one of these suggestions (now only "seemingly trivial") is the remedy to 'total scepticism' (T, 268).

In essence, therefore, it is because men, through custom, invariably associate discrete but repetitive experiences that the world is believed to be orderly. It is true that later in *Treatise* (in Book 1, Part 4) Hume does put forward the 'philosophical' argument that this orderliness cannot withstand the operation of the 'understanding' (T, 193) so that the existence of a continuing world outside our perceptions is in consequence problematic. However, there is no need here to follow Hume's argument. Suffice it to say that 'life' does not depend on the outcome of reasoning; nature triumphs. More particularly, the fictive capacity of the imagination, supplemented by memory, partakes of sufficient vivacity to produce the *belief* in the continuing existence of external bodies and represents the practical force of human nature in resolving "the manifold contradictions and imperfections in human reason" (T, 268).

We are now, finally, in a position to begin our discussion of the major theme of this chapter – social cohesiveness. It is a cardinal feature of Hume's philosophy that his theory of the 'external world' includes human activity – "there is a general course of nature in human actions as well as in the operations of the sun and the climate" (T, 402–3) so that, as we have already indicated, "no union can be more constant and certain than that of some actions with some motives and characters" (T, 404). This brings us back to Hume's treatment of human nature and its constancy.

On the basis of a constant human nature two points follow – one, this is, as we saw in the last chapter, how knowledge of any human practice, including that recorded by history, is attainable and, two, that human nature is constant is the assumption made in human practice itself. It is the latter of these which must now engage our attention.

The presupposition that makes social life possible is the expectation that the future will be like the past. This location of the possibility of social life, the cohesion of society, in custom will now be explored. Since this cohesion is based on custom or habit it also means, as we shall see, that it is based on internal, that is, mental or moral principles. To set the scene, as it were, we can at this juncture give an illustration of Hume's position in operation – "A prisoner who has neither money nor interest discovers the impossibility of his escape as well as from the obstinacy of the gaoler as from the walls and bars with which he is surrounded" (T, 406; U, 99, identically). Hume's point is that the regularity apparent from experience to the effect that the weight of the stone in prison-walls is immoveable by human strength alone is no different than the regularity apparent from experience concerning the behaviour of gaolers. Both of these regularities are constraints. What is of importance here is not only Hume's argument that "natural and moral evidence cement together" so that "we shall make no scruple to allow that they are of the same nature and deriv'd from the same principles" (T, 406) (to wit, custom) but also the repercussions that this has on Hume's understanding of the constituency and cohesiveness of social life.

This understanding will be examined in three broad areas: (I) a discussion of the place of 'general rules' in Hume's philosophy embracing, as it does, his theories of justice, property and government; then (II) a discussion of 'natural' social bonds in the form of familial affection and sympathy; and finally (III) a discussion of the role that Hume allots to 'manners', together with a concluding analysis of the significance of 'internality' in Hume. This third area will lead on to Chapter 6 and the discussion of Hume's account of social diversity.

I

Justice is an artificial virtue. This is the keystone of Hume's social and political philosophy. In outline his argument is that justice is a convention which arises from the inconveniences that ineluctably follow from the "selfishness and confin'd generosity" of men when coupled with "the scanty provision nature has made for his [man's] wants" (T, 495). As a convention it means that justice is not the immediate spontaneous product of natural sentiment but is the product of rules − hence the artificiality. These rules arise from the universal experience of the combination of selfishness and scarcity and their function is to restrain the passions in order to maintain society, since without them society "must immediately dissolve" (T, 497).

The motivation of justice is thus a concern for the public interest as well as one's own (T, 496). It is the fusion, in other words, of individual and collective rationality. This fusion, the non-existence of which Hobbes' depiction of the State of Nature as "solitary, poor, nasty, brutish and short", was designed to demonstrate, has been one of the abiding problems of 'modern' political philosophy. Hobbes' own answer was the ability of Leviathan, "that mortal God", to strike terror into the heart of everyman, which was effective because Hobbes had previously located the springs of human behaviour in a mechanistic and deterministic psychology. Hume's answer is two-fold; the operation of sympathy together with an insistence upon the inflexibility of general rules. This latter aspect will be discussed first.

The significance of these rules, and their inflexibility, can be seen in Hume's discussion of single acts of justice, which frequently (even) might appear to be contrary to the Public Interest. Hume believes this perspective is false because "however single acts of justice may be contrary either to public or private interest "tis certain that the whole plan or scheme is highly conducive or indeed absolutely requisite, both to the support of society and the well-being of every individual" (T, 497). In developing this theme Hume makes the important point (to which we shall return and upon which considerable weight will be placed) that it is through the convention of justice, a supposed sense of common interest, that any individual acts "in expectation that others are to perform the like" (T, 498). Once exceptions are made to the rules,[9] when they are flexible, then justice in the form of such expectations will break down and if justice breaks down then society breaks down or ceases to cohere. It is noteworthy, and another point to which

---

9. Cf. Hume's criticism of Cyrus (M, 111) for allowing the individual case to over-ride the general function of "general, inflexible rules, necessary to support general peace and order in society".

we shall recur, that the 'natural virtues' of pity etc. cannot fulfil the necessary task of social cohesion. In addition, since justice is fundamental to social existence, Hume believes all other conventions, including fidelity, obligation and rights generally, depend on its presence.

But, before developing these points it will be helpful to examine more closely, if schematically, what Hume means by 'general rules'. He declares it to be a principle of human nature that men are "mightily addicted to general rules" (T, 551). Hume's basic explanation of why such general rules are formed, and how they do influence conduct, is "habit and experience" (T, 147). This now connects Hume's discussion with the broad themes of his thought. General rules, in other words, are formed on the basis of expecting past occurrences to continue (cf. T, 362). This gives them a legislative function. General rules and custom are able to over-rule the passions (M, 95n). In particular, they restrain the "avidity and partiality of men" thereby promoting the constancy of expectation requisite for social cohesion (T, 532). This is an ability, so Hume believes, that increases with the development of society, and it is a belief that we will take up later. General rules, when based on "general and authentic operations of the understanding (T, 150) guide "wise men" and permit them to identify prejudices (themselves imaginative general rules) which prevail among the "vulgar". This is yet another point to which we shall return in the context of Hume's theory of rationality. A final function that Hume allots to general rules (and reflection thereon) is the correction of the senses in perception.[10]

To return now to justice: we have seen that justice is a convention necessary to support society. Men agree to restrain themselves by general rules and, for these to be effective, they must be inflexible. We stated in passing that, to Hume, property rights are dependent upon the presence of justice and, as such, he believes that for property to be stable it too must be fixed by general rules (T, 497). Hume's treatment of property will now be examined to the end of highlighting the importance of custom in the theory and also thereby demonstrating that the property relation is internal or mental and, as such, part and parcel of Hume's general position on the constitution and cohesiveness of society.

This examination will start by picking up a seemingly obscure point, namely, Hume's explicit references to causation in the context of property.

These references occur in three places. First, in Book II of the *Treatise*, where Hume, in fact, initially mentions property. There he defines property as "such a relation betwixt a person and an object as permits him, but forbids any other, the free use and possession of it, without violating the laws of justice and moral equity" (T, 310). This relation is a "particular species of causation" because, regardless of the theory of justice held (natural or artificial), the proprietor has the "liberty" "to operate as he pleases upon the object" and to reap advantages from it. The second reference occurs in Book III of the *Treatise*. There a definition of possession as "not only when we immediately touch it [anything] but also

10. This point had been made by Bishop Butler. *Analogy of Religion* (1736), Bk. 1 and Chap. 5, para. 6.

when we are so situated with respect to it, as to have it in our power to use it; and may move, alter or destroy it, according to our present pleasure or advantage" is immediately reported to be a relation which is "a species of cause and effect". Whereupon property, designated as "nothing but stable possession", is "to be considered as the same species of relation" (T, 506).

The final reference is to be found in the *Dissertation on the Passions* (a representation of Book II of the *Treatise*) which was first published in 1757, although the passage here in question was only included in a note appended to the 1760 edition. Hume there declares that "to be the proprietor of anything is to be the sole person who, by the laws of society, has a right to dispose of it and to enjoy the benefit of it" and such disposal and enjoyment "produces, or may produce, effects on it, and is affected by it. Property therefore is a species of causation" (P, 206).

The replication of terminology in these references is sufficient to dispose of any doubts about the deliberateness of Hume's remarks. What, then, does Hume mean by saying that property is a species of causation?

Though the answer to this question can be divined from the *Treatise*, Hume's fullest account of his position occurs in the later *Dissertation* (although its appearance in only later editions of that work suggests that he was aware of the somewhat cryptic nature of his remarks). Since property is defined as a *relation*, it follows that the answer to the above question hinges on Hume's account of relation or the association of ideas. Of the three principles of association – resemblance, contiguity, causation – the last is the most extensive. For Hume two objects are causally related when one is the cause of the existence of another, of the action or motions of the other and also when one has the power of producing a motion or action in the other (T, 12). It is in this last sense that property is a species of causation for "it [property] enables the person to produce alterations on the object and it supposes that his condition is improved and altered by it" (P, 206).

Now what is of general importance here is that in the *Treatise* Hume goes on to remark that causation as understood in this last sense may be observed to be "the source of all the relations of interest and duty by which men influence each other in society and are placed in the ties of government and subordination" (T, 12). As, for example, when a master has the power of directing the actions of his servant, that is, the master merely needs to exercise his will to bring about his end. it is this sense of cause as power, and its explicit application to 'social' relationships, that ties in with property, and moreover, explains Hume's claim that this relation is "the most interesting of any and occurs most frequently to the mind" (P, 206).[11]

Our property is something that we are able to do with what we will, is the power of using an object. The importance of 'power' here, and likewise the importance of defining possession as more than immediate tangibility, is that there

---

11. Passmore dismisses this declaration as a mere idiosyncracy on Hume's part not seeing how it does belong to Hume's chief preoccupations *Hume's Intentions*, rev. ed., p. 4.

is built into the notion of property a temporal dimension. Hume, in fact, declares that "property being produced by time is not anything real in the objects but is the offspring of sentiments on which time alone is found to have any influence" (T, 509) (the reference to property not being 'real' will be taken up shortly). Time operates "gradually on the *minds* of men" so that indeed "nothing causes any sentiment to have a greater influence upon us than custom" (T, 556, my emphasis). The temporal, and thence customary, element can also be seen in Hume's definition of property as "nothing but stable possession" and elsewhere as "constant possession" (T, 491; T, 503; T, 504n) and "fixed right" (T, 491).

Recalling that for Hume "the idea of cause and effect is derived from experience which informs us that such particular objects, in all past instances, have been constantly conjoined with each other" (T, 89 – 90), there is accordingly an implicit tie-up between, one, property and cause; two, custom and cause ("the mind is determined by custom to pass from any cause to its effect. . .their constant conjunction in past instances has produced such a habit in the mind" (T, 128)) and now, three, property and custom. Seeing property in the context of this complex of relationships helps to explain why it, for Hume, is an internal relation.

Property is 'nothing real in objects' in the same general way that causation is not a 'real' relation but "belongs entirely to the soul, which considers the union of two or more objects in all past instances. Tis here that the real power of causes is placed along with their connexion and necessity" (T, 166). More particularly, in the case of property this is so because the "sensible qualities" of any object continue "invariably the same while the property changes" (T, 527). Whereupon it follows that "property must therefore consist in some relation of the object", that is, a relation between objects and "intelligent rational beings" which means that "it is therefore in some internal relation that property consists" (T, 527).[12] It is an internal relation because its defining quality of constancy is a habitual mental relation. From this perspective it is now possible to look briefly at the well-known relationship, in Hume's thought, between justice and property.

Since property is an internal relation it follows (to Hume) that external relations, such as occupancy do not themselves constitute property. Occupation only "causes" property by having an "influence on the mind, by giving us a sense of duty in abstaining from that object", in other words, via justice (T, 527). Thus, as Hume had commented earlier, a man's property as the relation of an object to him is not "natural" but "moral and founded on justice" (T, 491). Hume is explicit that property is incomprehensible without "any reference to morality or the sentiments of the mind" (T, 515, cf. T, 523) and so it is that all the definitions of property given above refer to the 'laws of justice' or their equivalent.

Hume is here attacking Locke's theory of property.[13] Locke had held that a

---

12. Cf. T, 326, where animals are held to be incapable of right and property and thus the causes of their pride lie solely in the body and "can never be plac'd either in the mind or external objects".

13. Cf. J. Moore who 'suggests', in the light of Hume's early exposure to legal theory as a student,

man had property "in his own person" and also in whatever he "hath mixed his labour with" (*Second Treatise* (1689), Sect. 27). But neither of Locke's definitions square with Hume's own relational analysis. For Hume the property relation depends on the existence of other rational beings, who have instituted conventions to effect stability. In contrast, Locke's theory is individualist par excellence for in neither of his definitions do other rational agents directly figure, and, as such, it follows, on Humean premises, that Locke has merely provided a definition of possession and not property.[14]

Furthermore, Hume's subsumption of the property relation under that of causation entails (on his analysis of the genus) that the 'elements' are separable (cf. M, 26). This has a number of consequences. It is indeed because men can be separated from their property that instability arises (given scarcity and confined generosity). Locke, in other words, conflates what Hume considers to be "three different species of goods" – internal satisfaction of our minds, external advantages of our body and enjoyment of acquired possessions (T, 487). Another consequence of this separability is that the property relation, as a species of causation, comprises constant conjunction. Thus the earliest reference to property in the *Treatise* is as an example of the "perfect relation of ideas" whereby the "mention of property naturally carries our thought to the proprietor and of the proprietor to the property" (T, 310). That is, property is a species of causation as a natural relation, as producing an "union among ideas" (T, 94; T, 170). D.D. Raphael after drawing attention to Locke's discussion of the possibility of morality becoming a science 'capable of demonstration", wherein he cites, as an example, the relationship between property and justice (*Essay* IV; 3; 18), observes that just as Hume's general theory of causation is an attack on rationalist accounts of that relation so his theory of property is here an attack on Locke's rationalist pretensions in this quarter.[15] Finally, another consequence of he thesis of the separability of property concerns Hume's account of the principles of its distribution. Here Hume implicitly, though obviously, attacks Locke's 'labour theory'. We do not join our labour to a thing, but, rather, what

---

that his theory of causation is an attempt to produce a comprehensive response to the theory of power and property outlined in Locke's epistemology and in his political theory, 'Hume's Theory of Justice and Property', *PS* (1976), p. 115.

14. It is true that there are 'natural' limitations to property acquisition which are other-regarding (Sects. 31, 32, 36, 37) but these do not enter into the *definition* of property. Locke was exceptional in deriving private property without recourse to compact or consent, so that, in the sense that these practices point to other agents, Hume is here (as he acknowledged (M, 123n)) in line with Grotius and Pufendorf. On Locke's premises he has not confounded property and possession because the *right* to appropriation is enjoined morally by man's God-given free agency (his natural liberty) – on this point see M. Seliger, *The Liberal Politics of John Locke*, p. 194. These points are developed in C. Berry, 'Property and Possession' in J. Pennock & J. Chapman, eds., *Property*, pp. 89 – 100, on which I have drawn in the foregoing paragraphs. Locke's theory of property is discussed again in Chapter 11 infra.

15. 'Hume's critique of Ethical Rationalism' in W.B. Todd, ed., *Hume and the Enlightenment*, p. 18.

we do is make an alteration upon it (T, 505 – 6n; M, 126n). This alteration is a relation and this is, as we have seen, central to Hume's definition of property as a species of causation. In addition, Hume's general account of the principles of distribution is that they are "fix'd by the imagination or more frivolous properties of our thought" (T, 504n) and this accords with the basic theory of causality as the association of ideas in the imagination (T, 12). Thus, Locke's theory here is an example of the acquisition of property by accession, which itself is "nothing but an effect of the relations of ideas and of the smooth transition of the imagination" (T, 510n). We shall see that Hume's critique of Locke's theory of property is closely connected with his critique of Locke's theory of contract and that central to both critiques is Hume's own theory of justice.

Given that for Hume property is a mental relation and is dependent on justice then it is to be anticipated that justice itself will partake of a similar mental quality. Justice, as we have seen, is a convention, which takes the form of general rules that can only fulfil their function if they are inflexible, since only then are circumstances such that, to requote, "every single act is performed in expectation that others are to perform the like". Such expectations are so basic that only then will society cohere. Such expectations furnish the mutual expectations of a common sense of interest. This is established through "repeated experience" which is self-supporting, because "this experience assures us still more, that the sense of interest has become common to all our fellows and gives us a *confidence of the future regularity* of their conduct: And 'tis *only* on the *expectation* of this, that our moderation and abstinence are founded" (T, 490, my emphases). Accordingly, within a society all men in all their operations work on this assumption; thus, for example,

The poorest artificer who labours alone *expects* at least the protection of the magistrate to insure him the enjoyment of the fruits of his labour. He also *expects* that when he carries his goods to market and offers them at a reasonable price, he shall find purchasers and shall be able, by the money he acquires, to engage others to supply him with those commodities which are requisite for his subsistence. In proportion as men extend their dealings and render their intercourse with others more complicated, they always comprehend in their schemes of life a greater variety of voluntary actions, which they *expect* from the proper motives, to cooperate with their own. (U, 98, my emphases)

Society coheres then, for Hume, because of the presence of uniformities or regularities, of expectations deriving either directly from human nature, as we shall see in the cases of familial affection and sympathetic association, or indirectly, as in the case of justice. To have expectations capable of supporting actions depends on their having been constantly experienced, which is to say on them being habitual.

This, above all, is why Hume's social and political thought is conservative. If society depends on constancy, on habitually sanctioned expectations, then any 'break' or flexibility undermines the cumulatively acquired cohesiveness. Any innovations should be adjusted to the "ancient fabric" and "preserve entire the chief pillars and supports of the constitution'' (E (IPC) 499). If men are unable to form habits, then they will be unable to act in the foreknowledge of the actions of others and without this there can be no justice and thence no society. Justice is a universal habit – every society has the same rules (M, 33). These are the three indispensable principles of society (the rules of justice which, by virtue of their indispensability, are entitled to be called 'laws of nature') namely stability of possession; its transference by consent and the performance of promises (T, 526), and none of these is possible if habitual expectations are not built up. Thus Hume's conservatism is intrinsic[16] to his thought as a whole, since these expectations are basic to all knowledge, physical as well as moral.

This last point can be reinforced and clarified by noting, more particularly, Hume's employment of the principle of habit.[17] Habit, for Hume, operates on two levels. At a basic level there is what Hume calls "a general habit" (U, 114n). It is a necessary, uniform principle accounting for order and coherence (the uniformity of nature) in both the natural and social world. Thus, to utilise Hume's own example, the prisoner knows from experience (constantly confirmed habits) that prison-walls are too thick and prison-guards (given the lack of means to corrupt them) too zealous to permit his escape. But, the operation of the principle at this level in no way precludes (indeed it is presupposed in) the formation of more particular (social and individual) habitual behaviour patterns. For example, both the burglar and the police know habitually from constant conjunction that breaking glass makes a noise even though their 'professional habits' are very different.

The argument here pertains directly to Hume's comments on uniformity and variety discussed in the last Chapter. What history reveals are the 'varieties of circumstances', which is to say the particular habits, but because these habits are built up from regularities consequent upon the necessary relationships between man and his circumstances (the above 'laws of nature') then they will reveal the 'regular springs' and 'constant and universal principles' of human nature. Thus it is that evidence of variety is simultaneously evidence of uniformity.[18]

16. Cf. S. Wolin who draws attention to the importance of custom in what he terms Hume's "analytical conservatism", indeed, he aptly names it "social cement" but he does not develop the case for intrinsicality, 'Hume and Conservatism', *APSR* (1954), p. 1015. The argument for intrinsicality in the text is to be distinguished from that of D. Livingston and his general notion of 'past entailment', see, *inter alia*, 'Hume's Conservatism' in *Studies in C18th Culture*, 7, pp. 213–233.

17. Cf. H.H. Price (*External World*, p. 57) who, because of the fundamental importance of habit in Hume, questions if they "really are habits in the ordinary sense of the word". Though Hume may, indeed, use 'habit' with considerable latitude; this is a consequence of his thought and it is not incidental that it features so prominently in his social philosophy. This is seen by H.B. Acton, 'Prejudice', *Revue Internationale de Philosophie* (1952) 323–336.

18. This simultaneity is missed by G. Vlachos in his interpretation of Hume, since it is a prominent motif in his account that Hume's thought contains two contradictory methods: the one analytic and psychological emphasising the uniformity of human nature; the other concrete and sociological emphasising the variety of human nature, *Essai sur la Politique de Hume*, p. 115ff., 149, 232. G. Giarrizzo sees the tension between uniformity and variety dominating Hume's thought, *David Hume Politico e Storico*, p. 18, 29, 77.

Hence we can see, once again, the importance to Hume of allowing the ability to contract habits to be a universal constant property of human nature. This is a point of undoubted far-reaching importance in his thought as a whole. In his rejection of rational or natural necessity Hume was able, as we have seen, to explain the impression of coherence in this world through invoking the principle of custom. This principle is able to function in this way because it is anchored in human nature and is thus constant and universal. This anchorage in a non-contextualist theory of human nature explains, as will be illustrated, how in Hume's use of habit as a positive political principle, in his rejection of rationalistic and individualistic theories of politics, he is able to remain unconcerned with the societally specific and substantive questions of what these habits are and what effect their particular contraction has on the thus specified individual.

We can now continue our analysis of social cohesiveness by examining what Hume has to say about the origin and maintenance of government and its corollary the dismissal of the idea of a Social Contract. Hume Opens his essay *Of the Origin of Government* with the statement that "man, born in a family, is compelled to maintain society from necessity, from natural inclination and from habit" (E (OG) 35). We shall examine the role of the family and natural inclination and their connexion with habit later. Hume believes that such original familial groups could subsist without government but, of course as we have seen, they cannot subsist without justice – "though it be possible for men to maintain a small uncultivated society without government, 'tis impossible they should maintain a society of *any kind* without justice" (T, 541, my emphasis). Hume, in the *Treatise*, in accord with well-established convention, refers to America for verification of this hypothesis (T, 540).

How and why then do governments arise? In the *Treatise*, Hume provides a 'philosophical' account of the origin of government. Here the disposition of the imagination (a uniform trait of human nature) to prefer the contiguous (present advantage) to the remote (long-term benefit) is a source of disorder which is remedied by having a few men (governors) have for *their* contiguous interest the observation of the general rules of justice. These same few being indifferent to the rest constrain them to "a like regularity". Hume also provides a historical account of the origin of government. Here governments are said to "arise from quarrels" between different societies (T, 540; cf. E (OG) 37). Since war cannot be waged effectively without some one person being in charge such a contingency thrusts upon this person the role of leader (which is Hume's explanation of why governments are originally monarchical). The original establishment of government was thus, in 'fact', "formed by violence and submitted to from necessity" (E (OC) 461). Once government has been established, however, it becomes susceptible to the operation of the constantly present propensity in human nature to form habits – "a constant perseverance in any course of life produces a strong inclination and tendency to continue for the future" (T, 133). In this instance, a people growing accustomed to the rule of a particular man, and his successors, come to regard this situation as 'lawful' regardless of origin, even if that be usurpation or conquest. In short, "habit soon consolidates what *other* principles of human nature had imperfectly founded; and men once accustomed to obedience never think of departing from that path in which they and their ancestors have *constantly* trod" (E (OG) 37, my emphases). Such habitual recognition is moreover necessary to provide cohesiveness and stability to any society of any cultivation (that is, having a government) since,

human society is in perpetual flux, one man every hour going out of the world, another coming into it, it is necessary, in order to preserve stability in government, that the new brood should conform themselves to the established constitution, and nearly follow the path which their fathers, treading in the footsteps of theirs, had marked out to them. (E (OC) 463)

The need for stability in government is directly pertinent to its chief function – the execution and decision of justice (T, 538), that is, making men adhere inflexibly to the general rules. Government, as we have seen, and will note again below, is connected to the degree of cultivation and also to population size. On a small scale agreements to the mutual satisfaction of the participants can be carried out for "'tis easy for them to know each others mind" (T, 538) but, on the large scale, men are less able to be sure that "others will perform the like", that their expectation of the other's behaviour will be borne out. Government, by providing stability (it has the sanction of punishment at its disposal which works necessarily because it is part of the 'course of nature' in human affairs that men will avoid pain – see later), permits the establishment of such expectations so that large scale schemes, such as bridge-building, canal digging etc., can be effected (T, 539).

Though the location of the function of government in the provision of stability is a commonplace (Hume even uses the Lockean terms of 'remedying inconveniences' (T, 538)) his account of the *origin* of government is used to criticise the account proffered by the Contractarians. This criticism is part of a wider animus.

To elucidate if briefly: the Social Contract fell out of favour in the eighteenth century in so far as it was interpreted as a historical occurrence.[19] The increasing awareness in the eighteenth century of history as evidence, that we charted in Part I, consequent upon their modified Lockeanism, made many theorists disavow notions like the Social Contract and the State of Nature, because there was no evidence for their occurrence. The thought of Adam Ferguson is symptomatic, "if there was a time in which he [man] had his acquaintance with his own species to make. . .it is a time of which we have no record".[20] Though the seventeenth century, not without ambiguity, held or used these notions to arrive at a theory of the legitimate relationship between government and its subjects, the eighteenth century rejected them, because of this very ambiguity.[21] This is im-

19. I here utilise some material from my article 'From Hume to Hegel: The case of the Social Contract', *JHI* (1977) 691 – 703.

20. *Essay on the History of Civil Society* (1767), ed. d. Forbes, p. 6.

21. Though Hobbes and Locke refer to America, such references are independent of their argument. Hobbes admitted that there was never "a time in which mankind was totally without society"

portant because, as the very title of Hume's essay *Of the Original Contract*, indicates the question of the Social Contract thereby collapsed into an untenable historical theory of the original contract of government. Hence, an intrinsically de iure theory of legitimacy was dismissed on de facto grounds. To anticipate our discussion in Part III, we can here state that part of Rousseau's significance stems from his reformulation of the Contract as *theory*, and it was this theory that Hegel attacked. Accordingly, though Hume and Hegel both attack the idea of a Contractual origin of government their own positions are far from identical.

However, we must look at Hume's actual argument here more closely. The contract is "opposed by experience" (H, 225n); it is historically untenable.[22] Government arose by accident and was maintained not from consent, as such, but habit. In addition to this 'historical' argument Hume also supplies a 'philosophical' argument (explicitly in *Of the Original Contract*) to show the conceptual inadequacy of the Contract. This argument is based on Hume's position that justice is an artificial virtue and that it is absolutely necessary to society and upon which, consequently, other artificial virtues like fidelity and obligation are dependent. They are artificial, like justice, and for similar reasons, because they are not the spontaneous product of human nature but are the offspring of conventions.

One consequence of regarding fidelity as conventional is that it renders redundant the Contractarian argument that endeavours to make promises the basis of allegiance, of the obligation to obey government. Both fidelity and obligation have the same origin "the general interests or necessities of society" (E (OC) 468) so that there is no reason to subordinate one to the other. Moreover, it is possible to argue that because government provides sanctions to enforce fidelity then, in this regard, promise-keeping "is to be consider'd as an effect of the institution of government and not the obedience to government as an effect of the obligation of a promise" (T, 543). Indeed, as a final blow, Hume remarks that even if by some chance there was a situation where promises were unknown nevertheless government (in "all large and civiliz'd societies") would still be necessary (T, 546).

Again Locke is Hume's principal target (he is referred to as "the most noted of its [Contract] partisans" (E (OC) 473)). This critique of Contract is directly connected to the critique of Locke's theory of property noted above. Locke saw the

(quoted in J. Watkins, *Hobbes's System of Ideas*, p. 72) and for Locke's ambivalence see R. Ashcraft, 'Locke's State of Nature Historical Fact of Moral Fiction', *APSR* (1968) 898 – 915. Pufendorf is explicit that the State of Nature is an imaginative conception and "never actually existed", *On the Law of Nature and Nations*, tr. C.&.W. Oldfather, Bk. 2, Chap. 2, para. 2. The norm, however, was to take the history seriously, cf. M.P. Thompson, 'A note on "Reason" and "History" in late seventeenth century Political Thought', *Political Theory* (1976) 491 – 504.

22. Hume allows that the 1688 Revolution is a "singular exception" to the observation that revolutions are "commonly conducted with violence, tumult and disorder". But, although such violence is evidence against the view that there was an 'original contract' in its absence Hume is not committed to any acceptance of Contractarianism (HE, 868).

purpose or end of government as the preservation of property (*Second Treatise*, Sects. 124, 128, 221). This must mean that property is antecedent to government or civil society. Prior to this, in the natural condition of man (the State of Nature), there is justice and men enjoy property, both in their own persons and in the products of their labour, independently of any human artifice. But, for Hume as we have seen, men cannot co-exist without justice and this is a human artifice. Similarly, property, as a 'moral relation' between rational beings, is founded on justice and is not, as Locke's theory so interpreted holds, antecedent to human convention.

Finally, in this Section we can appreciate the significance of Hume's well-known remark that "it is therefore on opinion only that government is founded" (E (FPG) 29; cf. E (BGMR) 51). It is only opinion that can explain how the few can manage to govern the many, since in terms of strength the latter are all-powerful. Hume analyses the notion of 'opinion' into two kinds – of interest and of right, which is itself subdivided into of right to power and of right to property – that together constitute "the original principles of government" (E (FPG) 31) and which, as such, are presupposed by the principles of fear, self-interest and affection. These three 'secondary' principles are by themselves insufficient, because for some magistrate effectively to instil fear enough people need to be of the opinion that his edicts should be executed; without this opinion he is just another individual like any other. Similarly neither self-interest (the expectation of reward) nor affection, because they are both partial in their scope, can ever generate the authority needed for government over *all* members of a society; they can only operate once authority has been established.

A further aspect, and one that is especially significant in the present context, to this account is Hume's evocation of antiquity. Men in "all nations" are so attached "to their ancient government" that "antiquity always begets the opinion of right" (E (FPG) 30). The basis for this is to be found in habit, as we saw when discussing Hume's account of the origin of government. Men get accustomed to a certain state of affairs and the custom itself, its endurance or persistence, establishes a momentum of its own so that it becomes the effective basis of government. In his *History* Hume explicitly connects this argument, that opinion is the basis of government, with the "reverence" that the "multitude" thereby owe to authority; their conviction that they owe the duty of allegiance (H, 686).

More generally, Hume is putting forward here a principle of prescription. Indeed, in his discussion of property he explicitly establishes this point when he declares that "long possession or prescription" conveys a "title to any object" (T, 508). The same holds for political authority. Government is "sanctified by time" (H, 225n). Men now "willingly consent because they think that from long possession he [their prince] has acquired a title" when, in effect, this is the mere habituation of a state of affairs that originated in violence and was submitted to out of necessity (E (OC) 461; cf. HE, 868). The principle also applies more particularly to the Hanoverian succession (E (PrS) 498). Paul Lucas has demonstrated, chiefly with reference to Burke, but also to Hume in passing and by implication, the originality of such a conception of prescription, where longevity itself was legitimating and origins irrelevant.[23] There is, therefore, no need (contrary to Locke – *Second Treatise*, Sects. 1, 3) to locate the 'original of political power' in order to understand it 'aright'.

II

We can now turn to the second area identified above – the role of natural bonds in social cohesion. Here there are two points of concern – the family and the role of sympathy.

We have already quoted Hume's judgment that man is born in a family. He is thus born into a social state (T, 493). This simple point is fundamental to Hume's critique of individualism. If man is a social being then his experience is social and thus, given Hume's programme of basing the 'science of man' on the observation of experience, it follows that man is to be studied as a social animal.[24]

The basis of the family is two 'natural' principles – "the natural appetite between the sexes" (T, 486) and "natural affection", which is a technical term defining the "original instinct" shown by parents to their offspring (T, 486; cf. E (DMHN) 86; P, 212). It is, perhaps, worthy of note, in passing, that Hume here refers to both parents (T, 570; T, 518), though men seemingly need the added incentive of assurance of paternity, which is Hume's explanation of the demands for chastity and modesty in their women (T, 570). This 'natural affection' is the concomitant of the helplessness of the human infant. To this affection can be added the biological fact (also adumbrated by Locke – *Second Treatise*, Sect. 80) that conception can occur whilst the existing progeny are still 'helpless' and parentally dependent (M, 36). The family is thus an enduring institution, which gives it an important role as an agent of socialisation.

From what we have already discussed about the necessity of justice for 'any kind' of social existence, and from what we have just noted about man's familial condition, it should follow that justice must be a feature of familial relationships. Hume does on one occasion explicitly avow this – "every parent in order to preserve peace among his children must establish it [stability of possession] that these first rudiments of justice must everyday be improv'd, as the society enlarges" (T, 493; cf. T, 500; M, 21). Hume's position here seems redolent of patriarchalism, that is, families were the first civil societies (indeed Schochet attributes what he terms "anthropological patriarchalism" to Hume[25]) but Hume explicitly rejects the thesis that fathers have their authority from their biological role; instead, due to the origin of government in quarrels, it is their strength and ability which ensures them of this role.

23. 'On Edmund Burke's doctrine of Prescription', *Historical Journal* (1968), esp. 60–63.

24. Cf. R.D. Cumming, *Human Nature and History: A study of the development of Liberal Political Thought*, Vol. 2, p. 161. Cumming also maintains that Hume's theory is (in a general sense) relational – see Vol. 2, p. 164ff.

25. *Patriarchalism in Political Thought*, p. 278. Cf. H, 225, "patriarchalism is nonsense".

Although familial relationships are rule-governed and this is constitutive of their cohesiveness, because the 'natural bonds' alone are insufficient ('natural affection' is not reciprocal nor can it eliminate sibling rivalry), Hume is careful to argue that these relationships did not originate in convention. A father does have the *duty* to take care of his children but he also has a "natural inclination" to it (T, 519; cf. T, 478); indeed, "to kill one's own child is shocking to nature" (E (PAN) 399). This 'inclination', a natural objective fact about human nature, is necessary for the sense of obligation to arise in the first place, since "no action can be requir'd of us as our duty unless there be implanted in human nature some actuating passion or motive capable of producing the actions" (T, 518) and to locate this in a sense of morality per se is tautologous.[26]

This statement broaches two issues of wider significance. One, it intimates Hume's well-known theory of action, whereby reason is inert, and two, more immediately pertinent, it involves Hume's account of 'natural virtues'. Since these issues are connected a brief account needs to be given of both.

Hume opens Book III of the *Treatise* with an argument to the effect that moral distinctions are not derived from reason. The argument, in essence, is that morality has an influence on human passions, on the actions and affections of men (T, 457), and these are "original facts and realities, compleat in themselves" (T, 458). Reason, however, of itself is confined to the comparing of ideas and the discovery of relations and, as such, it can only direct judgments and never influence our actions (T, 414); to Hume, "actions may be laudable or blameable, but they cannot be reasonable or unreasonable" (T, 458) (it is a category-mistake to think otherwise). Reason is thus inactive or, as Hume puts it in his celebrated phrase, "reason is, and ought only to be, the slave of the passions, and can never pretend to any other office than to serve and obey them" (T, 415). If reason, or ideas, are not the source of moral distinctions that can only, on Hume's analysis, leave impressions and the necessary conclusion that "morality therefore is more properly felt than judg'd of" (T, 470).[27]

Accordingly, Hume's argument not only about the duty of fathers to their children being insufficient without some actuating principle (affection or passion) but also, by implication, for *all* virtues is central to his whole system of thought. This now raises the question of the relationship between artificial virtues (which are by definition necessary for society's cohesiveness) and Hume's theory of action. As we shall see this is where sympathy comes into play but, first, the basis of the distinction between artificial and natural virtues must be examined.

We have already seen why justice is artificial but we shall now see why it is a *virtue*. For Hume, it is the case that "the chief spring and actuating principle of

26. Hume does allow that a sense of duty can constitute a motive but he incorporates this into his theory since such circumstances are parasitic upon the existence of other motives, whose meritorious effects wish to be emulated (T, 479).

27. Cf. J. Harrison, *Hume's Moral Epistemology*, for a detailed examination of Hume's argument.

the human mind is pleasure or pain" (T, 574; cf. T, 188) and that "the mind by an original instinct tends to unite itself with the good and to avoid evil" (T, 438); good and pleasure and evil and pain are equivalents (T, 439; cf. T, 276). Now justice, because it maintains society, and because the maintenance of society is in our own interest (we are social beings), is pleasing or produces satisfaction and, due, as we shortly see, to the mediation of the principle of sympathy, this pleasure extends beyond our own direct interest to embrace the public interest. This is the source of the attachment to justice of moral approbation and its denomination as a virtue (T, 499 – 500). Conversely, injustice, because it is prejudicial to society and because through sympathy injustice to *anyone* is displeasing then it is regarded as evil and denominated a vice.

In the course of this general argument Hume distinguishes three meanings of the term 'natural' – as it is the opposite of miracles, of the unusual and of artifice (T, 474). We have already seen that the essence of artificial virtues is that they are conventional, that is, do not arise spontaneously. There are, however, sentiments in human nature, such as love, pity and gratitude (E (OC) 466), which are antecedent to any reflection. But when experience and reflection reveal that these sentiments make for a 'pleasant' society then "we pay them the just tribute of moral approbation and esteem" (Ibid.). These are the natural virtues.

In both artificial and natural virtues, then, the social factor is crucial. The decisive difference between them is that the latter occur as sentiments *prior* to any reflection whereas the former, because they are conventional, are the offspring of reflection. Though they are conventional these artificial virtues are in no way arbitrary. In fact, since they are necessary their creation "may as properly be said to be natural as anything that proceeds immediately from original principles" (T, 484) and thence the justification for calling them laws of nature, where 'nature' is now taken to mean "common to" and "inseparable from the species".[28] Hume is adamant, however, that the undoubted importance of the artificial virtues should not obscure the presence of the natural virtues. Indeed, he refers to them ("meekness, beneficence, charity, clemency, moderation, equity") as the social virtues because of their tendency to promote the good of society (T, 578; cf. M, 42, discussed below). Hume, whilst not denying a place for 'education' and the 'artifice of politicians', is accordingly critical of those philosophers (Hobbes and Mandeville for example) who would "extirpate all sense of virtue from among mankind" (T, 500) and make "all moral distinctions as the effect of artifice and education" (T, 578).

To return now to the duty of familial affection; we can see that it is a natural virtue – "of this nature are love of children. . ." (E (OC) 466) – and is at the root of man's natural sociability. However, this sociableness is discriminating. Hume subscribes to a theory of 'partial affection'. This theory is to be found in many of his contemporaries, though, of course, it has a long pedigree.[29] As

28. Cf. the list, in Chapter 4 supra, of the constituents of the constant content of human nature as inseparable.

29. Cf. Ld. Kames, *Sketches on the History of Man*, 1774 (3rd Edit.) Vol. 1, p. 388; A. Smith,

Hume expresses it — "a man naturally loves his children better than his nephews, his nephews better than his cousins, his cousins better than strangers, when everything else is equal" (T, 483 – 4). On to which is grafted the fact that man is selfish, so that it is rare "to meet with one who loves any single person better than himself" (T, 487). But, again, Hume counsels against a Hobbesian or Mandevillean depiction of human nature solely in these terms, because familial affection is powerful (T, 352) and men will put their wives and children first (T, 487).

There is here a point of wider import. It must not be thought that natural social bonds are coterminous with blood ties (another species of causation (T, 318; T, 12; A, 198)). To Hume "a perfect solitude is perhaps the greatest punishment we can suffer" and man, perhaps above all other creatures in the universe "has the most ardent desire of society" (T, 363). Significantly, this is more than rhetoric. On the contrary, it can be seen to be an important constituent in his thought.

The desire for society is a manifestation of a general human trait, namely that the mind "when left to itself immediately languishes" (T, 421; T, 224); it is "insufficient of itself, to its own entertainment" so that it "naturally seeks after foreign objects which may produce a lively sensation and agitate the spirits" (T, 352 – 3).[30] Chief amongst such 'objects' is other beings like himself. Man's natural state is the social. The mutual dependence of men is so great that no action is comprehensible without reference to the actions of others (cf. U, 98, quoted above); in fact, "we can form no wish which has not a reference to society" (T, 363). The individual is exposed to strong social pressures to conform (cf. P, 207; T, 479) and judges his own actions in the light of the reactions of others(cf. T, 292; T, 303).

The explanation that Hume gives of this social conformity is the principle of sympathy (T, 316). Hume declares that sympathy is a "very powerful principle of human nature" (T, 618; T, 577) and though, as many commentators have duly noted, Hume's treatment of this topic undergoes changes its basis in human nature is never doubted nor is its importance to social life. For current purposes what is important about sympathy is that it is used by Hume to close the gap between individual and collective rationality. The key to Hobbes' interpretation of the State of Nature is that therein it is in *every*man's best interest to do as he wishes and yet not be 'done by'. It is because this is not universalisable that a sovereign power is necessary to terrorise everyman so that it is in his interests 'to do as he would be done by'.[31] Hume's concept of sympathy obviates this remedy because it is through its operation that concern for the public interest is effected (thus accounting for the 'moral approbation' that attends justice) since by sym-

---

Theory of Moral Sentiments (1759) Pt. 6, Chap. 2, Sect. 1 (on final division in last edition 1790). See also Cicero, *de Officiis*, Book 1, Chap. xvii.

30. This is important to Hume's account of economic activity; cf. E. Rotwein, Introduction to his edition of *David Hume: Writings on Economics*, pp. xxxivff.

31. *Leviathan* (1651), Chaps. 13, 14, 17.

pathy alone is it that "the good of society, where our own interest is not concerned, or that of our friends, pleases" (T, 577).

We are now able to connect up this discussion with that given earlier concerning the inflexible observation of general rules. As we discussed above the exercise
of a rule on a particular occasion may be injurious but it is the whole system
which needs to be borne in mind — "tis only the concurrence of mankind in a
general scheme or system of action, which is advantageous" (T, 579). Justice requires that the *system* be inflexibly adhered to, and it is through sympathy that
the individual takes heed of more than his own interest, that he has a concern
with the system or the general interests of society — it "takes us so far out of
ourselves as to give us the same pleasure and uneasiness in the character of
others, as if they had a tendency to our own advantage or loss" (T, 579). This
combination of the inflexibility of justice and sympathy is vital because, to repeat
the gist of the earlier argument, it is Hume's understanding of social life that it
can maintain itself only if certain occurrences can be expected; if one can assume
the future will be like the past; since "in order to establish a general rule. . .there
is requir'd a certain uniformity in our experience" (T, 362). Society depends on
expectations which means that there must be stability, must be constants, since a
pragmatic, flexible or ad hoc approach would be unable to support the complex
of mutual dependencies.

III

Two final issues need to be covered. One, an examination of how Hume's treatment of manners, education, habit etc. contribute to maintain social cohesion
and, two, more abstractly, the significance of this reading of Hume, in this
Chapter as a whole.

We have already seen in Hume's rejection of Contractarianism that he believed
man to be a familial being and have seen also that for Hume the individual's actions are subject to strong pressures and performed in accordance with social
norms. Hume's account of the place of 'manners' in social life is an elaboration
of these points. 'Manners' is Hume's own general term in his *History* to
designate the whole formal and informal social complex and it corresponds to the
French term *Moeurs* (as in Voltaire or Montesquieu) and to part of what Hegel
means by *Sitten*. Once again we shall see that the principles that operate in the
determination of the influence of manners are those of constancy, regularity and
habit.

It is important to appreciate that although the argument hitherto has sought to
bring out Hume's theory of social cohesiveness in terms of expectations of
regularities, in internal relationships thus understood, this 'mental' argument is
not the same as a 'rational' argument. Societies, for Hume, are not based on a
high degree of citizen self-awareness, on a deliberate and deliberated principle of
cohesion, whereby each individual has assessed his role in society. Rather, as his
anti-Contractarianism illustrates in particular and as has been the motif of this

whole examination of Hume's treatment of habit, the unreflective is Hume's point of focus.[32]

Such a focus is intimately connected with Hume's utilisation of the notion of 'unintended consequences'. This notion figures prominently in Hume's analysis as it did also in a number of his compatriots, although most celebratedly in Adam Smith with his invocation of the 'invisible hand'.[33] Further as we shall discuss in Part III, Hegel's conception of the 'cunning of Reason' has been seen to have a certain affinity with this notion. What is important here is that society cannot be comprehended in terms of the actions of independently self-sufficient individuals, since not only do these actions only have sense in a social context (see above for Hume's critique of Locke's theory of property on these grounds) but also social practices and institutions are not simply the intended product of deliberate individual action.

Instead, once again, the notion of habit is crucial — "Habits more than reason we find in everything to be the governing principle of mankind" (H, 259). Habits are the work of time, they are not creations but accretions. This has bearing on both the location of explanatory principles in, and the content of, history. Regarding content, the historian, to make his history 'instructive', but also 'intelligible', must consider not merely political or constitutional matters but in addition "the state of the kingdom, with regard to government, manners, finances, arms, trade, learning" (H, 219). Regarding explanation, the 'social' (not the individual) should be attended to; thus, for example, in the augmentation of Henry VII's authority "the manners of the age were a general cause, which operated during this whole period, and which continually tended to diminish the riches and still more the influence of the aristocracy, anciently so formidable to the crown. The habits of luxury dissipated the immense fortunes of the ancient barons. . .the change in manners was the chief cause of the secret revolution of government and subverted the power of the barons" (HE, 546). Similarly, Hume's *Essays*, in addition, reveal much that can be justly designated 'social history'. In his essay *Of Money*, for example, he argues against attributing to the supply of money effects which are "really owing to a change in the manners and customs of the people" (E (Mon) 302).

Thus, in short, the important institutions and relationships in society are not simply those of the government and the individual but rather the "habits and

---

32. Cf. E (OG) 37, "though this progress of human affairs [origin of government] may appear *certain and inevitable*, and though the support which allegiance brings to justice be *founded on obvious principles of human nature*, it cannot be expected that men should beforehand be able to discover them or foresee their operation. Government commences more casually and imperfectly" (my emphases).

33. *Enquiry into the Nature and Causes of the Wealth of Nations* (1776) (Everyman edit.) Vol. 1, p. 400 — Smith also refers to the 'invisible hand' in his *Moral Sentiments*, Pt. 4, Chap. 1 (Bohn Library edit., p. 264). Cf. Ferguson, *Essay*, p. 122; J. Dunbar, *Essays on the History of Mankind* (1780) p. 175. The importance of this notion in the thought of Scots is brought out by D. Forbes, 'Scientific Whiggism', *Cambridge Journal* (1955) 643 – 670.

way of living of a people" (E (Int) 306). There is then here a sociological approach. Given (as we have seen and as we shall elucidate further) that man is a habit-forming creature it is the habits that he forms, and the constancy and interrelation of social experiences thereby implied, that constitute the social complex. Hence it is that societies do not subsist merely by virtue of a legal or political system. The law and government operate within a social context.

A general consequence of this is that the primacy of justice is not synonymous with the primacy of law and government,[34] understood as established social institutions; albeit that property and rank distinctions are the work of government and from which flow those diversifying features such as industry, manufactures, etc. (T, 402; see the full list quoted in the last chapter). Hume is clear that government is only instituted when society has experienced "encrease of riches and possessions" (T, 541) and has grown "numerous and civiliz'd" (T, 553; cf. T, 499). Again, we shall see in the next chapter, the establishment of a legal system has many beneficial consequences but it is the general rules of justice themselves that are the sine qua non of any social interaction. The definitive form these rules assume is inflexible or constant behaviour, which is to say habits of expectation.

In sum, society for Hume is composed of a network of habitual associations and behaviour patterns. These associations and patterns are the product of familial socialisation, education and the necessity of following the pre-established social ordering. This ordering is not the outcome of deliberate policy but is the offshoot of various accidental circumstances. This is where Hume's recognition of social diversity is crucial. On the one hand, he acknowledges that society is made up of habitual patterns of expectations, of rules which can be seen in the manners of a society, and, on the other hand, he is well aware that these manners etc. differ between societies. But, as we shall see in the following Chapters, Hume's broad theory of human nature, its constant character, operates so as to circumscribe the recognition of the full import of diversity and prevent it thereby from being an affirmation of relativism.

But before passing on to this discussion of social diversity we must consider the final issue, announced above, namely, the significance of this Chapter.

Society coheres because of mental relationships between its ultimate constituents, men. Whilst Hume is critical of the rationalistic individualism of his predecessors, with their postulated self-sufficient, independent agents, he is still himself a 'methodological individualist', because, in the last analysis, "a nation is nothing but a collection of individuals" (E (NC) 203). To locate social cohesiveness in internal relationships is, in essence, to say that society is rule-

---

34. This tends to be obscured by Moore (*PS*, p. 116) and D. Forbes, *Hume's Philosophical Politics*, p. 224, in their own arguments which emphasise Hume's divergence from the 'economism' of his compatriots (for this see the next Chapter). Hume's own amendments to his manuscript lend some credence to the difference here between 'justice' and 'law'; thus, at T, 450, line 18, the word 'laws' is changed to 'rules of Society' and again at T, 554, lines 19–20, 'laws of society' is changed to 'rules of justice' – as given in P.H. Nidditch, *An Apparatus of Variant Readings of Hume's Treatise of Human Nature*.

governed. Society operates and coheres because men have habit-sanctioned expectations that the future will be like the past, that life will be regular or rule-governed and not capricious. An individual's actions proceed on this basis and it thus follows that to understand these actions recourse must be had to the socially-sanctioned regularities (habits). In this context we can take up Hume's remark that "scarce any human action is entirely complete in itself or is performed without some reference to the actions of others, which are requisite to make it answer fully the intention of the agent" (U, 98). Elsewhere, Hume puts the general point graphically when he says men "cannot even pass each other on the road without rules" (M, 40).

There is here an issue of wider concern. This analysis of Hume which brings out, as it seeks to do, the internal dimension to society and the key role of habitual expectation, seemingly has affinities to the position of a number of modern social analysts, who, despite differences amongst themselves, unite in emphasising the importance of rules and meaning in attaining an adequate conceptualisation of social life. To these analysts such rules and meanings are *internally* related, which is to say that they are not observable or amenable to empirical methods. For example, Hume's illustration of road-users would be analysed along the lines that mere observation of the user's behaviour would yield no adequate answers, since their 'action' is only *intelligible* in terms of its conformity to the rule. It is this internal, non-observable, practice of rule-following that *explains* the action. It follows, though this is a considerable simplification, that the actors themselves must be aware that there is a rule to follow and that it is to this awareness that recourse should be had in explanation. The action is not, as is the case with a causal antecedent, something contingent or separate from its performance. The connexion between an intention and an action is intrinsic so that if the action does not 'materialise' it has not been performed. Raising one's arm, to give Melden's example, to indicate that the car one is driving is about to turn is an action (signalling) in accord with the public recognition of the rules of the road and, as such, it cannot be explained in terms of causal relationships. All that can be explained causally is the physiological happenings involved in an arm raising.[35]

The polemical aspect of this position is thus the rejection of empirical or 'causal' accounts of social life, which utilise an *external* analysis of what can be observed. In these polemics a number of writers, for example Melden himself and Winch and MacIntyre,[36] invoke Hume as the progenitor of the empirical/causal account. Since there is clearly a fundamental difference between these two approaches to the analysis of social life, and since in our interpretation Hume seems to adopt one but the subscribers to this approach *attack* him as adopting the other, where then does Hume belong?

35. *Free Action*, Chaps. 4 – 7 et passim. The 'Humean' view is, of course, not without its modern defenders.
36. P. Winch, *The Idea of a Social Science*, p. 16ff. et passim.; A. MacIntyre, 'A Mistake about Causality in Social Science' in P. Laslett & W.G. Runciman (eds.); *Philosophy, Politics and Society 2nd Series*, pp. 48 – 70.

First a minor but not a trivial point: the approach attacked by MacIntyre and the others is labelled 'Humean', that is, no exegetical claim is being made about Hume. Hume's analysis of cause is taken as the locus classicus and what is attacked is the application of this analysis by *anyone* to social life. But, Hume himself does wish, as we have seen, to extend his analysis in this manner − "we must certainly allow that the cohesion of the parts of matter arises from natural and necessary principles whatever difficulty we may find in explaining them: And for a like reason we must allow that human society is founded on like principles" (T, 401) so that "in judging of the actions of men we must proceed upon the same maxims as when we reason concerning external objects" (T, 403) since, as previously quoted, "there is a general course of nature in human actions as well as in the operations of the sun and the climate" (T, 402 − 3).

This conviction of Hume's that 'matter' and 'human society' are 'founded on like principles' is one of the fundamental tenets of his entire thought. As we have already demonstrated, expectations are the product of habit and this explains cohesiveness and coherence in both the social and natural worlds, since it is the basis of causal explanation itself, and that, moreover, it is only able to do this because it is anchored in human nature. Hume does believe that mental expectations are causally explicable.[37] he believes, in current terminology, that 'reasons are causes'.

Hume, thus, does seems a legitimate target for those writers who can be conveniently (if inelegantly) collectively termed 'anti-causalists' but this does not entail that the analysis thus far, demonstrating that Hume's account of social cohesiveness lies in internal relationships, is erroneous. Though it may well be that Hume was blind to the implications of his analysis, nevertheless the attempt to explain the world in terms of 'positive' principles alone − to excise all talk of quai-anthropomorphic entities like power, affinity, correspondence − is central to the Enlightenment view of the world and to Hume's own endeavour to establish a 'science of man'. But, more important, all that follows is that internality as Hume understands it and his underpinning assumptions, differs from how it is understood by the anti-causalists and their assumptions.

This can be brought out initially by noting H.L.A. Hart's distinction between the internal and external aspect of rules, especially since he develops this distinction in a discussion of habit.[38] For Hart, a habit is a merely observable general fact about the behaviour of a group but a social rule, in addition, has an internal aspect consisting of the group looking upon this behaviour as a standard to be followed by them. The observer can merely record habits, regularities but, as such, "he will miss out a whole dimension of the social life of those whom he is watching".[39]

37. For example (T, 78), "Passions are connected with their objects and with one another; no less than external bodies are connected together. The same relation, then, of cause and effect which belongs to one must be common to all of them" (Cf. A, 192).
38. *The Concept of Law*, p. 55 − 6.
39. *Concept of Law*, p. 87.

This dimension marks the distinction, alluded to in the previous Chapter, between formal and substantive accounts of social life. That is, to writers such as Winch the internality is societally specific. It is this factor that makes the question of 'understanding a primitive society' problematic; for if rules and their intrinsically attached meaning are societally specific then how is it possible for the member of another society (say an anthropologist or historian since the 'past is another place') to appreciate its 'meaning-impregnated' practices? A popular answer to this has been to maintain that there are "fundamental notions" which all human life involves and that there are distinctions, such as that between the real and the unreal, which the very concept of a language necessitates.[40] Although some necessarily formal trans-societal concepts of rationality are thus allowed by a number of anti-causalists this is insufficient to assimilate their position to Hume's

For Hume, the content or specificity of the rules is unimportant because of the basic constancy and uniformity of human actions and motives and *this* constancy *does*, in his lights, permit understanding (it makes history possible as we saw). This is not to say that Hume ignores social differences or localised social practices but, rather, that they are for him unproblematic. This is due to his necessitarianism. Since human nature is constant, its actions no matter where or when are comprehensible (motives and characters are constantly conjoined) so that, as we saw earlier, the causes of diversity bear witness at the same time to uniformity. It is in this sense, as we intimated in the last Chapter, that Hume's account of social life is formal. But, this is the converse of his substantive notion of rationality. Hume has no compunction about labelling savages stupid or superstitious. Thus, for example, whilst he gives an explanation of polytheism this in no way entails him attributing to its practitioners their own 'rationality' or standard of authenticity, because, as we shall see, this practice is explained by constant properties of human nature. These properties are the causes which the 'science of man' can elicit and the fact that the practitioners might not heed these is (pace Winch and the rest) irrelevant. Neither human nature nor (it follows) any study of it based on observation is societally specific.

In sum, then, there is a direct relationship between the upholding of a formal account of social life and a substantive account of rationality, as in Hume, and a converse, though equally direct, relationship between a substantive, or societally specific, account of social life and a formal notion of rationality, as in (despite

40. Winch provides an illustration of the point — "to say of a society that it has a language is also to say it has a concept of rationality. . .we imply formal analogies between their behaviour and that behaviour in our own society which we refer to in distinguishing between rationality and irrationality. This however is so far to say nothing about what in particular constitutes rational behaviour in that society", 'On Understanding a Primitive Society' in B. Wilson (ed.), *Rationality*, p. 99. Even modern critics of Winch still outline what can be fairly labelled a formal theory — see, for example, the contribution, in the same volume, by S. Lukes [pp. 194 – 213] who holds that there are some "fundamental and universal" criteria of rationality in contrast to other criteria (all that Winch allegedly accepts) which are context-dependent but Lukes allows that the former are not very informative.

their internal differences) Winch and the others. Hegel, it can be said here without elaboration, endeavours to have both a substantive account of social life and a substantive notion of rationality.

The crucial difference between Hume and the others lies in his account of human nature. We shall, in conclusion to this Part, develop this point in more detail but, generally, the anti-causalist approach itself flows, with Hegel perhaps as the chief, though as we shall demonstrate significantly attenuated, source, by various routes from the broadly 'idealist' interpretation of man and society.[41] Here is one of the interfaces of this study. Hume does, through his stress on habit, implicitly develop a theory of social cohesiveness, and social life generally, that sees this as a mental relationship, but Hume's notion of such a relationship is far removed from the Hegelian understanding of the interaction between thought or consciousness and social life or action.

41. Though Winch and Melden make great use of the later Wittgenstein it has not escaped the attention of recent writers on Hegel that there are noteworthy affinities between aspects of his thought and Wittgenstein − C. Taylor, *Hegel*, p. 567f.; R. Plant, *Hegel*, p. 202ff.

6. SOCIAL DIVERSITY

Hume recognises the 'facts' of social diversity. Crucially, however, this recognition is within a theory which holds that the causes of diversity "at the same time maintain such an uniformity in human life" (T, 402). Nevertheless, since different societies, across time and space, do enjoy different social customs and do exhibit different social institutions, the chief task to be undertaken in this Chapter is to see, given his theory of human nature, what explanation Hume provides for these differences.

But, first, briefly, in *what* does Hume see societies differing? In the passages, quoted above in Chapter 4, Hume merely provides a very general indication as to what constitutes the divergent or peculiar, namely, the "tempers and complexions of men" (T, 281); personal and national "characters" (T, 403) or "characters and prejudices and opinions" (U, 95). However, more concretely, Hume states, that societies differ as to their governments and laws (E (RPAS) 116; E (NC) 211; E (PAN) 410; M, 73); marital conventions (E (PD) 185); religious beliefs and practices (E (PG) 59; N passim); territorial extent (E (RPAS) 120); aesthetic accomplishments (E (RPAS) 116; E (ST) 231); treatment of women (E (RPAS) 133); criteria of moral evaluation (M, 79; M, 84; M, 149); language (E (NC) 214; T, 490; M, 55); economic mode of life (E (Com) 261; E (RA) 284); degree of civilisation (E (RA) 284, 278, 280). These, of course, are not mutually exclusive and we shall be picking up a number of them, and their interrelations, in the ensuing discussion.

It will be profitable to commence the examination of Hume's explanation of these differences by analysing his distinction between moral and physical causes. The former comprise "the nature of the government, the revolutions of public affairs, the plenty or penury in which the people live, the situation of the nation with regard to its neighbours and such like circumstances"; the latter comprise "qualities of air and climate" (E (NC) 202 – 3).[1] Hume is concerned to argue

---

1. 'Climate' in the eighteenth century did not have its present meteorological connotation; instead, Johnson defines it as "A space upon the surface of the earth, measured from the equator to the polar circles in each of which spaces the longest day is half-an-hour longer", *Dictionary*, 10th Edit. (1972); similarly for the *Encyclopaedia Britannica* (1771) climate is "a space upon the terrestrial globe".

against the *direct* influence of the latter. This does not mean that the physical location of a society has *no* effect only that it operates *indirectly*, that is, the institutions (moral causes) are adapted suitably to the physical circumstances.

In attacking the argument that climate has a direct deterministic effect Hume is rejecting the views of, amongst others, Dubos and Montesquieu. To present this view very briefly: the idea of climate as an explanation of social differences had had a long history prior to the eighteenth century but, as we saw in Chapter 1, it was then appropriated as an ordering principle.[2] Montesquieu's theory, in view of the popularity and influence of the *Esprit des Lois* (1748), was perhaps, the best known treatment. Though climate may well have had a long pedigree, nevertheless Montesquieu's treatment is presented with empiricist credentials in that he describes his experiments testing the reaction of a sheep's tongue to heat (*Esprit*, Book 14, Chap. 2). From the results he argued that cold air contracts the extremities of the fibres of our body, increases their elasticity and promotes the return of blood from these extremities to the heart, whereas warm air relaxes these fibres thus diminishing their elasticity. These physiological differences cause differences in *"sensibilité"* so that, for example, the inhabitants of warm lands are timid, like old men whereas those in cold lands are courageous, like young men. Quite simply the differences in climate, in temperature, by acting in different ways on the body, cause *"caractères bien différent"*. Though, as is obvious from the contemporary debate over his theory,[3] Montesquieu was identified as a proponent of the direct effect of climate, an analysis of the total of his writings suggests that he allowed a much more significant role to moral causes than is apparent from just Book 14 of the *Esprit*.[4]

Regardless, enough has been said to indicate what Hume was attacking in his critique of physical causes. However, the particular arguments that Hume gives in this critique are of less moment here than the reasons for the critique in the first place. Hume regards physical causes as "having no discernible operation on the human mind" (E (NC) 209). It is this mental aspect that is crucial. This is not because Hume puts any store by free-will (he is necessitarian, though he explicitly disavows (T, 410) the materialist view that fails to distinguish the will from 'senseless matter') but because, as the last Chapter argued, for Hume, society coheres by virtue of internal or mental principles. Physical causes are here ineffective. Rather, it is moral causes which are effective, because these are circumstances that "are fitted to work on the mind as motives or reasons and which render a peculiar set of manners habitual to us" (E (NC) 202). Thus, Hume's particular rejections of the physical or direct effect argument, along the lines that

2. For climate as an 'ordering principle' see C. Berry '"Climate" in the eighteenth century', *Texas Studies in Literature and Language* (1974) 281–292.

3. Cf. Berry, *TSLL*; R. Shackleton, *Montesquieu: A critical biography*, Chap. 14.

4. For example, climate is only one cause amongst several in his summation of the *esprit général* in *Esprit*, Bk. 19, Chap. 4, and see also his *Essai sur les causes* (published 1892) (in *Oeuvres*, Nagel Vol. III, pp. 398–430) wherein he writes that moral causes do more to shape the general character and more to fix the quality of a nation's *esprit* than physical causes (p. 421).

different manners are experienced in the same climate (and vice versa), a common ploy among his compatriots, make the point of contrasting "sympathy or contagion of manners" with the "influence of air or climate" (E (NC) 209; cf. T, 317).

In general terms, therefore, it is to moral causes that we are to look for Hume's explanation of social differences and variations (cf. E (PAN) 383). They are able to perform this explanatory function because, as just quoted, they are circumstances which operate by habituation and, as we saw in the last chapter, it is to habitual regularities that recourse must be had in social (and historical) enquiry in locating necessary uniformities. The uniformities are explained by the operation of the principles of human nature and this explanation necessarily explains the variations at the same time, since, otherwise, there could be no "science of man", no social science at all.

The first circumstance (moral cause) that merits further examination is progress or social development. As we saw in Chapter 1, in the eighteenth century, it was frequently noted that the effect of climate decreased in impact as society developed and, as we also discussed, 'progress' was one of the notions employed by the Enlightenment to make sense of social diversity. Hume, too, subscribes to it. This subscription comes in two not unrelated forms – changes in the economic mode of production and, more importantly for Hume, the growth of 'civilisation'.

To plot the development of societies in terms of changes in the prevalent economic mode was common in the eighteenth century,[5] though it perhaps finds its highest expression in Scotland. John Millar provides a neat précis of this argument:

Their [men's] first effors are *naturally* calculated to increase the means of subsistence, by catching or ensnaring wild animals, or by gathering the spontaneous fruits of the earth; and the experience acquired in the exercise of these employments, is apt, successively, to point out the methods of taming and rearing cattle, and of cultivating the ground. Accordingly, as men have been successful in these great improvements. . .the various branches of manufacture together with commerce its inseparable attendant. . .are introduced (my emphasis).[6]

Hume, too, sees as the earliest ('savage') state that dominated by hunting and

---

5. Cf., *inter alia*, Rousseau, *Discours sur L'origine de L'inégalité* (1755); Turgot, *Histoire Universelle* (c. 1750); Montesquieu, *Esprit* (Bk. 18, Chap. 11); Herder, *Ideen* (1784) Bk. 8, Pt. 3.

6. *Origin of the Distinction of Ranks* (1779 – 1st edit. 1771), ed. W.C. Lehmann, *John Millar of Glasgow*, p. 176. This same four-fold progress (hunting, herding, farming, commerce) occurs in A. Smith, *Wealth of Nations* (Everyman Edit., Vol. 2, pp. 182–5) and also, in significantly since this appears to be the major source of the notion, in his early (1763) *Lectures on Jurisprudence*; in A. Ferguson, *Institutes of Moral Philosophy* (1769); in W. Robertson, *History of America* (1777); in G. Stuart's *Historical Dissertation on the Antiquity of the English Constitution* (1768) Pt. 1, Sect. 3. For discussions see several writings by A. Skinner, e.g. in T. Wilson & A. Skinner eds., *Essays on Adam Smith*, pp. 154–178 and 'Natural History in the Age of Adam Smith', *PS* (1966) 32–48 and R. Meek, e.g. 'Smith, Turgot and the "Four Stages" Theory', *History of Political Economy* (1971) 9–27 and *Social Science and the Ignoble Savage*.

fishing (E (Com) 261). This is succeeded by the agricultural state, which, after its 'arts' have been improved by "time and experience", frees a number of men, who develop the "finer arts" (E (Com) 262). What is significant about the employment of this economic base to chart social development is the consequences that are held to follow from it. Again, it is in the Scots that this attains its highest sophistication. They linked together the economic mode with property relationships and these in turn with other social institutions.[7]

Although Hume does not ignore this analysis, his emphasis is placed on the second form under which he subscribes to the notion of progress, namely, the rise of civilisation, of stable government, of liberty.[8] Hegel, too, of course, read history as the actualisation of liberty. For Hume, 'civilised' Europe enjoys "great superiority" over "barbarous Indians" (M, 22). In broad terms he believes in progress away from superstition, characteristic of ages of barbarity and ignorance, towards the normatively superior order of liberty, moderation and humanity. The highest expression of such humanity is the Rule of Law and liberty — "the perfection of civil society" (E (OC) 39) — to which the chief opponents "in all ages of the world" have been priests (E (PGB) 65). This is because superstition derives from weakness, fear, melancholy and ignorance (E (SE) 75; cf. N, 55ff. and Chapter 7 infra) which, in turn, gives rise to priests (E (SE) 77), who instead "of correcting these *depraved* ideas of mankind, have often been found ready to foster and encourage them" (N, 95, my emphasis; cf. E (NC) 205n). In the 'uncivilised' teaching of the Koran, for example, "no steady rule of right" is followed and praise is bestowed on "treachery, inhumanity, cruelty, revenge, bigotry" if such are beneficial to true believers (E (ST) 233). Toleration has "proceeded from the steady resolution of the civil magistrate, in opposition to the continued efforts of priests and bigots" (N, 66). Hume, indeed, in his posthumous *Dialogues*, makes Philo declaim not only against the pernicious consequences of superstition on public affairs ("factions, civil wars, persecutions, subversions of government, oppression, slavery" (D, 195 – 6)) but also on its injurious effect on morality itself (D, 198; cf. H, 99). It is, of course, these and similar sentiments which gave Hume his high reputation amongst the

---

7. To outline this theory briefly; in the first stage there is no personal property (Millar, *Ranks*, p. 183), in the second there is a transition from common ownership of flocks to private herds (Millar, *Ranks*, p. 204). The agricultural stage sees the most significant stage when property in land, and ensuing permanency of possession, becomes established (Millar, *Ranks*, p. 252). The commercial stage witnesses a change in these property relations from land tenure to that based upon an exchange or market economy. These relations, in each stage of social development, determine to a large degree the 'mode of life' in that stage. Thus, when there is no property the only distinctions are personal, but once property becomes a private possession then "the ground of a permanent and palpable subordination is laid" (Ferguson, *Essay on the History of Civil Society* (1767), ed. D. Forbes, p. 98). The extent of this subordination determines for example, the form of government (Ferguson, *Essay*, p. 62). Finally, we might just note here that Hegel was 'influenced' to a noticeable extent by this analysis.

8. Cf. E.C. Mossner, 'An apology for David Hume Historian', *PMLA* (1941) 681; D. Forbes, *Hume's Philosophical Politics*, p. 298f.

philosophes,[9] and which also provides the justification for attributing to Hume a substantive theory of rationality.

The development away from superstition and priestly rule and toward liberty is, as we saw, the work of civil authorities (it is a feature of Hume's 'perfect commonwealth' that the clergy are dependent on the civil magistrate (E (IPC) 510)). Yet, in line with Hume's recognition of the impact of unintentional consequences on society, and, although he discourses at length on the relative merits of republican and monarchical governments, it is clear that it is the degree of civilisation that is decisive − "all kinds of government, free and absolute, seem to have undergone a great change for the better" so that "it may now be affirmed of civilised monarchies what was formerly said in praise of republics alone, that they are a government of laws not of men" (E (CL) 95). Hume's utilisation of the Rule of Law as a criterion of progress is directly linked to his emphasis on the inflexibility of the rules of justice requisite to engender stability and thereby social cohesiveness. Despotic rule (in Montesquieu's sense) is capricious, and caprice, above all else, induces uncertainty and precludes the formation of habits of expectation in social life. Finally, this view of the development of society *to* liberty is used by Hume polemically against the various manifestations of the popular argument that the ancient Britons were 'free' (cf. HE, 294).

The chief factor identified by Hume as being responsible for the development of civilisation is the growth in refinement. As well as invigorating the mind, industry and refinement in the "mechanical arts" produce advances in the "liberal arts" so that there is created a "spirit of the age" which leads to

improvements into every art and science. Profound ignorance is totally banished and men enjoy the privilege of rational creatures, to think as well as to act, to cultivate the pleasures of the mind as well as those of the body. The more these refined arts advance, the more sociable men become. . . they flock into cities; love to receive and communicate knowledge; to show their wit or their breeding; their taste in conversation or living, in clothes or furniture. . . so that beside the improvements which they receive from knowledge and liberal arts, it is impossible but they must feel an increase of humanity, from the very habit of conversing together, and contributing to each other's pleasure and entertainment. Thus *industry*, *knowledge* and *humanity*, are linked together, by an indissoluble chain, and are found, from experience, as well as reason, to be peculiar to the more polished, and, what are commonly denominated the more luxurious ages. (E (RA) 278, Hume's emphasis)

Now it is that, to supply another lengthy quotation,

knowledge in the arts of government beget mildness and moderation, by instructing men in the advantages of human maxims above rigour and severity. . . When the *tempers* of men are softened as well as their knowledge improved, this humanity appears still more conspicuous, and is the *chief characteristic* which distinguishes a civilised age from times of barbarity and ignorance. (E (RA) 280, my emphases, for their significance see below)

9. Cf. L.L. Bongie, *David Hume: Prophet of the Counter Revolution*, Chap. 1. Holbach (probably) translated Hume's essays 'on Suicide' and 'on Immortality of the Soul'.

We need now to address the above discussion to the matter chiefly at hand – Hume's explanation of social diversity. What both the degree of civilisation or liberty and the identification of the prevalent economic mode do is permit an ordering of history. The past can be subsumed under certain interpretative principles. In short, the degree of liberty or the dominant economic stage make history intelligible, they impose an order on the otherwise incoherent evidence of past social experience and they make judgment possible. This approach to the past was characteristic of much eighteenth-century speculation and, together with the attendant disparagement of chroniclers and annalists that we mentioned in Chapter 4, it led Dugald Stewart, at the end of the century, to remark on its distinctiveness – "To this species of philosophical investigation, which has no appropriate name in our language, I shall take the liberty of giving the title of *Theoretical* or *Conjectural* History; an expression which coincides pretty nearly in meaning with that of *Natural History*, as employed by Mr Hume, and with what some French writers have called *Histoire Raisonnée*".[10]

The work of Hume's referred to here is his *Natural History of Religion* (1757). This work is intended as an enquiry into the origin of religion in human nature (N, 31). Amidst all the variety of religious practices throughout history, supplemented by "our present experience concerning the principles and opinions of barbarous nations" (N, 33),[11] Hume sought the principles of human nature from which it is possible to conjecture ("according to the *natural* progress of human thought" (N, 34, my emphasis)) the development, or the natural history, of these practices. The opening sentence of the first chapter sets the tone – "It appears to me, that, if we consider the improvement of human society, from rude beginnings to a state of greater perfection, polytheism or idolatry was, and *necessarily must have been*, the first and most ancient religion of mankind" (N, 33, my emphasis).

Hume proceeds to outline the reasons why polytheism is the primary religion of men; how (mono)theism developed from this and how, thirdly, there is a "natural" tendency to sink again into idolatry. Thus, first, religion arose from "a concern with regard to the events of life and from the incessant hopes and fears which actuate the human mind" (N, 38). In a condition of ignorance these passions, abetted by the propensity in human nature to personify, lead to polytheism – "As the *causes*, which bestow happiness or misery, are, in general, very little known and very uncertain, our anxious concern endeavours to attain a determinate idea of them; and finds no better expedient than to represent them as intelligent voluntary agents, like ourselves; only somewhat superior in power and wisdom" (N, 54, Hume's emphasis). Second, from this it is "natural" that the vulgar should, when faced with increased fear and distress, invent "new strains of adulation" (N, 57) so that "a limited deity, who [is] at first supposed only the

---

10. *Life of Adam Smith*, prefixed to Smith's *Theory of Moral Sentiments* (Bohn Library edit.) p. xxv (Stewart's emphases). Cf. also his *Dissertation exhibiting the progress of Metaphysical, Ethical and Political Philosophy*, in *Works*, ed. W. Hamilton, Vol. 1, p. 69–70.

11. Cf. Chapter 1 supra.

immediate author of the particular goods and ills of life, should in the end be represented as sovereign maker and modifier of the universe. . ." (N, 58). But, third, since this is still based on superstition, and not reason, the "refined ideas" of unity, infinity, simplicity and spirituality require mediators and, hence, demi-gods arise which "being more familiar to us become the chief objects of devotion and gradually reveal that idolatry" (N, 63). Hume's account thus explains causally differing religious practices by viewing them as the effects of some constant principles of human nature. These principles are explanatory because they are "little or nothing dependent on caprice and accident" (N, 54).

This contrast between what is capricious and what is constant is important to Hume and recurs throughout his writings. For example, his essay on *Rise and Progress of the Arts and Sciences* (1742) opens by stating the 'classical' question as to the extent that human affairs are "owing to chance" and "what proceeds from causes" (E (RPAS) 112).[12] Hume then answers this question by invoking a general rule "what arises from a great number may often be accounted for by determinate and known causes". Accordingly, there are "common affections" which govern a multitude "in all their actions" and these affections are by their nature "stubborn. . .and less influenced by whim and private fancy" (E (RPAS) 113). In practice what Hume has done is take matters yet again back to human nature. The 'rise and progress of commerce' can be accounted for by reference to "avarice or the desire of gain" which is a "universal passion, which operates at all times, in all places, and upon all persons" (E (RPAS) 114) and the rise and progress of the arts and sciences is similarly reducible to "curiosity or the love of knowledge". Though the latter (like the related history of science and learning (E (EI) 98)) being more susceptible to chance is less constant than the progress of commerce or civil history it is still causally explicable because chance itself is nothing other than "secret or unknown causes" (E (RPAS) 112; cf. T, 130).

It is on this basis that Hume thinks a science of politics is possible. There are "general truths" in politics which are "invariable by the humour or education either of subject or sovereign" (E (PS) 17; cf. 22). Of course, due caution should be exercised yet, even given the imperfect nature of our knowledge (E (RC) 372; cf. E (CL) 89), certain universal axioms can be stated; for example, "a power, however great, when granted by law to an eminent magistrate, is not so dangerous to liberty as an authority, however inconsiderable, which he acquires from violence and usurpation" (E (RC) 378; for other examples cf. E (PS) 17, 19; E (IP) 40; D, 199; HE, 702). The science of man reveals uniformities in politics based on uniformities in human nature (cf. T, xx).

It is the explanatory force of a constant human nature that accounts for social diversity measured both as the progress of society from rudeness to civilisation and as the progress of religion from polytheism to mono-theism. Before examining other aspects of Hume's account of social diversity it should be noted that instead of, or as well as, Hume's espousal of progress a number of commentators

12. Cf. Machiavelli, *Il Principe* (1513) Chap. 25. Machiavelli himself, as so often, is utilising a 'pagan' convention.

have drawn attention to a cyclical theory in Hume's writings.[13] However, what Hume describe to is the commonplace idea of the exhaustion or decline of the fine arts (E (RPAS) 136).[14] This idea was a corollary of the acceptance of rules, and centrality allotted to imitation, in aesthetics. Once models have been established any young man will compare his own efforts unfavourably with them, as will the public, who will thus afford no encouraging praise, so that he will consequently be disposed to abandon his work; current work is thus judged to be inferior and the arts now in decline. More generally, Hume, and here again he is in line with his compatriots, does not subscribe to a uniform or necessary theory of progress (see his letter to Turgot – L II, 180; cf. Chapter 10 below). A survey of history, he believes, reveals periods of decline which are followed eventually by an upswing – "But there is a point of depression as well as exaltation, from which human affairs naturally return in a contrary direction, and beyond which they seldom pass either in their advancement or decline" (HE, 294). Hume instantiates this generalisation by referring to pre-Conquest England as darkness but from which period "the sun of science" began to re-ascend till the "full morning when letters were revived in the fifteenth century". This is not cyclicalism. Hume does believe that there has been progress in liberty, hence his encomia on the current British constitution (HE, 295, 898), and afore-mentioned criticism of 'ancient liberty', but he believes, also, that the passions of enthusiasm and ambition are an ever present threat. Liberty is a precious and precarious attainment; it should be protected from such passions, and from potentially 'unsettling' ideas; hence his well-known, if elusive, Tory bias.[15]

Further aspects of Hume's treatment of diversity still require examination. Like most of his contemporaries (see Chapter 1) Hume was exercised by the problem of differences in aesthetic judgments and, again like his contemporaries, he tackled this problem by utilising the notion of taste.

Hume opens his discussion by declaring that the variety of taste is undeniable; in fact, he goes further by saying that "it will be found on examination to be still greater in reality than in appearance" (E (ST) 231). Interestingly, in view of our discussion in Chapter 2, Hume sees in language one cause of this 'really greater' difference, since the word 'virtue', and its equivalent in every language, implies praise but there is a great difference in the application of this approbation be-

13. For example, J. Laird, *Hume's Philosophy of Human Nature*, p. 270; F. Meinecke, *Die Entstehung des Historismus*, 2nd Edit., p. 205; J.B. Stewart, *The Moral and Political Philosophy of David Hume*, pp. 292 – 5; F. Manuel, *The Eighteenth-Century confronts the Gods*, p. 178.

14. Cf. J.D. Scheffer, 'The Idea of Decline in Literature and Fine Arts in the Eighteenth Century', *MP* (1937 – 8) 109 – 142; H. Vyverberg, *Historical Pessimism in the French Enlightenment*, Pt. III.

15. As seen, for example, in his comment that "the doctrine of obedience ought alone to be inculcated and that the exceptions, which are very rare, ought seldom or never to be mentioned in popular reasonings and discourses" (H, 686). For debate on this issue see E.C. Mossner, 'Was Hume a Tory Historian?', *JHI* (1941) 225 – 232; M. Grene, 'Hume: Sceptic and Tory', *JHI* (1943) 333 – 348; G. Giarrizzo, *David Hume politico e storico*. But see D. Forbes for a convincing argument that Hume's *History* is to be understood as "establishment", and as neither Tory nor crudely Whig *Hume's Phil. Pol.*, p. 263f. et passim.

tween, say, Homer and Fénelon. Moreover, as a good empiricist, Hume goes on to remark that "beauty is no quality in things themselves: it exists merely in the mind which contemplates them; and each mind perceives a different beauty" (E (ST) 234 – 5). With these two arguments Hume seems to go beyond formal similarity to a recognition of substantive difference. But the significant point is that Hume's argument makes little or no capital out of them. It is this lack of concern on Hume's part that indicates the range of *his* assumptions and throws into relief the 'shift' that was to occur in conceptualisations about man and his culture, that is, the shift that this study as a whole is endeavouring to elucidate.

Hume faced with the evidence of this 'real' diversity neither accepts nor acquiesces in it. He does not accept the relativity of aesthetic judgment. Rather, it is to him "*natural* for us to seek a Standard of Taste, a rule by which the various sentiments of men may be reconciled" that is, confirmed or condemned (E (ST) 234, my emphasis). Whilst "exact truth" cannot be expected in poetry, it must be rule-governed, and these rules (recalling that Criticism is one of the sciences referred to in the Preface to the *Treatise*) are "founded only on experience, and on the observation of the common sentiments of human nature" (E (ST) 231) so that "amidst all the variety and caprice of taste, there are certain general principles of approbation or blame, whose influence a careful eye may trace in all operations of the mind" (E (ST) 238). Here is clear evidence of Hume's subscription to the tenets of neo-classicism. As early as the *Treatise* Hume had, in an illustrative aside, enunciated the doctrine that to mix in the one work profundity and humour is to neglect "all rules of art and criticism" which "are founded on the qualities of human nature" (T, 379). Such consistency is fundamental to one of the basic unities of criticism – the unity of action – and is traced to the operation of the association of ideas, to human nature (U, 34 – 9).[16] But, to return specifically to taste; the upshot is that "the principles of taste be universal and nearly, if not entirely, the same in all men" (E (ST) 246); they are "uniform in human nature" (E (ST) 249). Having established this Hume then, in a manoeuvre familiar from our discussion in Chapter 1, makes room for the role of the critic, since there are many imperfections under which "the generality of men" labour, so that the requisite qualities of "strong sense, united to delicate sentiment, improved by practice, perfected by comparison and cleared of all prejudice" (E (ST) 247) are (not surprisingly!) rare.

It is true that Hume closes this essay with another discussion of how the problem of diversity affects his 'solution' to the problem. There are two sources of variation – "the different humours of particular men" and "particular manners and opinions of our age and country" (E (ST) 249). Regarding the latter, it is again a fact of the human constitution that we are more pleased with resemblance to our own customs than a different set (a point Adam Smith was to make much of in his *Theory of Moral Sentiments* (Part 5, Chapter 2) published two years

---

16. Cf. M. Kallich, *Association of Ideas and Critical Theory in the Eighteenth Century*, p. 92. Hume's "defense of neo-classic dogma rests solely on the new philosophy of human nature, that of the mechanism of association".

(1759) after this essay). It is one of the characteristics of a man of learning that he can make allowances for different manners and customs, yet the gulf between Homer's rough heroes of antiquity and our own time means that we are unable "to enter into his sentiments" (E (ST) 252). But, despite these problems they are not so great as "to confound the boundaries of beauty and deformity" (E (ST) 249). This is what is important. It is Hume's conviction that human nature is constant which makes not only diversity intelligible but also provides a critical evaluative yardstick.

Having seen how Hume treats differences in aesthetic standards we can now turn to his treatment of different moral standards. Given that Hume is an empiricist then these standards must derive from experience. What constitutes that experience will seemingly differ over time and place. In a non-moral context Hume gives a clear indication of this principle at work – "The inhabitants of Sumatra have always seen water fluid in their own climate, and the freezing of rivers ought to be deemed a prodigy; but they never saw water in Muscovy during the winter, and therefore they cannot reasonably be positive what would there be the consequence" (U, 122). In terms of moral standards, similarly, experience is seemingly crucial –

It is indeed observable, that among all uncultivated nations who have not, as yet, had full experience of the advantages attending beneficience, justice and the social virtues, courage is the predominant excellence; what is most celebrated by poets, recommended by parents and instructors and admired by the public in general. The ethics of Homer are, in this particular, very different from those of Fénelon. (M, 79)

There are a number of points worthy of comment in this passage. There is testimony to the importance attached to the degree of social development (cultivation) in an explanation of social differences. Societies differ to the extent that the rule of law is effective, which in turn depends on stability, on the keeping of promises and the maintenance of commerce. There is further testimony, again, to Hume's awareness of evidence; how reading a society's literature can provide insight into that society's way of life. This is a point Hume makes elsewhere when criticising Fontenelle (and others) for their surprise at the toleration shown by the Athenians to Aristophanes, despite all his impieties, whilst they executed Socrates, since they (Fontenelle et al.) did not appreciate that Aristophanes' depictions of the gods "were the genuine lights in which the ancients conceived their divinities" (N, 46). Finally, from this passage, there is testimony to the role played by education and the family in the maintenance of social cohesiveness.

The sentiments expressed in this passage are not isolated. Later Hume writes "our ideas of virtue and personal merit" are diversified and varied as to whether a society is at peace or war (M, 153). Hume, here, develops the general principle that moral values relate to utility, so that it follows that in different societies or in the same society at different times, different qualities will be useful, and thence valued, – "in ancient times bodily strength and dexterity being of greater *use* and importance in war, was also much more esteemed and valued than at present'' (M, 69, Hume's emphasis). In similar fashion, the type of government (and here Montesquieu's influence is apparent) has an important bearing on what it is that is valued, that is, the sort of customs and values differ along with the constitution, with certain regimes favouring some more than other; honour and reputation in monarchies but riches and industry in republics (M, 73).

Yet Hume's conclusion is not relativist. His theory of moral sentiments, and behind that his presuppositions about a constant human nature, preclude such an inference.[17] As we saw, for Hume, actions and qualities are denominated virtues because they are pleasant or give satisfaction, and what is useful is a source of satisfaction. The basis of satisfaction is the constitution of man himself. Man is so made that pleasure and pain actuate him. This susceptibility is independent of societal context.

Hume's writings are full of instances of this position. The fullest discussion is to be found in *A Dialogue*, a piece appended to the *Second Enquiry*. Hume's own assessment of this argument in this piece is revealing – "I have surely endeavoured to refute the Sceptic with all the force of which I am master; and my refutation must be allowed sincere, because drawn from the capital principles of my system" (L I, 173). The theme of this dialogue is precisely the relativity of moral standards. After the sceptic (Palamedes) has sketched out the customs of the Athenians and the 'I' those of contemporary Europe, Palamedes declares that his intention all along has been

to represent the uncertainty of all these judgments concerning characters, and to convince you that fashion, vogue, custom and law were the chief foundation of all moral determinations. . .What wide difference, therefore, in the sentiments of morals must be found between civilised nations and barbarians, or between nations whose characters have little in common? How shall we pretend to fix a standard for judgments of this nature? (M, 179)

Hume's reply (in the guise of 'I') to this question is first to note that Palamedes has omitted "good sense, knowledge, wit, eloquence, humanity, fidelity, truth, justice, courage, temperance, constancy, dignity of mind" (M, 150) and instead, has, insisted "only on the points in which they [Athenian and contemporary standards] may by *accident* differ" (M, 150, my emphasis). Moreover, these differences, and this is the decisive point, can be accounted for "from the most universal established principles of morals" (M, 150). There is one general foundation of the moral sentiments – "never was any quality recommended by anyone, as a virtue or moral excellence, but on account of its being *useful* or *agreeable* to a man *himself* or to *others*" (M, 152, Hume's emphases; cf. T, 591) so that "the principles upon which men reason in morals are always the same, though the conclusions which they draw are often very different" (M, 151).

17. Cf. J.W. Chapman, 'Political Theory; Logical Structure and Enduring Types', in *L'Idée de Philosophie Politique* (annales de philosophie politique no. 6) p. 86f.; L. Strauss, 'Relativism', in H. Schoeck & J.W. Wiggins eds., *Relativism and the Study of Man*, p. 158 – 9.

Hume, now, invokes different customs, because they give an "early bias to the mind" (M, 153), to explain the differences that do occur. They are "particular accidents" so that of the four sources of moral sentiments (utility, agreeableness, to self, to others) one may overbalance the others at any one time. Hume does allow that chance also has a great influence and that many manners are not subsumable under this general rule (M, 156). Regardless, the important point stands – "different customs and situations vary not the original ideas of merit (however much they may some consequences) in any very essential point" (M, 156). Nor are these customs of equal value. Again, Hume's judgment of the Koran is apposite; it is "a wild and absurd performance" and the actions it praises (inhumanity, bigotry etc.) are "utterly incompatible with civilised society" (E (ST) 233).

Hume's rejection of ethical relativism is an important indicator of the tenor of his thought, because it shows the definite limits to his acceptance (and appreciation) of the significance of social differences. In this regard, Duncan Forbes drives too substantial a wedge between Hume's sociological relativism and his (admitted) abjuration of ethical relativism.[18] In terms of Hume's intellectual situation, this abjuration signals the attenuated character of his sociological relativism. Though Hume's position (as interpreted by Forbes) is of course defensible, it requies a sophistication in distinguishing the ethical from the social for which Hume himself had no need. As noted above, Hume is able to treat the whole issue of understanding an alien culture as unproblematical for, as this study is aiming to show, it is the post-Humean development of a contextualist theory of human nature that makes this issue contentious by rejecting the uniformitarianism that made all human activity explicable (comprehensible) on the same non-societally specific principles.

We have seen how Hume's theory of moral sentiments is premised on his uniformitarian view of the constancy of human nature and how, indeed, his argument, in *A Dialogue*, does, thereby, flow from 'the capital principles' of his 'system'. There is further evidence of this connexion in the key chapters on 'Liberty and Necessity', where Hume writes

The same motives always produce the same actions; the same events follow from the same causes. Ambition, avarice, self-love, vanity, friendship, generosity, public spirit – these passions, mixed in various degrees and distributed through society, have been, from the beginning of the world, and still are, the source of all actions and enterprises which have ever been observed among mankind. Would you know the sentiments, inclinations and course of life of the Greeks and Romans? Study well the temper and actions of the French and English: you cannot be much mistaken in transferring to the former *most* of the observations you have made with regard to the latter. (U, 92 – 3, Hume's emphasis)

There remains two topics to consider. First we can note Hume's one allusion to

---

18. *Hume's Phil. Pol.*, Chap. 2, esp. p. 110, 117.

Race.[19] He declares "I am apt to suspect the Negroes to be naturally inferior to the Whites" (E (NC) 213n). The basis of this suspicion is the lack of accomplishment from either a Black nation or individual. Nor is this attributable to differences in social development since "the most rude and barbarous of the Whites, such as the ancient Germans, the present Tartars, have still something eminent about them, in their valour, form of government, or some other particular"; consequently "such a uniform and constant difference" must be put down to an "original distinction between these breeds of men". But although Hume thus accepts this distinction he makes nothing of it and does not see in it any wider repercussion. Though racial difference is 'original' Hume's use of this difference, or rather his indifference to it, indicates that it, too, seemingly pertains quite literally to the 'tempers and complexions' of men.[20]

Finally in this Chapter, we turn to Hume's remarks on language. In view of the significance of attitudes towards language, as seen in Part I, Hume's own attitude is of especial interest. Perhaps, the most important point is that language is not a subject to which Hume devotes any special attention, it is not an issue he regards as problematic. Though there was, as we discussed in Part I, a lively debate, in the eighteenth century, on the origin of language, and on the explanations given to account for the different languages spoken, this is a debate in which Hume does not engage.

What remarks Hume does make indicate that he subscribes to the school (whose members include Adam Smith, Priestley and Condillac) which sees language as a convention.[21] Language is given, by Hume, as an instance of the general point that human experience is such that mutual interest is promoted through acting in harmony and that this is possible without the need for promises (T, 490). Languages are thus "fixed by human convention and agreement" (M, 123) and in his *Letter from a Gentleman* (1745) Hume illustrates his natural/artificial distinction by declaring that "Sucking is an Action natural and Speech is artificial".[22] To say that language is a human convention is not, of course, to say that it is arbitrary, since, for Hume as we have seen repeatedly, there are constancies which hold at all times and in all places. Accordingly, there are universal

19. It is true that in another place Hume avers that "The difference of complexion is a sensible and real difference" (E (PG) 57) which is contrasted with absurd differences over articles of faith. For discussion of the influence of Hume's racism, see R. Popkin, 'Hume's Racism', *Philosophical Forum* (1977/8) 211 – 226.

20. Hume's use of the term 'complexion' here can justifiably be read as referring to skin-colour since, one, this meaning had become current by the eighteenth century, two, Hume uses the word in this connexion at E (PG) 57 and, three, his discussion of 'Race' is, in fact, in terms of colour. Human nature is thus basically unaffected by any factor seemingly superficial by definition. Incidentally, this aside by Hume was picked up by Beattie, in his general assault, for being nothing other than assertion and, as such, not proved; indeed, it is falsified by the example of the Peruvians. *Essay on the Nature and Immutability of Truth*, 7th Edit. (1807) p. 424 – 5.

21. Cf. C.J. Berry, 'Adam Smith's "Considerations" on Language", *JHI* (1974) 130 – 138.

22. Ed. E.C. Mossner & J.V. Price, p. 31. Contrast this with the opening sentence from Herder's prize-winning Essay on language discussed in Chapter 2.

elements in language – "The epithets sociable, good-natured, humane, merciful, grateful, friendly, generous, beneficent or their equivalents, are known in all languages and universally express the highest merit which human nature is capable of bestowing" (M, 9). Human nature is such that the susceptibility to pain and pleasure is uniform and thus the moral distinctions expressed in language are uniform in their associations.

It is important to note the element of priority here – "The distinction therefore between these species of sentiment being so great and evident, language must soon be *moulded upon it* and must invent a peculiar set of terms in order to express those universal sentiments of censure and approbation which arise from humanity, or from views of general usefulness and its contrary" (M, 95, my emphasis). Though language derives from certain universal constants (including the operation of the principles of association (T, 10; U, 32)) it can still be imprecise so that it may well happen, as we saw earlier in the case of taste, that men "differ in the language and yet agree in their sentiments or differ in their sentiments yet agree in their language" (E (FPG) 34n). In addition, language, as befits a convention, is itself subject to caprices which turn disputes into "merely verbal" ones (T, 262).

Hume, of course, is aware that the existence of different languages does have consequences. He does link together language and manners. This has incidental social repercussions, as he observes in his critique of Locke's theory of tacit consent – "can we seriously say that a poor peasant or artisan has a free choice to leave his country when he knows no foreign language or manners. . ." (E (OC) 462). More generally, as we saw above, Hume does conjoin language and manners in his discussions of national character (E (NC) 208, 214) and sympathy (T, 318). Hume even extends this conjunction on one occasion to noting that a different language "keeps two nations inhabiting the same country from mixing with each other" (E (NC) 210). But all that Hume does here is cite, as an illustration of this observation, the contrast between the Turks and the Greeks. Thus, although Hume does see an association between language and manners this is not necessary, for "we may often remark a wonderful mixture of manners and characters in the same nation, speaking the same language, and subject to the same government" and the converse is also possible (E (NC) 212, 214). All of this is pertinent to comments made in Chapter 5. There we remarked that though Hume seemingly sees the composition of social life in terms of human interactions and expectations, which solidify into habits, the relationship between the societally specific character of the habits and the individual is not pursued. This point (together with the operation of sympathy) we shall discuss again but here what is germane is that the same holds for Hume's discussion of language.

Though men interact and language is recognised as part of this process it is not accorded any special status. As such, Hume's treatment of language fits simply and straightforwardly into the broad structure of his thought. All languages exhibit formal similarities derived from the constitution of human nature. Indeed, as we saw in Chapter 5 and have just seen again, the similarities are put down to the operation of association. Mandelbaum has noticed how associationism was

110

used to explain similarities instead of, as might have been expected, differences.[23] Though it is true, as Mandelbaum also points out, that Locke did emphasise the divergency of social practices[24] this, as we noted in Chapter 1, was part of his programme in his attack on innate ideas. But, Locke's commitment to Natural Law precluded acceptance of such different practices as each of equal value, hence as we mentioned in Chapter 4, his use of custom to explain error (divergence).

Although Mandelbaum does not put it in quite these terms, it is the assumptions about human nature that operate to account for the (unexpected) use of associationism to explain similarities between social practices. For Hume, as we have seen, the susceptibility to pleasure and pain is independent of societal context and, because *all* men are in that manner susceptible, then, for example, the condemnation of crime or immorality "arises entirely from the sentiment of disapprobation which by the *structure of human nature* we *unavoidably* feel on the apprehension of barbarity or treachery" (M, 111, my emphases). As we shall see later, one consequence of this position is that men are not held to be entirely malleable. Thus, to return specifically to language; although different men speak languages this does not make a *fundamental* difference. Moral (and aesthetic) distinctions still hold in such a manner that they are open to the comprehension, and hence evaluation, of any observer.

There is one final aspect of Hume's approach to language that needs to be considered. In fact, it is the *absence* of any discussion that is significant. The context at issue here is Hume's discussions of animals. It is one of the characteristics of the *Treatise* that Hume includes chapters on the bearing of his analysis of human nature to that of *animal* nature. Moreover, this is no merely trivial characteristic because he includes a chapter on 'Of Reason in Animals' in the *First Enquiry*. In all his discussions of animals and their relationship to men Hume does not once regard language as a differential. Here Hume is perhaps more exceptional than ever. The utilisation of the ability or inability to use a language, to speak, as a criterion to distinguish man from the brutes has been a persistent theme in Western thought from the Greeks onwards. Admittedly in the eighteenth-century, this criterion was a subject of intense speculation, of which Monboddo's *Origin and Progress of Language* (1771 – 1791) was only the chief, and most notorious, representative, with his argument that language is not decisive evidence of humanity, so that accordingly, the Orang Outang can, and should,

23. M. Mandelbaum, *History, Man and Reason*, p. 157. Cf. C.W. Hendel, *Studies in the Philosophy of David Hume*, p. 111; J. Chapman, *Political Theory*, p. 86.

24. Thus in Mandelbaum's quotation from Locke (*History, Man & Reason*, p. 150 though with wrong reference) "He that will carefully peruse the history of mankind, and look abroad into the several tribes of men, and with indifference survey their actions, will be able to satisfy himself that there is scarce that principle of morality to be named, or rule to be thought on. . .which is not somewhere or other slighted and condemned by the general fashion of whole societies of men [governed by practical opinions and rules of living quite opposite to others]" (*Essay* I; 3: 10). The elision contains the important comment – "those only excepted that are absolutely necessary to hold society together".

be given the status Man.[25]

Hume's theme, in his discussions is, in fact, to stress the similarity of the operation of his principles in both men and animals. In Hegel, on the other hand, the dis-similarity between men and animals is stressed. The fact that Hume is able to attribute to animals "a reasoning that is not in itself different, nor founded on different principles, from that which appears in human nature" (T, 177) is testimony to a conviction that mental operations do not require language, which by implication, is to demote its significance. Thus, if language is not used to differentiate men from animals, it is scarcely remarkable that Hume does not use it to differentiate *between* men.

25. See Vol. 1, Bk. 1, Chap. 14; Bk. 2, Chaps. 8 & 9. He further discussed the point in his other major work *Antient Metaphysics* (1779 – 1799), Vol. 3, Bk. 2, Chap. 1 & Appendix; Vol. 4, Bk. 1, Chaps. 2, 5. The *Origin and Progress of Language* was partly translated by Herder.

7. HABIT HUMAN NATURE AND SOCIETY

This concluding Chapter, to this Part, will draw together and further develop some of the threads of the earlier discussion. It will be concerned with two related issues. The first is an examination, once more, of the role the principle of habit plays in Hume's thought, and why it is crucial to his entire thought that habit-forming is a principle of human nature. To this end, after examining Hume's explanation of the process of habituation, a number of passages will be analysed more minutely. To assist this analysis a stipulative distinction will be drawn between the operation of the principle of habit and a process of acculturation. The second issue will relate this distinction to a fuller discussion of Hume's account of sympathy, and its implications for his theory of human nature.

As we saw in the last Chapter, it was to moral causes that Hume attributed the constitution of 'national character'. We also saw that these moral causes (the factors to which reference should be made in the explanation of diversity) operated by rendering "a peculiar set of manners *habitual* to us" (E (NC) 202, my emphasis). It is this process of habituation that we must now examine.

We have seen that Hume subscribes to a theory of 'partial affection' but that, even so, he upholds, in his later work, the position (it is experientially certified) that a principle of humanity cannot be denied (M, 93). Man is a sociable creature and this propensity to associate with our fellows "makes us enter deeply into each other's sentiments" (E (NC) 208). This is a bond of union so that, in a passage we have already utilised, "where a number of men are united into one political body, the occasions of their intercourse must be so frequent for defence, commerce and government, that, together with the same speech or language, they must acquire a resemblance in their manners, and have a common or national character, as well as a personal one, peculiar to each individual" (E (NC) 208). What is decisive in the establishment of such a character is the endurance of the union. It is here that habit comes into play. It maintains the coherence necessary for a character to form — "whatever it be that forms the manners of one generation, the next must imbibe a deeper tincture of the same dye; men being more susceptible of all impressions during infancy, and retaining these impressions as long as they remain in the world" (E (NC) 208 – 9; cf. U, 95; T, 116).

Here, by inference, can be seen once again, the importance of socialisation, as provided by the family and education. Hume's treatment of education is closely related to his treatment of habit. It is important and, significantly, moreover, its influence (accounting for "more than half of those opinions that prevail among mankind") is "built almost on the same foundation of custom and repetition as our reasonings from causes and effects" (T, 117). Though Hume does lay stress on education, and custom, the import of his argument *here* is to mitigate the scope and significance of this stress. This mitigation is expressed more fully elsewhere, though for a similar reason, in his argument against the "sceptical" position that "all moral distinctions arise from education" (M, 42). That, whilst of course, education does have this "powerful influence", the view to the effect that

all moral effection or dislike arises from this origin will never surely be allowed by any judicious inquirer. Had nature made no such distinction, founded on the original constitution of the mind, the words honourable and shameful, lovely and odious, noble and despicable had never had place in any language, nor could politicians, had they invented these terms, ever have been able to render them intelligible or make them convey any idea to the audience. . .The social virtues must, therefore, be allowed to have a natural beauty and amiableness, which at first antecedent to all precept or education, recommends them to the esteem of uninstructed mankind and engages their affections. (M, 42 – 3, Hume's emphasis)

Again, we can see not only Hume's abjuration of ethical relativism, but also an implicit denial of the radical malleability of man. This latter point will be developed below.

This aspect of education and custom in Hume's discussion echoes Locke, even to the extent that Hume comments that "custom may lead us into some false comparison of ideas" (T, 116). Moreover, the very tenacity of opinions imbibed in infancy means that there is recalcitrance to future (more informed) amendment, so that the maxims of education "are frequently contrary to reason and even to themselves in different times and places" (T, 117). This fact, when coupled with the anti-sceptical argument outlined above, has the important consequence that it gives Hume a perspective from which to accept and explain diversity whilst still being able to adopt an evaluative stance.

This can be developed by taking up from Chapter 5 Hume's distinction between two sorts of general rules. First, there are imaginative, customary, general rules or 'prejudices', such as the view that "an Irishman cannot have wit and a Frenchman cannot have solidity" (T, 146). According to Hume, 'human nature' is "very subject to errors of this kind" (T, 147), because, owing to the "nature of custom", it associates those similar in some degree – such as, to continue the example, being born in Ireland. Against this first sort of general rule, which prevails among the 'vulgar', Hume sets the second sort, which are "form'd on the nature of our understanding and on our experience of its operations in the judgments we form concerning objects" (T, 149). It is these latter rules (themselves, of course, the product of habit and experience) by which "wise men" (T, 150) are guided, and by which "we learn to distinguish the accidental circumstances from the efficacious causes" (T, 149).

The principle behind this distinction here between the rules of the wise and those of the vulgar is an important one in Hume's thought, because, besides being an explanation of the role of the 'scientist' (moral, as well as 'natural'), it throws considerable light on the meaning and significance of his theory of human nature. Crucially, it enables Hume to pass judgment on habitual practices; in particular, to see and designate superstitions for what they are, to wit, "false opinion" and a "pestilent distemper" (E (Sui) 585) — inferior beliefs produced by ignorance and barbarism. There is no suggestion that they might be the expression of a distinct self-authenticating way of life; instead, they are "frivolous, useless and burdensome" (M, 30).

What is at issue here is the relationship between a formal account of social life and a substantive account of rationality. To recapitulate: for Hume, habit forming is part of human nature; it is a constant uniform principle and so everybody contracts habits. Habit must be a constant principle because of the 'work' it has to do in explaining the world's evidentially apparent orderliness. This applies to the social as well as to the natural world. Amidst the variety of particular social habits is the uniformity of habituation, which, due to the uniformity of human nature and inescapable relative scarcity of resources, in all societies, is responsible for the rules of justice. This line of argument, since it yields all the requisite information about social life, permits Hume to regard as unimportant the question as to what effects having particular habits has on an individual. In other words, Hume's non-contextualism separates the habituating from the particular habits habituated. It is a contingent variable about one group of men that it has one particular set of habits, for example, worshipping their ancestors, and, similarly, it is a contingent variable that another group has another set. The particularity of the society, and of the beliefs of its members, make no difference to the operation of the 'regular springs' of human behaviour, or to the operation of 'the constant and uniform principles of human nature'. This is why history (and anthropology) can "give us a clue" (U, 94) or 'furnish us with materials' as to their operation; materials that can be gleaned without prejudice from the reported experience of the ancient Germans, the contemporary tribes of the Americas as well as the observation of eighteenth-century Scotsmen. The 'science of man' does not have a parochial subject-matter. Indeed, like the other sciences, it is enabled to penetrate beneath the "pretexts and appearances" (U, 94) that deceive the vulgar and to reveal the causes at work — the uniform principles of human nature. It is this general indifference to specific social location, when seeking a comprehension of human nature, that supports the claim that Hume's account of social life (its internality) can be denominated formal and it is his conviction that the 'science of man' can reveal the true springs of human nature that justifies the attribution to Hume of a substantive theory of rationality.

Both of these are involved in Hume's labelling of particular habits as superstitions. The fact that Hume's 'science of man' has elicited the proper basis of human nature means that he has a benchmark (what the 'wise' habituate) which enables him to 'order' the diverse social practices evident to experience (recall his judgment of the Koran cited in the last chapter). Kemp Smith, indeed, sees Hume here, in his distinction between the wise and the vulgar, using 'experience' in a normative sense.[1] This relates not only to the general thesis as to the Enlightenment's 'situation', as outlined in Chapter 1, but also, more particularly, to the substantive account of rationality within Hume's thought. Habits such as parental infanticide which, as noted earlier, are seen by Hume as being 'shocking to nature', may 'fit' the specific culture, but Hume's assumptions and thinking make him see only superstition and barbarism.[2] Although this may well be an extreme case the principle holds good for all the various customs that Hume dismisses derogatively as superstitions, which includes "a considerable ingredient in all religions" (E (SE) 77). Superstition is exposed by the "scrutiny of sense and science" (M, 29). In all superstitious practices a proper (universalist) scientific study of human nature reveals that the practitioners have a *false* picture of the world. These are not different pictures, self-validating 'forms of life', but false ones that can be legitimately so judged. It is from this perspective, and bearing in mind the argument in Chapter 1, that Hume can be seen to be a 'man of the Enlightenment'. This is despite his undeniable epistemological atypicality and his resignation to the knowledge that these customs are too deep-rooted for their eradication to be expected at some future dawn.

This interpretation of the connexion between Hume's evaluative theory of habit and his theory of human nature will now be developed by drawing a distinction between 'habit' and 'acculturation'. This stipulative distinction serves a dual heuristic purpose – as an analytical perspective and a historical context. Hume's emphasis upon the necessarily uniform, the presupposition of the 'science of man', means that he does not have a contextualist theory of human nature. The process of acculturation, as here understood, is a by-product of this theory. This process is a radical one in the sense that it makes a man concrete by specifying, or individuating, his conceptions, his identity, his very nature as a result of his total but specific, and individual, socio-cultural context – in Hegel's terms, as we will demonstrate in Part III, what the individual *is* is his culture. It is a consequence of acculturation that as the context changes so too does the man. Man is thus malleable, so that he now becomes intrinsically a cultural being. The point to be made here is that Hume's use of habit is not radical in this sense, since he does not, for all his recognition of social interaction and inter-dependence, outline a process of acculturation, as here stipulated.

However, it is true that Hume does, on a number of occasions, seemingly connect the mental abilities of men with their cultural situation, and it would be *possible* to read these as his subscription to the view that human nature is radical-

---

1. *The Philosophy of David Hume*, p. 382f.

2. Though not put in these terms J. Noxon's interpretation of Hume's belief as philosophical, in that it provides an evaluative criterion, and the close connexion he sees between this theory and Hume's antipathy to religion, appears to be making a similar point. *Hume's Philosophical Development*, Pt. 5 passim. Cf. also J. Passmore, 'Hume and the Ethics of Belief', in G. Morice (ed.), *Hume: Bicentenary Papers*, pp. 77–92, esp. p. 90.

ly malleable or acculturated. These apparent connexions will now be examined to the end of confirming the above analysis in the light of what would be counter-evidence.

Hume's most systematic treatment of this topic is in the *Natural History of Religion*. At several places in that work he remarks on the capacity of the rude or vulgar mind – enquiries "concerning the frame of nature" are "too large and comprehensive for their [savages'] narrow capacities", they cannot "comprehend the grandeur of its author" (N, 42). The notion of a perfect being is reached not by "any process of argument but by a certain train of thinking more suitable to their genius and capacity", they are not guided by "reason, of which they are in a great measure incapable" (N, 57, 58) so that they are "incapable of conceiving those sublime qualities [of the Deity]" (N, 60).

Such sentiments occur elsewhere in Hume's writings. In the *First Enquiry*, again referring to religion, Hume mentions that speculative dogmas "could not possible be conceived or admitted in the early stages of the world, when mankind being wholly illiterate formed an idea of religion more suitable to their weak apprehension" (U, 143). In the *Second Enquiry*, the savage is declared to have "but faint conceptions of a general rule or system or behaviour", a situation that is contrasted, two sentences later, with "we, more accustomed to society and enlarged reflections. . ." (M, 95). The first point here is echoed in the *History*, in the Appendix on Anglo-Saxon manners, where an explanation of the irregularities of succession is put down to the Saxons being "not sensible of the general advantages attending a fixed rule" (HE, 46). In the *Treatise*, Hume remarks, that "it is impossible" that men in their wild, uncultivated state are able by study and reflection alone ever to attain the knowledge that society is advantageous (T, 486). Finally, with perhaps one of the clearest presumptions of the radical construction, in the essay *Of the Original Contract*, Hume avers that the idea of a compact for general submission was "an idea far beyond the comprehension of savages" (E (OC) 455).

Despite the radical construction (that Hume adheres to a notion of acculturation so that human nature is contextual) that can be put on these quotations it can be shown both internally and historically that such is not Hume's meaning. What there is in Hume, as we sketched out in the previous chapter, is a general theory of cultivation or the development of civilisation. Hume depicts the savage as prone to superstition, as stupid (N, 55; D, 129) and most commonly as ignorant (N, 55; 35, 43; E (SE) 75; E (PG) 59, 61; U, 126, 140; HE, 425; E (RA) 280; etc.).[3] Further, savages being subject to the pressure of "numerous wants

---

3. Hume frequently juxtaposes sound 'philosophy' and superstition, E (Sui) 585; T, 271; U, 21; U, 25; H, 665. This connexion between superstition and ignorance ("from the grossness of its superstitions we may infer the ignorance of the age" (H, 252)) is a well-established 'classical' sentiment – see, for example, Plutarch's essay *On Superstition* or Cicero's *de Divinatione* (Hume explicitly refers to Cicero in this regard (E (Sui) 585)). More recently, it had been a prominent motif in the Deist movement in England to decry superstition; again, the same sources were drawn upon – Toland planned a book 'Superstition Unmasked' of which the first part would be a commentary on Plutarch's 'admirable treatise' (cf. J. Redwood, *Reason, Ridicule and Religion*, p. 142): Trenchard wrote a work *The Natural History of Superstition* (1709) of which both the title and content suggest to F. Manuel that Hume "probably perused" it, *The Eighteenth Century Confronts the Gods*, p. 72.

and passions" have no leisure. Thus, the savage's inability to attain knowledge of society's advantages by reflection alone is a concomitant of the *lack* of leisure. Hume does not argue that the extent of social development has any direct effect on the cognitive capacities and techniques of man. Human nature does not change along with society. The "chief characteristic" that distinguishes civilisation from barbarism is the "indissoluble chain" of industry, humanity and knowledge (E (RA) 278 – 80) but this correlates positively with a sociological variable (extent of leisure) and, moreover, pertains to the 'tempers' of men which means that it provides merely "a very inconsiderable" variation in human nature (T, 281).

Similarly, both quotations just given from the two *Enquiries* should be understood in this light. The 'enlarged reflections' that 'we' enjoy are consequent upon our cultivation but that *that* in itself entails fundamental change, as the radical argument decrees, is not warranted by the quotation. The religions of the savages are as they are because of their illiteracy and attendant '*weak* apprehension'. In like fashion, in the account of the Saxons, their insensibility to the advantages of a fixed rule is tied to their being "so little restrained by laws and cultivated by science" (HE, 46). The passage from the essay on the *Original Contract* is part of Hume's argument that the origin of government happens on a much more piecemeal basis than the Contractarians allow. Hume is not here making a positive statement about the primitive mind. Rather, indeed, recalling that the argument is against the notion of '*general* submission', his thrust is the same as in the *Second Enquiry* concerning the 'faint conception' that a savage has of framing 'general notions', which is attributable to the savage being 'rude' and 'untaught'. The presence of such 'generality' is the hall-mark of the Rule of Law and civilisation. In like manner, the incapability of the savage to comprehend the sublime qualities of the 'author of the frame of nature' is explicable by the persistence of superstition, and its attendant causes of ignorance and lack of refinement. In fact, Hume's designation of polytheism, quoted in the last Chapter, makes this very point, since it is "the primitive religion of *uninstructed* mankind" (N, 37, my emphasis). When society has developed and superstition been banished then there is time "to admire the regular face of nature" and search for the true causes of everyday phenomena (N, 35).[4]

In sum, therefore, Hume puts no weight on historical and cultural differences between men, other than the *degree* of cultivation and that, as we have seen, is an 'accident' or contingent variable. Hume does not, as the principle of acculturation requiries, and as Giarrizzo seems to suggest,[5] tie together the degree of social

---

4. Adam Smith argued the same in his posthumously published essay *The principles which lead and direct Philosophic Enquiries illustrated by the History of Astronomy* (1795 – written in the 1750s). This similarity is probably not coincidental and Dugald Stewart connects this work in its approach with Hume's *Natural History*. *Life of Adam Smith* prefixed to Smith's *Moral Sentiments*, p. xxxv ff.

5. He writes "cosi la storia naturale dell'umanita diverta. . .storia delle 'revolutions of the mind' che accompagno e seguono i progressi della societa civile", *David Hume: politico e storico*, p. 115. Cf. Meinecke who sees the *Natural History* opening the door to a developmental history of the

development with a distinctive 'intellect'. Indeed, such a position would render untenable the very idea of a *natural* history of religion. Hume *because* of the constancy of human nature is enabled to write history. He can conjecture the behaviour of savages by placing himself imaginatively into their situation. Such a procedure is licensed because human nature is uniform 'in all nations and ages'. Hence it is that Hume (along with conjectural or natural historians generally) is able to say what 'naturally' or 'necessarily' takes, or has taken, place (see the quotations from Hume on p. 59n, 101 and Millar on p. 98).

This procedure makes no judgment about the intrinsic quality of the primitive mind. To argue that such a judgment is implicit in Hume requires not only an unwarranted exegetical licence, especially when faced with the overwhelming explicit evidence of Hume's conviction that human nature is constant and uniform, but also, in addition, some explicit evidence somewhere that Hume was sensible of such a conception as the 'primitive mind'. But, there is no qualitative concept of the 'primitive' in Hume. There are, of course, sound historical reasons why this should be so. The recognition effectively of the principle of acculturation was, as we outlined in Part I, not (with the ever exceptional Vico) formulated until the end of the eighteenth century by Herder and, as Hume himself said, constancy was "universally acknowledged" (U, 92). As a final observation, it is worth commenting that the attributes of the savage, his ignorance and superstition, do not belong to some far away, in either time or space, society but are attributable to a considerable portion of eighteenth-century British society (the vulgar or rabble).[6] In contrast, the idea of acculturation is that *all* men in a society share the same individual and distinct *Weltanschauung*.[7] In other words, if man is analytically differentiated from his culture then in *any* culture men can exhibit putatively 'primitive' behaviour patterns. Hume has a non-contextualist theory of human nature; he does not see man's behaviour (its intelligibility) as societally specific.

Thus, Hume's recognition of malleability is not to be understood in any definitionally pervasive sense. The examination of another passage can demonstrate this finally. Hume writes that "the prodigious effects of education may convince us that the mind is not altogether stubborn and inflexible, but will admit of many alterations from its original make and structure" (E (Sc) 173). However, in light of both the above argument and what Hume *says* here, extreme malleability or

human mind but who seems Hume's psychology as inhibiting him from carrying through his own developmental thinking, *Die Entstehung des Historismus*, 2nd Edit., p. 211 – 2. For discussion of Hume's alleged 'developmentalism' see infra.

6. Cf. Manuel, *Eighteenth Century and Gods*, p. 129, who comments that Hume's (Baylian) conclusion was that "the vulgar and the primitive mind were the same".

7. Cf. E (NC) 203, where Hume writes "A soldier and a priest are different characters, *in all nations*, and *all ages*" (my emphasis). Not only are there similar functions performed in all societies but the attendant characters, discernible by the science of man, are also not societally specific. All soldiers are generous and all priests, *because* their way of life is contrary to that of the military, have the opposite character.

recognition of acculturation is not countenanced. The phrase 'not altogether' is indicative of mitigation and the alterations do not effect the original structure as such. True, alterations are admitted but these, as we saw in Chapter 4, are dependent upon the necessary presence of constant uniformities, and it is their presence, and their basic explanatory force, that means that Hume cannot be held to subscribe to the radical argument as here outlined.[8]

What then does this tell us finally about Hume's understanding of habit? It is possible to say that the role 'habit' plays in Hume's thought is an attack on rationalism, rather than an awareness of pervasive personality and conceptual change. Thus, although Hume is aware of a temporal dimension in the modification of behaviour through habit, this dimension structured as it is within a uniformitarian framework, is only partially exploited. Thus, history, for example, is premised on man's uniformity and the content of history is not held to have fundamental individuating or specifying consequences, because such inconstancy between actions and characters would entail, on Hume's premises, the overthrowing of 'the very essence of necessity'. Hegel, as we shall see, on his premises, was only able to retain necessity (and substantive rationality) by making it synonymous with the historical process.

Bearing this general conclusion in mind we can now turn to the second issue announced in the opening paragraph. Men live in society and they are, as we noted in Chapter 5, subject to strong pressures to conform to the standards of their peers and compatriots. Hume's account of this social interdependence of men, together with his use of the concept of sympathy, we can term his account of 'socio-psychical dynamics'.

In one place Hume characterises these dynamics as "the minds of men are mirrors to one another" (T, 365). By this he means not only that men 'reflect' each other's emotions, but also that these 'rays' 'reverberate'. He goes on to provide an illustration of his meaning, and of these dynamics, – "the pleasure which a rich man receives from his possessions, being thrown upon the beholder, causes a pleasure and esteem; which sentiments again, being perceiv'd and sympathiz'd with, encrease the pleasure of the possessor; and being once more reflected become a new foundation for pleasure and esteem in the beholder". To gloss this: there is an 'original satisfaction' from riches and the 'pleasures of life' thereby bestowed; from this is generated, by virtue of sympathy with the possessor's pleasure, love and esteem in others; yet this esteem is now a 'secondary satisfaction' for the possessor and, indeed, it becomes "one of the principal recommendations of riches" even to the extent of being "the chief reason" for desiring them. Thus the value we place in 'things' is not independent of the responses of others.

---

8. The same may be said of another statement from the paragraph immediately following the last quotation – "Habit is another powerful means of reforming the mind and implanting in it good dispositions and inclinations" (E (Sc) 173). It is worth noting that this Essay is one of a series wherein Hume puts forward notions to which he does not necessarily subscribe – even in one entitled 'The Sceptic'.

This passage has been analysed because it is important to appreciate the principles, and their assumptions, that operate here for Hume. Charles Hendel has argued that this passage is an instance of Hume's position whereby we know our self to be real through "intercourse with others who define it for us by their living presence".[9] This comment will replay speculation.

Aside from the fact that this view of Hume's is itself, in a large measure, traditional,[10] both Hume's premises and his intellectual paradigm (see Chapter 4) serve to delimit the sense in which the Humean 'self' may be said to be 'defined'. If all that is signified is that men as social beings are inter-dependent, so that the very notion of a self is only comprehensible in a social matrix, then this is undeniable and our own account of the operation of socio-psychical dynamics in Hume's thought has implicitly brought it out. But, if Hendel's wording is construed to mean that 'definition' by 'intercourse' is that which makes a self *what* it is then different forms of (social) intercourse, which is to say, different habits, should entail different selves. On this stronger construction of 'define' this would mean that Hume has articulated a concept of an acculturated self. However, and this is the point of issue, Hume's account of the operation of sympathy, as a constant principle of human nature, means he possesses no such concept.

The sympathetic process is the conversion of an idea into an impression. From the observation of another's behaviour it is causally inferred (as "in any other matter of fact" (T, 319)), given the constancy of human nature, that they are experiencing certain passions or sentiments. This is an idea in our mind. Yet, because of this very constancy in human nature, men are similar and, thus, we can sympathise with the inferred passion, so that "we enter into the sentiments of others and embrace them with facility and pleasure" (T, 318). Given the general importance of sympathy in Hume's account of morality, that we outlined in Chapter 5, these inferences cannot be exceptional; indeed, Hume provides an explanation of their universality. He holds that "ourself is always intimately present to us" (T, 320; cf. "with us" T, 317; "conscious of" T, 339) thus giving us "a lively conception of our person" so that "whatever object therefore is related to ourselves must be conceived with a like vivacity of conception" (T, 317). Since other men are related to us (they are similar to or resemble us) then the idea of them experiencing the passion is enlivened into an impression (the sympathetic conversion) so that we experience "the very passion itself" (T, 317, 319).

9. *Studies in the Philosophy of David Hume*, p. 269. He is seemingly followed by Forbes *Hume's Philosophical Politics*, p. 106.

10. Cf. F. Hutcheson, "The Pleasure of the Proprietor depends upon the admiration of others: he robs himself of his chief Enjoyment if he excludes Spectators", *Essay on the Nature and Conduct of the Passions and Affections* (1728), p. 172. The general sentiment can be read back into Cicero − "for where there are many of the same humour and same inclinations everyone sees, in some measure, his own self and is accordingly delighted in the person of another", *De Officiis*, Bk. 1, Chap. 17. Finally, Hume's point is repeated virtually verbatim by Bentham (*Principles of Morals and Legislation* (1789) ed. W. Harrison, p. 174): a fact which is not entirely superfluous because it *suggests* that this position is based on assumptions far removed from a recognition of a socially plastic human nature − see infra.

But, although Hume puts this emphasis on personal inter-relation, it is unwarranted to proceed to claim that the individual becomes self-conscious as a *consequence* of sympathetic interaction. This is explicit; in sympathy there is nothing "that fixes our attention on ourselves" (T, 340). Furthermore, we are "at all times" conscious of ourselves and this consciousness is presupposed (is "determined by an original and natural instinct") in the passions of pride and humility (T, 286; cf. T, 277).[11] Thus, whilst we may enter "so deep into the opinions and affections of others" (T, 319) there is nothing, strictly understood, in Hume's account to say that we thereby know ourselves to be 'real'. Hume allows that similarity of manners, character, country or language "facilitates" the process of sympathetically entering into another's affections. But this is not definitional; it is only a facilitation which operates "besides the general resemblance of our natures" (T, 318). If the self were (following the 'strong' construction) defined through social intercourse (acculturated) this would restrict the scope of sympathy but Hume, because of his non-contextual view of human nature, believes that it is possible to sympathise with any man – "the pleasure of a stranger, for whom we have no friendship, pleases us only by sympathy" (T, 576). Moreover, given the importance of sympathy to Hume's ethical theory, such a restricted view would seem tantamount to an espousal of ethical relativism, which is a position that Hume openly rebuts. Though it may well indeed, be the case as Forbes holds that anthropology (he cites Kluckhohn) presupposes a universal human nature, that does not mean, to repeat a point made earlier, that Hume's eighteenth-century (pre-contextualist) understanding of human nature and *his* argument against relativism is assimilable to that of a twentieth-century social scientist[12] who must come to terms with a different (post-contextualist) range of arguments.

Hume's whole approach is far removed, as we shall now, in conclusion, demonstrate, from what has been variously described as the developmental, active or dynamic theory of the self. To claim that such a theory is implicit in Hume is uninformative and, in a strict sense, unhistorical for, as this study is aiming to convey, such a theory (as well as the related theory of self-consciousness) was only articulated by virtue of the prior enunciation of the premises of a contextualist theory of human nature. As a prior requirement to examining in what sense the

11. Cf. also Mercer's argument that the Humean process of sympathy presupposes that the sympathiser has experienced the impression of which the other's experience is, in the sympathiser's mind, a 'faint image', *Sympathy and Ethics*, p. 34.

12. *Hume's Philosophical Politics*, p. 112n. Additionally these social scientists are not agreed. See, for example, the well-known work of B.L. Whorf who, from studies of Hopi language in particular, sees linguistic differences as constituting different 'thought-worlds', *Language, Thought and Reality*, ed. J.B. Carroll, p. 147, 158, 239 – 40, 252, 262 – 3 et passim; or Clifford Geertz, 'The Impact of the Concept of Culture on the Concept of Man', in his *The Interpretation of Culture*, pp. 35 – 54, who regards the drawing of a line between the universal or constant and the local or variable in man as a falsification of the human situation; there is no such thing as human nature independent of culture – man is 'finished off' by culture but this finishing is highly particular. Incidentally, Geertz links the rise of a scientific concept of culture with the overthrow of the Enlightenment's theory of human nature.

Humean 'self' is dynamic, it is necessary to say a brief word about his theory of
the self in its own right. This is one of the most intensely debated aspects of
Hume's whole philosophy but here only a cursory summation of his argument is
in order.

Much of the academic debate on this topic stems from Hume's own explicit
hesitations. He admits, in the Appendix to the *Treatise* (published with Part III
in 1740 — a year after the first two Parts) that his account of personal identity (in
Part I) is "very defective" (T, 635). The defect concerns the incompatibility that
Hume personally finds ("this difficulty is too hard for my understanding. I pretend not, however, to pronounce it absolutely insuperable" (T, 636)) between his
analysis of self and any subsequent principle of synthesis. It follows from his
analysis of perception, and its discreteness, that "we have no impression of the
self or substance, as something simple and individual" for "I never can perceive
this self without one or more perceptions" (T, 634). The upshot, as he puts it in
the text, is that "mankind. . .are nothing but a bundle or collection of different
perceptions" (T, 252). Nevertheless, it is obvious that there is a "propension to
ascribe an identity to these successive perceptions and to suppose ourselves
possest of an invariable and uninterrupted existence through the whole course of
our lives" (T, 253). The principle of synthesis is required to account for this.

In the text this synthesis, or unity constitutive of identity, is put down to the
associative quality of the imagination. There is nothing 'real' in identity to bind
together the discrete perceptions. Instead, the synthesis is fictitious being comprised in the imagination by the three principles of association — resemblance,
contiguity and causation — so that "our notions of personal identity proceed entirely from the smooth and uninterrupted progress of the thought along a train of
connected ideas" (T, 260). It is this account that Hume declares to be unsatisfac-
tory in the Appendix for he now regards this explanation as incapable of accounting for the fact that we do attribute to the self 'real' simplicity and identity (T,
635). Accordingly, since Hume is unwilling to jettison his associationism, with its
inherent contingency consequent upon the doctrine that perceptions are discrete,
he is forced to declare his account defective.

Hume's own doubts about his treatment of the self, as witnessed not only by the
Appendix to the *Treatise*, but also by the absence of any discussion of this issue in
the later *First Enquiry*, together with his abandonment of the elaborate mechanics
of association in his discussions of sympathy in the *Second Enquiry*, all point to
the problematic nature of this issue in his thought. The significance of this, for this
study, is that despite this, and because of his unwillingness to jettison his theory as
a whole over this issue, Hume's own theory of socio-psychical dynamics is con-
structed from his own premises. This conclusion is all the more justified when it is
borne in mind that throughout Hume's discussion in Book 1 of the *Treatise*, of
personal identity (and its attendant and consequent problems) he is explicitly dealing with it "as it regards our thought and imagination" (T, 253). The question of
the self as it regards the "passions or concern we take in ourselves" is not subject to
the same problems and it is this latter sense which figures in Book 2 in the discussions of pride etc., that is, it figures in the arena of socio-psychical dynamics.

Hume never abandons his belief in human nature as constant. The dynamics, the social/individual interplay, can never be allowed to be so far-reaching as to be constitutive of human nature. Man is not radically malleable. When Hume talks of the need of the human mind to be active he is *not* saying that through activity the human mind is made. This latter position has historically been associated with the contextualist view that men create their own socio-cultural situations and because these situations differ so too do the men who made them. Thus human nature itself is now seen to have a history, to be itself part of history and not 'outside' it. The unity of the self is *now* to be found in activity; it makes itself what it is and is not the passive recipient of external formative forces.

As a final elaboration of this point we can see that Hume does not subscribe to the idea of development. This idea is Aristotelean in origin (*Metaphysics*, Book ⊖) and is based on the distinction between Form and Matter, where the latter lies potentially in the former and development is the actualisation of this potential. Such a schema does, therefore, in its own terms, incorporate change *within* constancy. Hume's theory of human nature and change is implicitly assimilated to this schema by J.B. Stewart — "the potentialities of human nature always are the same, but in the beginning they are not realised, so that civilisation may be described as the development of man's attributes".[13] However, Hume does not see matters in this light. It is a matter of more than incidental importance that it is Hegel who adopts this idea.

Hume had shown the unintelligibility of the concept of power or potential in the *Treatise* (T, 171) — a concept of Scholastic and thence Aristotelean provenance — although that does not preclude him (especially considering his much commented upon inconsistency[14]) from utilising the idea. But, Hume's distinction between the constant and the variable in human nature is static in that man does not have 'attributes' that develop. The variable element ('character', 'temper'; the manners, habits etc.) is a local contingency explicable by the 'science of man'; the diversity is simultaneously evidence of uniformity. Though men might behave differently in different circumstances there is no need in order to explain these differences to have recourse to Aristotelean or evolutionary perspectives. G. Giarrizzo, therefore, misreads the Humean position when he attributes to it the notion of a politico-social organism that has an evolutionary capacity towards *perfettibilità.*[15] For Hume, the development of liberty is merely metaphorically organic. It is the offspring of knowledge and refinement, but, though more is now known in 'enlightened' and 'refined' societies, the men who comprise these societies are the same as those of an earlier epoch. Thus, in his at-

---

13. *The Moral and Political Thought of David Hume*, p. 291 – 2. On p. 297 Hume is said to have placed "extensive reliance on the idea of development".

14. Cf. J. Passmore, "Hume. . .had a quite extraordinary insensitivity to consistency", *Hume's Intentions*, revised ed., p. 131. He repeats the point on p. 152.

15. *David Hume*, p. 121. However, Giarrizzo attributes this to Hume only in his 'liberal phase' for it is a leading theme of Giarrizzo's interpretation that Hume becomes increasingly conservative (and relativist), a movement that is put down to his "paura della perfezione" (p. 48).

tack on the grounds of belief in miracles, Hume remarks that the accounts of miracles "chiefly abound among ignorant and barbarous nations" but

in proportion as we advance nearer the enlightened ages, we soon learn that there is nothing mysterious or supernatural in the case but that all proceeds from the usual propensity of mankind toward the marvellous, and that, though this inclination may at intervals receive a check from sense and learning, it can never be thoroughly extirpated from human nature. (U, 12)

In conclusion, implicit in this distinction between the Humean and the developmental view is a conception of mankind. The developmental (Hegelian) view defines mankind temporally; it assimilates the history of mankind to a process, so that it now 'makes sense' to employ organic language or talk of this 'whole' possessing attributes. Mankind is progressive. To Hume, mankind is defined atemporally; it enjoys certain propensities etc. which are ever present, though their exercise will, as history shows, vary with circumstances — Hume does not employ the language of organicism. Mankind is constant and uniform. It is indicative of their respective philosophies of human nature that for Hegel mankind is the 'subject' of history whilst for Hume mankind is an 'object' for history.

III. HUMAN NATURE AND SOCIETY IN HEGEL

INTRODUCTION

The world has meaning. It signifies something. Hegel's philosophy is the systematisation of this affirmation: an affirmation that is itself necessitated by the world being significant. Thus (and here is the aptness of the circularity that Hegel frequently and persistently designates as the proper characteristic of his philosophy) the affirmation is at once the premise from which the world's significance stems and the product of the world having significance.

Hegel is certainly one of the most self-consciously systematic of all philosophers. The corollary of this is that in studying his philosophy, whilst a start can be made at any point, the comprehension of this point entails the comprehension of the system that gives it meaning. Hence, although our concerns with Hegel are, as they were with Hume, limited, it does mean that explication of this concern will involve and invoke putatively 'wider' issues.

The nub of our concern is this: Hegel sees man as socially (historically) defined and he regards any discussion of man outside society as meaningless; yet the meaning of man's socio-historical nature is to be found in the universality that constitutes the significance of the world. Man is thus concrete and culturally specific or contextual. However, the relativism seemingly implied thereby is rendered inappropriate by seeing both man and the cultures in which he is found as the bearers of the world's meaning.

Our point of entry into the circle is Hegel's understanding of human nature and our perspective the connexions drawn in his thought between this understanding and his interpretation of society and history. As such the treatment formally mirrors that given to Hume in Part II and we shall on occasion indulge in a comparative analysis of certain specific issues dealt with by both thinkers. We shall first examine Hegel's conceptualisation of human nature (Chapter 8). The relationship therein theoretically implied between human nature and society will then be analysed in terms of the major categories (the *Volk* and the State) that can be seen to effectuate this relationship (Chapter 9). The fact that full comprehension of this relationship requires a universal or absolute perspective within an explanation of social diversity is next elucidated in the context of Hegel's philosophy of history (Chapter 10) before finally the bearing of the meaning of this perspective on the individual in interaction with his fellows and environment is examined (Chapter 11).

As with the exposition of Hume, the argument, in this Part also, will require the introduction of certain themes at one place in the argument and their postponement until a more appropriate juncture where they can be discussed in full.

128

The following abbreviations are inserted in parentheses in the text throughout this Part.

WL   *Sämtliche Werke*, ed. G. Lasson (& J. Hoffmeister) (1921).

WG   *Werke*, ed. E. Gans et al. (1840).

WJ   *Sämtliche-Werke (Jubiläumsausgabe)*, ed. H. Glockner (1927.

Ph   *Phänomenologie des Geistes*, tr. as *The Phenomenology of Mind* by J.B. Baillie.

PhK   *Phänomenologie des Geistes − Vorrede*, tr. as *Hegel: Texts and Commentary* by W. Kaufmann.

EL   *Encyclopädie des Philosophischen Wissenschaften − Logik*, tr. as *The Logic of Hegel* by W. Wallace.

EN   *Encyclopädie. . . − Natur*, tr. as *Philosophy of Nature* by A.V. Miller.

EG   *Encyclopädie. . . − Geistes*, tr. as *Philosophy of Mind* by W. Wallace & A.V. Miller.

SL   *Wissenschaft der Logik*, tr. as *Hegel's Science of Logic* by W.H. Johnston & L.G. Struthers in 2 vols.

PR   *Grundlinien der Philosophie des Rechts*, tr. as *Hegel's Philosophy of Right* by T.M. Knox.

PHS   *Philosophie der Weltgeschichte*, tr. as *Hegel's Philosophy of History* by J. Sibree.

PGN   *Philosophie der Weltgeschichte − Einleitung*, tr. as *Lectures on the Philosophy of World History (Introduction)* by H.B. Nisbet.

VG   *Ibid.*, tr. as *Reason in History* by R.S. Hartmann.

PW   *Hegel's Political Writings*, tr. T.M. Knox.

TW   *Early Theological Writings*, tr. T.M. Knox.

TJ   *Hegels Theologische Jugendschriften*, ed. H. Nohl.

GA   *Vorlesungen über die Aesthetik (Einleitung)*, tr. B. Bosanquet in G. Gray, *Hegel on Art, Religion and Philosophy*.

GR   *Vorlesungen über die Philosophie der Religion (Einleitung)*, tr. E.B. Spiers & J.B. Sanderson in Gray.

GPG   *Vorlesungen über die Geschichte der Philosophie (Einleitung)*, tr. E. Haldane & F. Simson in Gray.

PRel   *Vorlesungen über die Philosophie der Religion*, tr. as *Lectures on the Philosophy of Religion* by Spiers & Sanderson in 3 vols.

GP   *Vorlesungen über die Geschichte der Philosophie*, tr. as *History of Philosophy* by Haldane & Simson in 3 vols.

JRI   Jenenser Realphilosophie (1803/4), ed. J. Hoffmeister (= WL, Vol. XIX).

JRII   Jenenser Realphilosophie (1805/6), ed. J. Hoffmeister (= WL, Vol. XX).

8. THE CHARACTERISATION OF HUMAN NATURE

We have seen that the general characterisation of human nature as found in Hume, and in the Enlightenment more generally, as constant and uniform and of its content as particularised into faculties, can be read to have been criticised on those grounds, amongst others, by Herder and his successors. Instead, human nature was now seen, especially in Germany, as an 'organic unity' and as contextual or integrally social. Hegel's own intellectual biography reflects this transition. Thus, according to the exhaustive examination of Hegel's youthful career undertaken by H.S. Harris, the schoolboy Hegel subscribed to the Enlightenment's notion of human nature as possessing a fixed essence but the gradual emergence of a historical conception of human nature can be traced back to an essay of 1787. Indeed, from the evidence of Hegel's remaining juvenilia, Harris argues that "the true focus of Hegel's researches throughout his life was always, properly speaking, man".[1]

We shall commence our examination of Hegel's conceptualisation of human nature, which is as Mandelbaum has observed "one of the least developed aspects of the whole Hegelian system",[2] by returning to his discussion of the actual organisation of the human mind. For Hegel the mind is a living unity or system of processes. The full comprehension of Hegel's meaning can be best gauged by examining the explicit juxtaposition between this definition and its chief alternative – faculty-psychology. This examination will entail a more general discussion of the distinction in Hegel's thought between Reason (*Vernunft*) and Understanding (*Verstand*) and this, in turn, will require an examination of the overall structure and purpose of the Hegelian system.

We saw in Chapter 2 that Herder was severely critical of faculty-psychology and that he, too, saw the human mind in unitary terms. We shall look at Hegel's relationship to Herder shortly but, as we also noted in Part I, faculty-psychology was regarded (not without some justification) as part and parcel of Kant's critical philosophy. Hegel himself, when at his most sympathetic and receptive to Kant,

---

1. *Hegel's Development: Toward the Sunlight 1770 – 1801*, p. 30.
2. *History, Man and Reason: A Study of Nineteenth-Century Thought*, p. 177.

did subscribe to this psychology. For example, the structure of a sketch on Psychology in 1794 is in terms of mental faculties which are heavily indebted to Kant's distinctions.[3] A year earlier in another sketch Hegel had spoken of *Seelenkräfte* and distinguished between theology and religion in terms of the operation of different psychological faculties, namely, understanding and memory in the former and feeling (a matter of the heart) in the latter.[4] However, a few years later at the time of his early (1802) Jena writings Hegel was criticising any such representation of the mind as a bag full of faculties (WJ I, 275); a criticism he was to repeat and elaborate upon in his subsequent writings.

The general tenor of the complaint that Hegel has of the faculty approach is that it misconstrues the mind's living quality; by hypostatising its activities, by separating them into individual faculties, it reduces this living unity to a confusing motley of inter-actions (EL, 238: WG VI, 138). In the *Phänomenologie*, in the discussion of observation as applied to self-consciousness, this motley is again compared to a bag, which contains in it "all sorts of faculties, inclinations and passions" but which happen to be alongside one another; a situation that is all the more incongruous since the ingredients are seen (self-observed) to be "not lifeless inert things but restless active processes" (Ph, 332 – 3; WL II, 200 – 1).

On a number of occasions Hegel's critique is more far-reaching and extreme. In the *Encyclopädie* he explicitly distinguishes between Rational and Empirical Psychology. The former is concerned with abstractly universal determinations or, more simply, unmanifested essence. It is a branch of metaphysics of the pre-Kantian variety. Though Hegel had little time for such speculation, for it treats the mind as a "dead essence" (EG, 6: WG VII, 11), he reserves most of his scorn for the empirical approach to the mind. This approach treats the mind in the same way that it treats any other part of reality. Hegel explicitly connects this approach with post-Baconian science which based itself upon observation and experience. Empirical psychology anatomises the mind (EL, 246: WG VI, 267). It identifies a number of different mental operations which it then proceeds to denominate as particular faculties (*Vermögen*). The result is that the mind is turned into an aggregate of separate independent forces (*Kräften*) which can only be externally connected. The effect of this is so far to misunderstand the mind's organic, systematic, living quality that it kills it "by tearing it asunder into a manifold of independent forces" (EG, 6: WG VII, 11). Thus, Hume's explicit intention to anatomise human nature means that he can only treat it as something lifeless so that he must, perforce, produce a profoundly inadequate account.

Hegel's own comprehension of the mind's organic quality is explicitly contrasted by him to a mechanical approach. Indeed, the view of the mind as a mere aggregate of isolated mental faculties is described as making the mind a "mechanical collection" (EG, 189: WL V, 385). Mechanism in general terms for

3. Harris, *Hegel's Development*, p. 176.

4. Harris, *Hegel's Development*, p. 485, 48. The term *Seelenkräfte* was a commonplace in eighteenth-century German aesthetics, cf. P.H. Reill, *The German Enlightenment and the rise of Historicism*, p. 62ff.

Hegel is a "shallow and superficial mode of observation" (EL, 337: WG VI, 368), in fact, it fails even to explain such 'physical' phenomena as heat, light and magnetism so that it is still more inadequate when it attempts to apply its own principles (pressure, impact) to organic nature. For Hegel it is a defect of contemporary science that it persists with mechanical principles in areas where they are manifestly inappropriate (a general point made by Kant in conjunction with a 'blade of grass' as we saw in Chapter 3). Moreover, it is indicative of the importance that Hegel attaches to the proper apprehension of the mind that, in this same passage, he chooses to illustrate the inappropriateness of the mechanical principle, whereby things are only externally associated, by referring to its consequential conception of the soul as "a mere group of forces — faculties subsisting independently side by side".

What the mechanical approach does, and what it shares with the approach of empirical psychology is that it treats the mind as a thing, as an entity susceptible to (Humean) causal analysis and, as such, as explicable externally (or what Hegel calls finitely) like any other particle of 'dead matter' (EG, 6 – 7: WG VII, 12). This conclusion is symptomatic of the employment of *Verstand*. This point, already made in 1802, is put unequivocally in the *Encyclopädie*, "Though psychology might not expressly talk of the parts of the soul or mind, yet this discipline, by its use of Understanding, is based on the idea (*Vorstellung*) of that finite relation in so much as the different forms of mental activity are enumerated and described merely in their isolation one after another, as so-called special powers (*Kräfte*) and faculties" (EL, 246, amended: WG VI, 268).

Since Hegel's critique of faculty-psychology and his own conception of the mind as a living unity crucially involves the distinction between *Verstand* and *Vernunft*, and since this distinction is basic to his thought as a whole, and hence pertinent to much of the ensuing discussion, it will be profitable at this juncture, though at the risk of some loss of continuity, not only to elucidate the basis of this distinction but also to sketch the salient outlines of the Hegelian system itself.

As Hegel himself pointed out on more than one occasion (EG, 226; EL, 92: WG VII, 356; VI, 96) the distinction between *Verstand* and *Vernunft* was not made prior to Kant. For Kant they were two distinct faculties of the mind. Their distinctness derives from their precise inter-relationship. To Kant the process of knowledge falls into three phases: it "starts with the senses, proceeds from thence to the Understanding and ends with Reason" (RV, 300: W III, 237). It is the task of *Verstand* to correct the 'manifold of appearances' by means of concepts and to reduce them to empirical laws. It is the task of *Vernunft* to systematise the unity of all possible empirical acts of *Verstand*; in short, "the Understanding is an object for Reason, just as sensibility is for the Understanding" (RV, 546: W III, 439). This means that *Verstand* alone applies immediately to the objects of intuition, which it unifies, whilst *Vernunft* applies to *this* unity and orders it into a totality (RV, 533: W III, 427). In summary, *Verstand* is the 'faculty of rules' whereby the unity of appearances is secured and *Vernunft* is the 'faculty of principles whereby the unity of these rules is secured (RV, 303: W III, 239).

From what we already know, this sharp differentiation of the mind into distinct faculties is unacceptable to Hegel.[5] But, though *this* differentiation is unacceptable, Hegel still retains a distinction. Indeed, Hegel's own particular utilisation of this distinction has been traced back to his juvenilia[6] and it features prominently in his *Differenz* (between Fichte and Schelling) (1801). For Hegel, *Verstand* is concerned to establish the fixed, separable and mutually exclusive character of phenomena. It deals with finite or external, mechanical relationships and, as such, it is the appropriate 'vehicle' to convey empirical 'truth'. Since these relationships separate form from content, and the universal from the particular, then *Verstand* can also be said to deal with abstract universals or formal identity (EL, 143; EG, 226: WG VI, 147; VII, 356). This further means that *Verstand* is the appropriate 'instrument' for mathematical deductions based as they are on the laws of contradiction and identity – "This maxim [that A = A and A cannot simultaneously be A and not A] instead of being a true law of thought is nothing but the law of abstract understanding" (EL, 213: WL V, 129).

In contrast, *Vernunft* is concerned to establish the unity not the separateness, of phenomena. Accordingly, this means that for *Vernunft* both form and content, and the universal and the particular, comprise a conceptual whole, because "in Rational thought the content produces its form from itself" (EG, 226 amended: WG VII, 356). Crucially, there is a distinctive dynamic element in this depiction. This dynamism is characteristic of what Hegel calls the true infinite. In contrast to infinity as understood by *Verstand*, where it is merely the negation of finitude (an endless progress: ad infinitum), the true infinite is a process – the production of content's form from itself. It is the process of "coming to itself in its other" (EL, 175: WG VI, 184). This key phrase conveys the distinctive character of the dynamism for it implies an internal development not an external addition. It is by virtue of this internal dynamism that the 'other' is recognised to be at home in, at one with, its supposed (by *Verstand*) opposite. This 'being at home with itself in the other' is the crux of Hegel's vision of his philosophical system as expressed in his maxim that "The truth is the whole. But the whole is only the essence perfecting itself through its development" (PhK, 32: WL II, 14).

It is because the truth is an internally dynamic totality or unity that it is also said to be concrete, that is, to contain differentiations within it (SL II, 472: WL IV, 490). *Vernunft*, which grasps this totality, thus deals with concrete universals, again in contrast to the formal abstractness of *Verstand*. This concreteness also marks the difference between Hegel's and Kant's employment of the distinction between *Verstand* and *Vernunft*. Kant's employment (in Hegel's interpretation) was vital to his maintenance of the distinction between the phenomenal (how things appear to us) and the noumenal (things in themselves). But this latter

5. It is thus infelicitous to talk of *Vernunft* as "a special and distinct mental faculty" from *Verstand* as Z.A. Pelczynski does in his Introduction to *PW*, p. 114. Similarly, G.D.O'Brien, *Hegel on Reason and History*, p. 70.

6. To his amendment whilst making an abstract of Garve's *Prufung der Fähigkeiten* in 1787, cf. Harris, *Hegel's Development*, p. 37n.

realm, according to Hegel, comprises the pure negativity of "utter abstraction" and Kant's *Vernunft* is similarly negative and abstract — "a mere stepping stone beyond the finite and conditioned range of Understanding" (EL, 93: WG VI, 96–7). On the contrary, the truth is the whole; there are no distinguishable realms of phenomenality and noumenality. For Hegel the dynamic process of the whole-coming-to-be is itself (given the concrete identity of form and content) the activity of *Vernunft*, wherein lie 'the true laws of thought'.

This activity is dialectical. It is here that the key between *Verstand* and *Vernunft* in Hegel's own thought is to be found. The dialectic is the process of emanation (*immanente Hinausgehen*) whereby the one-sided partiality and limitation of *Verstand* is revealed and overcome (EL, 147: WL V, 105). Hegel employs the verb *aufheben* to depict this dialectical process. In so doing he was deliberately exploiting the resources of the German language (a favourite ploy) for, as he acknowledged on more than one occasion, the word means not only to clear away, annul or let finish but also to keep and preserve (EL, 180; Ph, 163–4; SL I, 119: WG VI, 191; WL II, 76; III, 94).

Thus, although *Vernunft* goes beyond *Verstand*, this does not mean that the latter is thereby rendered redundant; rather, it is retained, but its partiality is recognised for what it is. This means that *Verstand* is inadequate rather than wrong; Hegel is not saying anything so silly as that mathematical deductions or mechanical laws are 'wrong'. Instead, they are correct (*richtig*) and Hegel stresses the importance of their findings because "apart from Understanding there is no fixity or accuracy in the region either of theory or practice" (EL, 144: WG VI, 148; cf. *Differenz* WL I, 26). But 'correctness', which depends solely on form or abstract identity (EL, 305: WL V, 166), is not the same as Truth, which, as the whole, is concrete. Truth is the identity of form and content when the process of coming-to-be is fulfilled. Hegel cites, as an example of the 'philosophical' meaning of Truth, the meaning of a 'true friend' as expressed in common speech, namely one whose conduct conforms with the concept of friendship. It is harmony or coherence, or again, as expressed at the close of the *Logik*, it is "self-coincidence" (*Zu-sich-selbst-kommen*) (SL II, 484: WL IV, 503), which marks the wholeness of Truth. Moreover, friendship is not an abstract mathematical relationship but a 'living' complex inter-relation.

In sum, *Verstand*, with its abstracting qualities is unable to grasp the active, dynamic whole which can only be apprehended by the dialectical *Vernunft*. Rather, *Verstand* only grasps what Hegel invariably calls a *Moment* in this dynamic process. This is an active or life-process; but there is only life where there is contradiction (SL II, 68: WL IV, 59). Accordingly, for the dialectic to operate at all there must be contradictions (propositions that *Verstand* would hold to be mutually exclusive). These contradictions are nothing other than the "very moving principle of the world" (EL, 223: WG VI, 242). Once again, given the identity of form and content, just as *Verstand* has its place and appropriate sphere so these contradictions are in the world and remain so.[7] This movement

7. That Hegel's philosophy does not abolish tensions or contradictions is stressed by J.N. Findlay, *Hegel: A Re-examination*, p. 77ff.

engendered by contradiction is the whole-coming-to-be or, what is the same process, the whole becoming concrete, since it is these partial Moments that constitute its intrinsic differentiation.

To pursue matters further, this notion of a concrete, dynamic whole bears directly on the important concept of *Wirklichkeit* (actuality).[8] For Hegel, the actual is to be distinguished from 'mere appearance'. It is another distortion by *Verstand* to separate 'thought' and 'actuality' and, moreover, to view the latter as synonymous with external or sensible existence (EL, 258: WG VI, 282). The actual is correctly apprehended by *Vernunft*. This means that it comprises a concrete unity. Just as 'true friend' in common parlance expressed the 'philosophical' meaning of Truth so the depiction of someone as a '*wirklichen Dichter*' excludes anyone who is unable to perform anything meritorious. In both examples the relationship in question is one of harmony. Since there can be (can exist) individuals who are neither truly friends nor actually poets, it follows that the fact of something or somebody existing does not of itself say anything about its actuality. This now goes to the nub of Hegel's philosophical system for it has two important, closely related, repercussions, namely, on his theory of necessity and on his theory of Rationality or Reasonableness (*Vernünftigkeit*) (to maintain clarity and to indicate the direct connexion between *Vernunft* (Reason) and *Vernünftig (keit)* (Rational(ity)) the initial letter will be capitalised when it is Hegel's concept that is under discussion).

"Genuine actuality is necessity; what is actual is inherently necessary" (PR, 283: WL VI, 354). From what we already know it now follows that not everything that exists does so necessarily. This explains the role that Hegel allots to contingency. The contingent or fortuitous exists (EL, 11: WL V, 37) but does so only as an aspect of actuality (EL, 265: WG VI, 290). Hegel, indeed, counsels against the attempt to demonstrate that everything is necessary. Such attempts are the work of a priorism and word-mongering characteristic of what Kant called dogmatism. Whilst it is the work of *Vernunft* (as we shall shortly see) to elicit necessity from beneath the semblance of contingency, it is part and parcel of this elicitation that a legitimate sphere of contingency is recognised – it has, as Hegel puts it, its "due office (*Recht*) in the world" (Ibid.; PR, 137: WL VI, 173). An example that he provides more than once of this 'office' is the decision in the execution of corporal punishment as whether to give forty or thirty-nine lashes (PR Ibid.; PRel II, 337: WJ XV, 200).

However, it is clear that the contingent is analytically tied to the necessary.[9] The contingent is thus linked with the merely existent as the necessary is linked with the actual. But, we have still to explain positively Hegel's concept of necessity. This leads to the question of Rationality, because having seen that actuality is necessary we can now note that "what is Rational is actual and what is actual is

8. Cf. T.M. Knox, Editorial preface to *PR*, p. vi. In all future quotations *Wirklichkeit* will be rendered as 'actuality'.

9. Cf. D. Henrich, 'Hegels Theorie über den Zufall', *Kant-Studien* (1958/9), p. 135.

Rational" (PR, 10: WL VI, 14; EL, 10: WL V, 36[10]) — "there is nothing irrational about actuality" (PR, 283: WL VI, 355).

This is central to Hegel's vision of the world as a meaningful totality and it brings us to the prime Hegelian concept — *Geist* or Spirit. It is intrinsic to Hegel's philosophy that *Geist* cannot be defined, that is, limited from without — there is nothing outside *Geist*. The meaning of the world, which is to say the meaning of all its 'contents' including, preeminently, mankind, is to be found in the world for ultimately all that has meaning in the world is *Geist*; this (to be explicit) is the interpretation of this prime concept put forward in this study. It is *Geist*, as the world's actualising purpose, that is the subject of the whole-coming-to-be, Truth is when *Geist* as subject is identical to itself as substance — "what moves itself, that is *Geist*; it is the subject of the movement and it is likewise the moving process itself or the substance through which the subject passes" (Ph, 782: WL II, 505 — I shall leave this key term in the German in all translations).

This movement or process falls into three Moments. As expressed in their utmost generality (that is, as the articulation of the Concept — see below) these Moments are universality, particularity and individuality (EL, 291: WL V, 159). The universal 'represents' simple identity, but this is only potential, it is only identity in-itself. The intrinsic dynamism of the organic takes the form of actualising this potential (the Aristotelean language is no imposition). The identical particularises itself or engenders contradictions (it is the basic error of *Verstand* to take these particulars as self-subsistent wholes). Finally, the particulars are known to be at one with the universal and the Concept thereby returns to itself. This union of the universal and the particular constitutes the individual or actual (or, again, the concrete universal). This is the process of dialectical supersession (*Aufhebung*) so that at this new higher level the identity is now for-itself as well as in-itself. This basic triadic process of simple union, differentiation and union enriched, or made concrete, with the explicit (actualised) incorporation of its differentiation (potential) is "the rhythm, the pure eternal life of *Geist* itself and had it not this movement it would be something dead" (GA, 182: WJ XII, 76).

As such this rhythm recurs throughout Hegel's writings as the basic structural model. For example, there is the basic triad of Logic, Nature and Spirit. But further within Spirit, for example, there is the triad of Subjective, Objective and Absolute Spirit and, again, each of these has three Moments; thus in Subjective Spirit is to be found Soul, Consciousness and Mind; in Objective Spirit there is Abstract Right, Morality and Ethical Life and in Absolute Spirit there is Art, Religion and Philosophy.

These triads, as the work of *Geist's* self-unfolding, are hierarchical or progressive. Thus, as we shall see, it is philosophy that constitutes the acme, it is the thought of the world (PR, 12: WL VI, 17). The content of this thought is what Hegel terms the Concept (*Begriff*) or that which constitutes the "Reason of that which is, the truth of what we call the mere thing" (SL I, 48: WL III, 19) — the

---

10. For the significance of the second citation see E. Fackenheim, 'On the Actuality of the Rational and the Rationality of the Actual', *Review of Metaphysics* (1969/70) 690–98.

basic proposition in Hegel's idealism. It follows that this 'thought' is progressive, as *Geist* comes to *knowledge* of itself. *Geist* comes to know itself and when it does, when substance and subject are identical, it means that knowledge and the object of knowledge are the same (Ph, 566: WL II, 355). But, further, this means that in the process of so doing *Geist*'s "thinking self-comprehension" (GPG, 240; WJ XVII, 62) is simultaneously the progression of actuality. Everything that has happened (the meaning of the world) is this work of *Geist* (GPG, 230: WJ XVII, 52; cf. EG, 18: WL V, 335). What is actual is so for a reason or purpose; it constitutes a necessary phase in the process of *Geist*'s coming-home-to-itself. Necessity is thus purposive.[11] It is that which holds in giving the world meaning; in short,

> this unity with the world [man's recognition of it as complete and self-dependent] must be recognised not as a relation imposed by necessity but as the Rational. The Rational, the divine, possesses the absolute power to actualise itself. . . the world is this actualisation of divine Reason. (EG, 62: WG VII, 100)

Necessity then for Hegel is the realisation that the Truth is the whole, that the world's actuality, its meaning or purpose, is the coming-home-to-itself of *Geist*. As a process of internal development it is self-contained. A necessary relation is thus one that exhibits this same character. Accordingly, whilst the contingent is derivative − is merely what is "not through itself but through something else" − the necessary is "what it is through itself" (EL, 268: WG VI, 293). It is self-determining. Again, the organic (teleological[12]) image is the appropriate one; the apple-seed necessarily grows into its telos, an apple-tree (and not a cherry-tree), for it contains what it is going to be. The tree (the source of the seed) is its own premise. With the decisive difference that this is truly a question of Spirit (self-consciousness) this (albeit hackneyed) image does convey the import of Hegel's own frequent description of his philosophy as a circle.

Further aspects of these ideas of actuality, Rationality and necessity will be covered and refined as we proceed but a basis has been established so that we are now able to return to the topic of human nature.

Thus, though Hegel rejects faculty-psychology for dividing and separating the living whole of the mind, the above discussion makes it possible to see how Hegel is able nevertheless to make distinctions. That is, within the living process there are Moments, which represent partial perspectives, or the internal differentiations, within the concrete whole. Accordingly, Hegel is able to write that "the truly philosophical grasp of these forms [mutually independent powers and faculties] just consists in comprehending the Rational connexion existing between them in recognising them as stages in the organic development of intelligence" (EG, 202: WG VII, 323).

11. Cf. F. Bergmann, 'The Purpose of Hegel's System', *JHP* (1964) 189 – 204; C. Taylor, *Hegel*, p. 345.
12. Cf. Findlay's argument that Hegel is properly to be dominated a 'teleological idealist', *Hegel*, p. 23.

Additionally, it is this emphasis on organic development that serves to distinguish Hegel's critique of faculty-psychology from that of Herder. Though there is clearly much in which Hegel and Herder are in agreement, Hegel is seemingly critical of the Herderian alternative formulation. This apparent criticism is to be found in Hegel's discussion of *Kraft*, which, it will be recalled from Chapter 2, was the unifying force in Herder's account of the mind. Hegel remarks that the multiplicity of the forces (*Kräften*) of empirical psychology – the faculties of memory, imagination, will etc. – creates the desire to see these different forces as the manifestations of a single whole. However, to invoke a primary force (*Urkraft*) to account for these manifestations would be to invoke little more than an empty abstraction, for it would lack content (EL, 249 – 50: WG VI, 272 – 3). Force as such is defective because it is externally, not internally, determined, that is, there is absent the characteristically organic principle of intrinsic determination. Hence, force, too, lacks the identity of form and content and Hegel explicitly cites Herder's concept of God as Force as an exemplification of this deficiency (EL, 247: WL V, 142). In other words, Herder's own alternative to faculty-psychology is still an expression of *Verstand*, because 'force' is a mechanical (Newtonian) concept. Only *Vernunft* is capable of grasping the concrete and this is achieved, as we have seen, by the apprehension of the dialectical process of coming-to-be.

Thus far we have concentrated on the negative aspect of Hegel's theory of human nature, having simply asserted his own positive belief in active organic unity in juxtaposition to the passive mechanical approach. We must now consider the positive side in more detail.

As a preliminary we can note the importance Hegel attaches to 'animal magnetism' or hypnotism (EG, 115: WG VII, 185). Drawing on the researches of Mesmer, Hegel regards this phenomenon as giving "even in experience" a confirmation of the underlying unity of the soul and as contributing to the dismissal of the mechanical interpretation proffered by *Verstand*. This is so because, by its operation, hypnotism illustrates the emancipation of the mind from the externality of spatio-temporal relationships (EG, 4 – 7: WG VII, 9 – 12). Hence, to this same end, Hegel's deep interest in other such phenomena as somnambulism, clairvoyance, ante-natal life and insanity (EG, 99 – 125: WG VII, 159 – 200). All of these illustrate aspects of the mind's corporeity. The seriousness with which Hegel treats these subjects is indicative of his own understanding of the cosmos for it sheds some light on the working assumptions upon which he erected his system. Of course, the significance of these phenomena in the system itself is limited. They properly belong to what he calls Anthropology, that is, the study of subjective mind or soul, or the mind within the confines of Nature.

But to move to the positive question directly at issue; wherein consists the living unity of the mind? Hegel's answer is Thought. The various faculties identified and separated by *Verstand* are to be properly understood as specifications of thought (EL, 47: WG VI, 47). Thought is present in every mental activity. This means quite literally that man is always thinking: in all human perceptions thought is present (EL, 48: WG VI, 48) even when he is asleep man is thinking

(EG, 69: WG VII, 111). This is the distinctive characteristic of man for only man is *denkende Geist* (EG, 14: WG VII, 24) and *this* radically distinguishes him from Nature. This, as we shall see, is the most important 'fact' about human nature, on Hegel's interpretation. It is entailed by this interpretation that man cannot have developed out of a state of animal sensibility, since "animal humanity is altogether different from animality proper" (PGN, 133: WL VIII, 142). What man has that the brute lacks is thought. Everything that is human is so because it contains within it thought (GPG, 213: WJ XVII, 31). It is because, in essence, that man knows himself to be animal that he ceases for that very reason to be an animal (Hegel gives as an example here man's ability to turn the animal function of digestion into a self-conscious science (GA, 115: WJ XII, 120)).

Hegel, therefore, explicitly regards man's ability to think as "the fundamental characteristic of human nature" (PGN, 50: WL VIII, 35). However, to appreciate Hegel's full position it is necessary to enquire as to the distinctive quality of thought. In the passage just quoted Hegel goes on to say that this 'fundamental character' is that man can think of himself as an I. The importance of this further specification is that it introduces the vital factor of universality – "man is a thinker and is universal: but he is a thinker only in that he is a universal for himself" (EL, 47, amended: WG VI, 47). Man knows himself as a universal whereas the animal does not, it never goes beyond the individual thing. Man's self-conscious universality first happens when he knows he is 'I' since when "I call myself 'I', though I undoubtedly mean the single person myself, I express a thorough universal" (EL, 48: WG VI, 48). This whole process is, of course, elaborated in the opening chapters of the *Phänomenologie*, wherein the dialectic of sense-certainty issues forth into (has its truth in) universality. Language (absent in the brute: it cannot say 'I') is the living truth of this, since the particular is the ineffable – "When I say 'an individual thing', I at once state it to be really quite an universal, for everything is an individual thing" (Ph, 160: Wl II, 74).

The upshot of this, to simplify drastically, is that "thought. . .is knowledge of universals" (PGN, 49: WL VIII, 34) which reaches its self-completion in the Absolute Idea. Since thought is *the* characteristic of man it follows that he has (contrary to Kant's noumenal 'I think' – see Chapter 3) knowledge of himself. But there is more. This universality – knowledge by man of himself as man – must always be *Geist* (EG, 1: WL V, 332).

It is because man's universality lies in thought that man is Spirit; that he is removed from Nature, because "natural objects do not think" (EN, 7: WG VIII, 13). This means that Nature has no meaning either in or for itself; rather its meaning or purpose is to be as 'other' through which *Geist* comes-to-be: *Geist* is logically prior to Nature (EN, 19: WG VIII, 32). In Nature *Geist* is present in its immediacy, as 'there', but in its coming-home-to-itself *Geist* realises that Nature is in fact its own creation. When *Geist* knows that the 'otherness' of Nature is its own creation then it has reached the level of self-comprehension. Man as spirit (the self-conscious universal) is the subject, or vehicle (as it were) of this self-comprehension; it is in man that *Geist* comes to know itself as *Geist*. More precisely, as we stated above and as we shall develop, it is because man's universality lies in thought "in the whole of its universality. . .is the Idea or Absolute" (EL, 24: WL V, 47), that it is in the history of thought (philosophy) that the meaning of the world (its actualising purpose) is to be discerned. But, when man recognises this then, in Charles Taylor's phrase, his 'centre of gravity shifts' as he ses that he, too, is the vehicle of *Geist*'s process of coming-to-be and thus that his meaning or purpose and that of the world are one.[13] The full implications of this will be developed as our argument proceeds.

We can now turn to a more particular examination of Hegel's general characterisation of human nature and its relation to society.

On two separate occasions Hegel explicitly addresses himself to this question. The first of these is to be found in the new introduction to one of his early 'theological' essays.[14] Hegel wrote this essay (known as *The Positivity of the Christian Religion*) in 1795 but in 1800 he re-wrote the introduction and it is in this new version that Hegel explicitly addresses himself to the present topic. The theme of the Essay as a whole as originally written, is an enquiry into the institutionalisation of religion, that is, how the teachings of Christ became formalised into a Church. The disjunction is between the purely moral religion as taught by Christ, which as such was not grounded in external authority, and a positive religion, which is authoritative and thus of inferior value (TW, 71: TJ, 155). That is, Christ's teaching was made obligatory as Christ's teaching, as commanded by him, with the consequence that the content of his teaching lost its meaning and the teaching itself became another "positive doctrine about virtue" (TW, 85 – 6; TJ, 166).

However, in the new Introduction the implications of the simple disjunction between a positive religion and what is now called a natural religion are expounded more critically. The very distinction between positive and natural religion presupposes there is only one natural religion "since human nature is one and single, while there may be many positive religions" (TW, 167: TJ, 139). Such a view of human nature characterises it in terms of a few universal abstract concepts. But, it is the meaning and utilisation of these universal concepts of human nature with which Hegel is now concerned. As universal these concepts become necessary conditions and characteristics of humanity as a whole. The consequence of this is that "the variations in national (*Völker*) or individual manners, customs and opinions become accidents, prejudices and errors" (TW, 168: TJ, 140).

The significance of this to Hegel's present theme is that these variations are held to constitute positive religion but, and this is now the crucial point, this is to misconceive religious feeling. What from the perspective of a universal human nature is merely a modification or accident is for the living individual "perhaps

---

13. Taylor, *Hegel*, p. 91. Cf. L. Colletti, *Marxism and Hegel*, p. 207 – 8.

14. There has been considerable debate – not all of it very fruitful – as to the proper characterisation of these essays; see *inter alia* R. Kroner's Introduction to *TW*; W. Kaufmann, 'The Young Hegel and Religion', in *Hegel: A Collection of Critical Essays*, ed. A. MacIntyre; G. Lukacs, *The Young Hegel*.

the only thing which is natural and beautiful" (TW, 169: TJ, 141). Though Hegel explicitly and importantly for our general argument disclaims that this approach is a justification for superstition, church despotism and the obtuseness of pseudo-religious institutions (TW, 170: TJ, 142), nevertheless he is critical of the facile Enlightenment view, as represented here most probably by Lessing and Mendelssohn, whereby "understanding and reason may claim to sit in judgment on everything; they readily pretend that everything should be intellectual and rational" (TW, 171: TJ, 142). This attitude is restated later in both *Glauben und Wissen* (1802) and in the *Phänomenologie* where it characterises that stage in *Geist*'s estrangement which Hegel terms *Aufklärung*.

Hegel is here echoing Herder's reaction to the intellectual arrogance of the Enlightenment, by seeing these beliefs in their own terms. For Hegel the positivity of a religion is more concerned with the *form* in which it authenticates the truth of its doctrines rather than with the *content* of the doctrines themselves, since he declares "there is no doctrine which might not be true in certain circumstances" (TW, 172: TJ, 143). Hence, the proper approach to positivity must proceed on the assumption (lacking from the facile judgment of the Enlightenment) that "the convictions of many centuries regarded as sacrosanct, true and obligatory by the millions who lived and died by them in those centuries were not, at least on their objective side, downright folly or plain immorality" (TW, 172: TJ, 143).

Two general points can be seen as emerging from this discussion. One, Hegel has developed a distinct historical sense – history makes a difference.[15] He rejects notions of a universal human nature as unhistorical, as too empty or abstract. Such notions can tell us nothing about specific men. But, further, by using universal human nature as a standard by which to judge men and their culture, it is simultaneously self-supportive and distorting, for in seeking the truth of religion (in this case) in *abstraction* (Hegel's emphasis) from the manners of the people in question it comes up with the answer that their religion is superstitious and deceitful (TW, 173: TJ, 144). Secondly, as the corollary of this, Hegel sees that what men live by is no incidental fact about them and that any assessment of their 'culture' must take this into account. We shall see this involves directly Hegel's interpretation and understanding of history.

This can be observed clearly on the second occasion when Hegel discourses in general terms about the appropriate characterisation of human nature since this is to be found in his theoretical introduction to the philosophy of history. We shall treat Hegel's philosophy of history in detail in Chapter 10, but in outlining his conception of the subject he touches directly on the relationship between a notion of human nature and a particular understanding of history. As we saw in Part II it was in elucidating the possibility and scope of historical knowledge that Hume delivered his most forthright characterisation of human nature and, as we illustrated in Chapter 1, Hume was not singular in this respect.

It is to this Enlightenment understanding of human nature that Hegel

---

15. Cf. W. Dilthey, *Die Jugendgeschichte Hegels*, in *Gesammelte Schriften*, Vol. 4, p. 31.

animadverts when he declares "the expression 'human nature' is usually taken to represent something fixed and constant. Descriptions of human nature are meant to apply to all men, past and present. The general pattern is capable of infinite modifications, but, however much it may vary, it nevertheless remains essentially the same" (PGN, 44: WL VIII, 28). This approach will thus ignore these modifications and emphasise the common factors. Hegel gives an example of this approach in operation – when seeing someone worshipping an idol although the content of the prayer is "contemptible in the eyes of Reason" nevertheless it is possible to respect the feelings that animate it and regard these as valuable as Christians' own worship of truth for (in words that echo those of Voltaire quoted in Chapter 1) "only the objects of such feelings are different; but the feelings themselves are one and the same". Indeed Hegel is explicit that he has in mind as practitioners of this approach to history those "French and English writers who describe their works as 'philosophical history'" PGN, 45: WL VIII, 28 – 29).

Just as the Enlightenment's approach to positivity condemned as superstitious nonsense what men have actually believed and lived by, so their approach to history, with its use of a notion of a constant human nature, "abstracts from the content and aims of human activity". By abstracting in this way Hegel alleges that they ignore what he calls the "objective situation". Simply to fasten on to the passions, that is the uniform, constant elements, is to ignore what is of real interest (the criterion of which for Hegel is world-historical – but see Chapter 10) which is inseparable from the determinate objective situation, since each individual "exists in a particular country (*Vaterlande*) with a particular religion and in a particular constellation of knowledge and attitudes concerning what is right and ethically acceptable" (PGN, 46: WL VIII, 30). This specificity of the individual's context and its implications for an understanding of human nature will be developed shortly.

However, leaving aside Hegel's own philosophy of history, it is clear that he rejects the Enlightenment view, based on the constancy of human nature, for being indeterminate and also for being, in consequence, anti-historical. If the determinate circumstances and modifications are ignored, if it is feelings qua feelings that are focused upon, then this tantamount to saying "there is no need to refer to the great theatre of world history at all" since indeed "the same motives and aspirations can be found in a small town as in the great theatre of world events" (PGN, 45: WL VIII, 29). If the premise is that all men are the same no matter where or when then clearly history can (in Hume's words) 'inform us of nothing new or strange'. Men are not historical creatures; but it is fundamental to Hegel's own understanding of human nature that history does make a difference.

The upshot of these two discussions of the general character of human nature clearly expresses Hegel's rejection of the adequacy of the Enlightenment's depiction of human nature as constant and uniform. Of course, there are, common features, such as the satisfaction of basic needs, that are shared by all men (cf. PR, 127: WL VI, 160) but these are animalistic and thus say nothing about *human* nature. More generally, Hegel distinguishes between common-ness and universality. The true universal operates as the "ground and foundation, the root and the substance of the individual'' whereas common-ness is only something that attaches externally to all individuals. Hegel provides an example of his meaning: although only men (as opposed to animals) have ear-lobes and this is thus something common to them all, yet "it is evident" that the absence of ear-lobes would not affect the rest of "his being, character or capacities". On the contrary, it would be nonsense "to suppose that Caius without being a man, would still be brave, learned etc." (EL, 309: WG VII, 340; cf. EN, 10: WG VIII, 32). The upshot of this is, then, that "the individual man is what he is in particular only in so far as he is before all things a man as man" and this (concrete) universality as such "permeates and includes in it everything particular". The ultimate location of man's universality lies, as we have seen, in his possession of thought and self-consciousness; possessions that enable man to transcend animalistic needs.

To ignore this distinction between the superficially common and the truly universal is to commit serious mistakes in political theory (see next Chapter) and history. In history this mistake is typically made by one of Hegel's favourite targets – the pragmatic historian. Pragmatic history is a species of Reflective History, which is typified generically as going beyond the confines of the period under consideration (see Chapter 10). The pragmatic historian, specifically, is one who is concerned to learn lessons from the past. He thus practises that typically humanist approach to the past, which was present in much eighteenth-century historical writing, including, as we saw in Chapter 4, the work of Bolingbroke and Hume. The entire enterprise assumes that human nature is constant. It is this unhistorical assumption to which Hegel is alluding when he remarks (in what is perhaps his most widely known dictum) that "what experience and history teach is this – that peoples and governments have never learned anything from history or acted upon any lessons they might have drawn from it" (PGN, 21, amended:[16] WL VIII, 179) and this is because each age is peculiar and unique. But, more particularly, Hegel reserves most of his scorn for the pragmatic historian in the guise of the 'petty psychologist'. This individual endeavours to explain historical events by subjective motives, by consideration of contingent particularities, by the "casual and private features shown in isolated instincts and passions" (EL, 256: WG VII, 280). Although the pragmatic psychological account is especially inappropriate when dealing with world-historical individuals (see later) it, more generally, fails to heed the distinctively (truly universal) human quality in men's actions.[17]

That this is so can be established through an examination of the theoretical underpinning of this criticism of pragmatic history and psychology. This examination will lead us, once again, to the core of Hegel's system but, in so doing, it enables us to reveal the theoretic basis of Hegel's theory of the contextualisation of human nature.

16. I shall consistently amend *Volk* to 'people' (Nisbet gives 'nation') without notification in future quotations – for a discussion see Chapter 9 infra.

17. For Hegel's critique of psychologism see H.B. Acton, 'Hegel's conception of the study of Human Nature', in *The Proper Study*, ed. G. Vesey, pp. 32 – 47.

The misapprehension under which the pragmatic psychologist labours is his acceptance of the separation (made by *Verstand*) between the inner and the outer. More precisely, the emphasis is placed on the former; the inner is held to be the essential whilst the outer is regarded as superficial and trivial (EL, 253: WG VI, 277) (thus the petty psychologist looks at the agent's inward disposition to explain what he does outwardly). The chief application of this thinking is in ethics when a premium is placed upon good intentions and conscience. Hegel closely associates conscience (*Gewissen*) and certainty (*Gewissenheit*). The certitude of conscience is that of the subject's absolute inwardness; it is an individual's certainty that *his* conscience alone is the criterion of truth (Ph, 654: WL II, 415).

This has two related consequences. Firstly, there is a lack of any objective content (PR, 91: WL VI, 115). Morality is reduced to an empty formalism, to the doing of duty for duty's sake. But, secondly, and more seriously, to leave morality at this abstract empty level is to undermine morality itself. If the individual's conscience is the test of moral rectitude then its deliberations will not necessarily be the same as any other individual's. I can do my duty and be thereby self-consistent but if *I* decide what are in fact to be *my* duties then they lose their character of dutifulness. In other words, the truth of self-certainty is "altogether the caprice of the individual and the accidental content of his unconscious natural existence" (Ph, 654: WL II, 416). Accordingly, what is fulfilled by one individual with a clear conscience as a duty others may call violence or wrongdoing. Since this emphasis on intention is empty it means that in the individual's construction of his duty he can just as easily make the particular (as opposed to the universal) his guiding maxim.

The upshot of this is that the individual is potentially evil (PR, 92: WL VI, 117). When the individual, in fact acts in the world the abstract form of his morality is unoperational − hence, in the *Phänomenologie*, immediately after his discussion of conscience, Hegel depicts the 'beautiful soul', who "flees from contact with actuality and steadfastly perseveres in a state of self-willed impotence to renounce a self which is pared away to the last point of abstraction" (Ph, 666: Wl II, 425). But, since, to Hegel, it is impossible to will without willing something positive then "simply to will the good and to have a good intention in acting is more like evil than good, because the good willed is only this abstract form of good and therefore to make it concrete devolves on the arbitrary will of the subject" (PR, 97: WL VI, 123). Against this emphasis on intention (characteristic of that Moment in the *Philosophie des Rechts* denominated *Moralität*) Hegel stresses the concreteness, the content-filled character of true moral action, as found in Ethical Life (*Sittlichkeit*) which, as we shall see, provides the adequate ground of 'genuine individuality'.

This adequacy is also to be found in a proper appreciation of the relationship between the inner and the outer. As correctly apprehended by *Vernunft*, the inner and outer are identical. They are a whole, a unity. In exactly the same way that Hegel is critical of the language of *Kraft* for seemingly having a 'force' distinct from its manifestation, so the inner distinct from the outer (and vice versa) is empty and meaningless.

This bears directly on Hegel's ethical theory and also on his criticisms of pragmatic historians discussed above. It follows, for Hegel, once the inner and the outer are seen as one then "we are thus justified in saying that a man is what he does" (EL, 255: WG VI, 279). Whilst allowing for the unpredictable contingent, it does not make sense to say that a person's intentions are excellent but his deeds are worthless. Men cannot conceal the whole of their putatively inner self for "infallibly" it betrays itself (EL, 256: WG VI, 280). What an individual does, so does he intend; for "the man himself is the sum total of his deeds" (PGN, 57: WL VIII, 44) (the same significantly holds for cultures as we shall see). Thus in the case of great men or heroes we cannot in any way lessen an appreciation of their actions by examining, in the manner of the pragmatic historian, their supposed internal motivation or disposition. Great deeds can only be carried out by great characters (EC, 2: WG VII, 5). Indeed, we must acknowledge that great men willed what they did, and that they did what they willed (EL, 257: WG VI, 281) and not indict them in terms of private virtues like humility, charity etc. (PGN, 141: WL VIII, 154).

That a man is what he does is the key to Hegel's contextual theory of human nature and also serves to tie this theory into his philosophical system. This is so because the denial of the distinction between inner and outer is an integral part of his concept of actuality, for this concept is defined as "the unity become immediate of essence with existence or of inward with outward" (EL, 257: WL V, 145).

The crucial question now is – in what does a man's actuality consist? In the *Encyclopädie* he writes,

All the general determinations of the soul individualised in me and experienced by me constitute my actuality and are therefore not left to my caprice but, on the contrary, are powers controlling my life and just as much belong to my actual being as my head or my heart belong to my organic existence. I am this whole circle of determinations. (EG, 110: WG VII, 176)

The important point here is the specificity of these determinations. This quotation immediately follows (and generalises upon) the observation that one cannot be a friend in general but one is necessarily "for these particular friends a particular friend living in a particular place at a particular time and in a particular situation". A little earlier in the same work, Hegel had emphasized that the concrete existence of the individual lay in the empirical ties that connect him with other men and the world at large and this totality forms his actuality, so that it "has its threads in him to such a degree that it is these threads which make him what he actually is" (EG, 102: WL, V356). The example that Hegel gives of this is the suicide of Cato – after the fall of the Roman Republic he could not live when his actuality was dead (Ibid.; cf. TW, 155: TJ, 222; PW, 222; WL VII, 114). Though these comments occur in Hegel's discussion of Anthropology they are of general significance.

This can be borne out by looking at his discussion of individuality in the *Phänomenologie*. The theoretical basis of this discussion we have already covered — "the true being of a man is. . .his act; individuality is actual in the deed" (Ph, 349: WL II, 212). This means, crucially, that the world or circumstances generally cannot be juxtaposed as external to the internality of individuality; for what the individual *is* is his world (Ph, 336: WL II, 203). Had the "circumstances, style of thought, customs, the whole state of the world in short" not have been as they are then the individual would not have been what he is —

what is to have an influence on individuality and what sort of influence it is to have — which properly speaking mean the same thing — depend entirely on individuality itself: to say that by such and such an influence this individuality has become this specifically determinate individuality means nothing else than saying it has been this all along. (Ph, 334: WL II, 202)

We cannot meaningfully separate a man from his cultural context. Hegel explicitly enunciates this cardinal tenet of contextualism when he writes "for the individual exists as a determinate being, unlike man in general (*nicht Mensch überhaupt*) who has no existence as such" (PGN, 72: WL VIII, 63).

Thus far we have merely seen that the individual is specific or exists in context but the crucial factor in Hegel's account of contextualisation is the relationship he sees between the individual and his context. Or, more precisely, in what does this context consist? The individual we have seen is universal. He is universal because he is thought or spirit. Given that there is no distinction between inner essence and outer accidence it follows that the context in which the individual dwells is also spiritual (*geistig*). The individual is at one with the world (*Geist*) when he recognises that it not only sustains him but also specifies and identifies him and is thus responsible for both his spiritual universality as well as his own individuality.

The individual knows himself in other individuals and vice versa. In his context man thus confronts himself not an alien other, for in actuality both the individual and the context are the work of *Geist* — "*Geist* is the immovable irreducible basis and starting point for the action of all and everyone, it is their purpose and their goal. . .is likewise the universal product wrought and created by the action of each and all, and constituting their unity and likeness and identity of meaning" (Ph, 458: WL II, 285). The universality of human nature thus lies in the universality of *Geist*. But this is no abstract quality for it is concrete through and through. Man is a concrete universal. This is the crux of Hegel's concept of human nature but, as this chapter has aimed to demonstrate, this concept cannot be understood unless it is first appreciated that the purpose of man's (mankind's) existence is inseparable from the delineation of *Geist* as the purposive explanation for their being existence at all. Each individual is part of this purpose; he is

the son of his people and also in so far as the State to which he belongs is still developing, the son of his age for no one can remain behind the age he lives in, let alone transcend it. This spiritual being (*geistige Wesen*) is his being and he is its representative and he arises out of it and exists within it. (PGN, 103: WL VIII, 102)

This quotation provides the germ of the next Chapter, were we shall examine the relationship between the individual and his State and his *Volksgeist*. Additionally, this quotation intimates the importance of history to these relationships, because the spiritual context in which man exists is the 'stuff' of history. This means that human nature is radically historicised[18] — "we are what we are through history" (GPG, 210: WJ XVII, 28).

---

18. Cf. Mandelbaum's conclusion — "the very nature of man changes as the world-spirit develops and in order to understand men at one time or another one must place them in their appropriate historical contexts, viewing them in terms of their place in a larger process of spiritual development. Thus Hegel's organicism and his historicism merged with one another", *History, Man and Reason*, p. 187.

9. MAN IN *VÖLKER* AND STATES

The previous chapter outlined the theoretical underpinning of Hegel's contextualist theory of human nature. This chapter will examine the agents by which human nature is 'contextualised'. The 'agents' in question are the individual's people (*Volk*) and State. It must be emphasised at the outset that these agents can only be distinguished analytically because it is important, in Hegel's eyes, to realise that they act in concert. By so doing they constitute a whole or totality (the context) to which the nearest approximation is perhaps 'Culture', understood in its wide anthropological sense as "that complex which includes knowledge, art, belief, morals, laws, custom and any other capabilities acquired by man as a member of society",[1]

The individual lives in a context. But whilst animals live in a passive predetermined environment men qua spiritual, concrete universals are active self-determining, self-conscious agents, the meaning of whose activity is that it comprises as the self-same activity of *Geist* (*Geist* is pure activity (EG, 3: WG VII, 7)), the meaning of the world. This entails and this is the key to the argument of this chapter, that the *Volk* and State (the work of men) have to be understood, like man himself, as agents of *Geist*. They are, therefore, not external to the individual but as 'his' own creation, internally constitutive of him.

We shall first examine the meaning and significance that Hegel attaches to the *Volk*. The various *Völker* are "the concepts which *Geist* has formed of itself" (PGN, 51: WL VIII, 36). Since *Geist* is dynamic, is the process of coming-to-be which constitutes the meaning of the world, the significance of the various *Völker* is historical. Bearing this always in mind throughout the ensuing discussion, we shall postpone until the next chapter an examination of Hegel's philosophy of history and deal here with the *Volk* and the State synchronically.

For Hegel, *Geist* is the Substance which underlies the *Volksgeist*. The individual lives within this substance and he cannot transcend it, that is, although

1. E.B. Tylor, *Primitive Culture* (1871), p. 1. Tylor is credited with the introduction of this meaning of 'culture' into English and, in fact, he took it from the German, with Herder usually cited as the locus classicus – see W.H. Bruford, *Culture and Society in Classical Weimar 1775 – 1806*, p. 6f.

he "may be able to distinguish himself and others of his kind, he can make no distinction between himself and the *Volksgeist*" (PGN, 52: WL VIII, 37 – I shall leave the key term in the German in all translation). The reasoning behind this statement we covered in the previous chapter, when *Geist* was seen to be the ultimate source of the meaning of both the individual and his context. The *Volksgeist is Geist* in a particular form (PGN, 53: WL VIII, 37). The identity is crucial. From what we already know of the character of *Geist*, the configuration of the *Volk*, for Hegel, can be easily appreciated. Thus, he affirms that a *Volksgeist* is a "concrete whole" (PGN, 55: WL VIII, 42), a "spiritual totality" (PGN, 103: WL VIII, 102) and the *Volk* is an "organic totality" (*System der Sittlichkeit* [1801/2] WL VII, 464). The fact that an entity is a concrete organic whole means, for Hegel, that it contains within it internal differentiation. On a number of occasions Hegel specifies these differentiations; thus, for example in one place he lists the following – "its [*Volksgeist*] religion, ritual, manners, usages, art, constitution and political laws – indeed the whole range of its institutions, events and deeds – all this is its own creation and it is this which makes the *Volk* what it is" (PGN, 58 – slightly amended: WL VIII, 44).[2]

Now because these are internal differentiations then they are, as the work of *Geist*, necessarily inter-related. In one of his striking metaphors Hegel depicts the *Geist eines Volks* as a cathedral "divided into numerous vaults, passages, pillars and vestibules all of which have proceeded out of one whole and are directed to one end" (GPG, 259: WJ XVII, 84). This view that a *Volk*'s institutions are inter-connected Hegel attributes to Montesquieu (PGN, 102: WL VIII, 101; PR, 16: WL VI, 21) though he goes on to remark that this notion of all aspects of life as interwoven has been done to death. These remarks call for brief comment.

A number of commentators have drawn attention to Montesquieu as a source for the conception of a *Volksgeist*. The well-known passage from *De l'Esprit des Lois* (Book 19, Chapter 4) is quoted – "Mankind are govered by various factors – climate, religion, laws, maxims or government, precedents, customs and manners; which constitute a general spirit" – and attention is drawn to the title of the following Chapter – "How it is necessary to be aware of changes in *l'esprit général d'une nation*".[3] Montesquieu certainly was known to Hegel at an early age and did have an impact.[4] Indeed, in one of his earliest writings (a fragment

---

2. Cf. elsewhere in the same work – the particular *Volksgeist* "is the common denominator of its [the *Volk*'s] religion, its political constitution, its ethical life, its system of justice, its manners, its learning, art and technical skill and the whole direction of its industry" (PGN, 138: WL VIII, 149). E. Gombrich regards this passage as definitive of the enterprise of cultural history, *In Search of Cultural History*, p. 9.

3. These passages are quoted by F. Rosenzweig, *Hegel und der Staat*, Vol. 1, p. 23; H. Jendreiek, *Hegel und Jacob Grimm*, p. 155; H. Kantorowicz, 'Volksgeist und Historische Rechtsschule', *Historische Zeitschrift* (1912) 296.

4. Cf. G. Planty-Bonjour, 'L'esprit général d'une nation selon Montesquieu et le Volksgeist hégélien', in *Hegel et le siècle des Lumières*, ed. J. d'Hondt, pp. 7–24, though the case is somewhat overstated. In 1802 Hegel referred to Montesquieu's "immortal work", *Über die wissenschaftlichen Behandlungsarten des Naturrechts* (WL VII, 406).

from 1794), when he was engaged speculatively in studying, amongst other issues, Christianity as a folk-religion, Hegel quotes from the *Esprit* (Book 24, Chapter 2) (TJ, 40) and, in another fragment he comments, already, that the *Geist des Volkes* is to be found in its history, religion and degree of political freedom and that these are interwoven into a single band (TJ, 27).

However, the systematic employment of the term *Volksgeist* itself is generally traced back to Herder, though he too, of course, was familiar with Montesquieu's work, and these early discussions by Hegel of the *Volk* have been characterised by one commentator as having been written under "deep Herderian influences".[5] Yet, as Hegel acknowledges, these ideas had become a commonplace, Meinecke, indeed, distinguishes three usages − that of Hegel himself, that of Savigny and the Romantics and also that of non-Romantic liberals.[6] It is, however, in the usage of the Romantics and the Historical School of Jurisprudence that particular emphasis was placed on this idea.

Hegel was severely critical of both these movements. We shall cover this critique later in the chapter but we can here note in this particular context, his criticism of that Romantic yearning for an earlier state of collective unity, as seen in their version of the Middle Ages. Hegel is well aware of the attractiveness of a tightly knit community of which the Greek polis was the supreme exemplar. Indeed as we shall shortly see, it is in his depiction of the polis that Hegel spells out his notion of *Sittlichkeit* (Ethical Life) which is vital to his idea of both the *Volk* and the State. But, the very factors (customs, traditions, religious ritual, etc.) that made the Greeks a *Volk*, which made *them* what they were, disqualifies these specific institutions from performing the same function for another *Volk*. Moreover, given the inter-relation between all these institutions they can only endure as a whole; once one ingredient is lost then so are the rest. Accordingly, Hegel, like Herder, never wished for nor believed in a return to the Greek ideal (that the simplicity of Greece has gone for ever is a keystone in his philosophy of history). Similarly, the Romantic idea of returning to medieval Germany, by revivifying its cultural cohesion, is naive, because we are now living in the modern age (post French Revolution) and such a return is always doomed to failure − "the old German imagery has nothing in our day to connect or adapt itself to; it stands as cut off from the whole circle of our ideas, opinions and beliefs and is as strange to us as the imagery of Ossian or of India" (TW, 149: TJ, 217).[7]

5. S. Avineri, 'Hegel and Nationalism', in *Hegel's Political Philosophy*, ed. W. Kaufmann, p. 116, though Avineri's argument is that Hegel is freeing himself from Herder's preoccupations − see infra. J. Shklar argues that the undoubted political dimension (see text infra) to Hegel's theory of the *Volksgeist* witnesses the Montesquieuian rather than Herderian provenance of this concept in Hegel, *Freedom and Independence: A study of the political ideas of Hegel's Phenomenology of Mind*, p. 142. E. de Seade sees Rousseau as the source, 'State and History in Hegel's concept of People', *JHI* (1979) 369.

6. *Cosmopolitanism and the National State*, p. 159n.

7. The examples at the end are a possible gibe at Herder and his followers and also at F. Schlegel

More generally, it is because of this emphasis on the inter-relation of social institutions, on the *Volk* as a totality, that the term Culture is a defensible translation. It must always be remembered, however, that this Culture, this underlying Substance, is ultimately *Geist* and cannot thus be defined (have its meaning) in purely mundane terms (*Weltliche*) (PGN, 52: WL VIII, 36).[8] Since for Hegel human nature cannot exist outside a cultural context, we can say, to repeat the terminology from Part II, that 'man' is societally specific. We can now proceed to elaborate the significance of this in Hegel's writings.

We can commence with his theory of language. We saw in Chapter 2 the crucial importance that Herder attached to language in the definition of a *Volk* and how in Fichte, as one example, the speaking of the same language was held to constitute an internal bond between men and thus a barrier to those with a different language. This location of cultural identity in language had, as a concomitant effect, the consequence of dismissing the universality that the Enlightenment was wont to attribute to human nature. Men who speak different languages are in a meaningful sense different. A clear implication of this acceptance of the specificity of human nature and culture is the relativist denial of the tenability of cross-cultural appraisal. We have seen that Hegel, too, rejects the Enlightenment's theory of a universal constant human nature in favour of a radically contextualist notion. But, as the last Chapter brought out, since Hegel's theory of human nature is an integral part of his system then this entails, as the next Chapter will bring out more fully, his rejection of the relativist implication of contextualism. Furthermore, given that the existence of different languages, and thence different constructions of 'reality', is a major prop of this relativism (as seen in the modern writings of Whorf for example) then the place that Hegel allots to language is clearly germane.

Hegel does not ignore the differences between languages. The significance of the 'discovery' of Sanskrit is not lost on him; indeed, he calls it a "great historical discovery" through its linkage of the German and Indian *Völker* as both having spread outwards from Asia (PGN, 135; WL VIII, 144). Of course, such a family resemblance is insignificant (they are 'pre-historical') given the vast differences in religion, constitutions, ethics, etc. That is, though they may belong to the same family of languages they are different languages; a point that F. Schlegel, the chief publicist of Sanskrit in Germany, had himself made.[9]

Perhaps, the most succint comments that Hegel makes on the differences be-

---

who was one of the leading expounders of Indian Mythology as well as being a leading exponent of the 'return' to the Middle Ages — see his *Philosophie der Geschichte* (1828), Lecture XIV.

8. Cf. L.J. Goldstein, "The Meaning of 'State', in Hegel's 'Philosophy of History'", *Philosophical Quarterly* (1962) 60 – 72, who stresses the parallels between Hegel's theory of the State and 'configurationist' anthropology (e.g. Ruth Benedict) to the extent of stating that Hegel's theory "is not particularly different from that of recent authors who think of a culture as expressing or embodying patterns or ideals" (p. 66). In his endeavour to defend Hegel against crude misrepresentation Goldstein is too eager to extract Hegel's theory from the wider philosophical context of his thought.

9. See his *Über die Sprache und Weisheit der Indier* (1813), Bk. II, Chap. 1.

tween languages occurs in speech, given in 1809 in his capacity as Rector of a Gymnasium in Nüremberg. In this speech he refers to the argument that the teaching of Latin is now obsolete, because the intimacy that characterises the possession of our own language is lacking in our possession of a foreign tongue; so much so that knowledge of this tongue is "separated from us by a barrier which prevents it from genuinely coming home to our minds" (TW, 322: WG XVI, 136). But the tenor of Hegel's remarks suggests a partial rejection of this thesis, because, in his general vindication of the continued study of Latin and Greek, he remarks that perfunctory acquaintance is insufficient and instead "we must take up our lodging with them. . .and become at home in this world [that is, the Greek world, which is 'the fairest there has ever been']" (TW, 325: WG XVI, 139). Thus it is possible seemingly to break through the alleged barrier. Yet, at the same time, Hegel is dismissive of translations (TW, 326: WG XVI, 141). Translation is indeed possible (always the lynch-pin against linguistic relativism)[10] but, as the cliché has it, something is lost thereby. Nevertheless, mastery of a language particularly when coupled with comparative knowledge of other languages does enable the individual to discern "the great spirit and culture of a people" (SL I 68: WL III, 39). This is to be found in their grammar. Significantly for Hegel this is no mere contingent by-product, since in grammar can be recognised "the expression of *Geist*" (SL I, 68: WL III, 39).

Hegel's discussion now takes on a deeper significance. Language is the work of thought (EL, 38: WL V, 55). We saw in the last chapter, in passing, that it was via language that man's universality, his thought, was made evident. The commonplace (though Hume rejected it) that man was distinguished from the brutes because he alone has articulate speech is thus, for Hegel, a product of man's distinctive possession of thought. Man by his speech (not sounds) turns his thoughts into words. But this is no accidental process because it is only in the guise of words that man knows his thoughts, that is, as something definite or objective; as external but, crucially, as an "inward externality" (EG, 221: WG VII, 249; cf. Ph, 729: WL II, 466). To wish to think without words is thus irrational. Hegel uses this point to attack the intuitionism of the contemporary Romantics, who held that the true meaning of life and the cosmos was beyond words. It is fundamental to Hegel's vision that this meaning is exhibited, that actuality consists of *Geist*'s coming-to-be. The meaning of the cosmos is *Geist*'s self-fulfilment in man's ultimate progressive knowledge of himself and his world as *Geist*. The ineffable is thus for Hegel not the sublime but the confused. The ineffability of sense-certainty, referred to in the previous chapter, bears witness not to the inadequacy of words but to the inadequacy and confusion of such a philosophy.[11]

Language then is the medium of expression whereby each man actualises and

10. Cf. G. Steiner, *After Babel*, p. 94; S. Lukes, 'On the Social Determination of Truth', in *Modes of Thought*, ed. R. Horton & R. Finnegan, pp. 230–248.

11. The point is well made by D.J. Cook, *Language in the Philosophy of Hegel*, p. 157–8 & p. 49–50.

manifests himself or lets "the inner get right outside him" (Ph, 340: WL II, 205). Incidentally, Hegel sees labour (*Arbeit*) in this same light. Indeed, in his earlier writings he had discussed at some length now language like labour was an act of appropriation.[12] Unlike the operation of imagination, which remained internal, language, by bestowing names made the internal existent. Adam by naming took possession of the whole of Nature and this (symbolically) was the first creative act of *Geist* (JR II, 183).

The significance of this externalisation (*Entäusserung*) is the role it plays in Hegel's account of self-consciousness. For self-consciousness to have definite or real existence it has to alienate (*entfremden*) itself from itself (Ph, 514: WL II, 319). The dialectic of self-consciousness will be examined in some detail in Chapter 11 but here we can draw attention to the role language plays in this process. The Jena writings had tied together language and mutual recognition with the *Volk*. Language only exists in the shape of a *Volk* and it is through its language that a *Volk* expresses its essence and being (JR I, 235). It is via their language that the members of a *Volk* come to recognise each other. The *Phänomenologie* later expresses the point thus − "In speech the implicit singleness of self-consciousness comes as such into existence, so that its particular individuality is something for others" (Ph, 530 − slightly amended: WL II, 330). This process whereby the self is recognised by others establishes a unity between them, since the whole process is mutual − other selves recognise me as me and I recognise each of them as each of them. Accordingly, the self attains universality − "language is self-consciousness existing for others, it is self-consciousness which as such is there immediately present and which in its individuality is universal" (Ph, 660: WL II, 421).

The attainment of self-consciousness thus requires a community of like selves, which by embodying this universality, Hegel calls, in the *Phänomenologie*, an ethical world. This world is the work and creation of the individuals themselves. This brings us back to our earlier discussion for this work is 'actually' the process of *Geist* coming-to-be. The individual only is what he is (a universal self-conscious agent) because he inhabits a *Volk*. This is the meaning of the statement quoted above that the individual can make no distinction between himself and the *Volksgeist*. The individual's world is his own world: they are as one the expression of *Geist* and *Geist* is at first (that is, in its immediate truth) a people's ethical life (Ph, 460: WL II, 286; cf. JR I, 233).

The most important aspect of this ethical life is its political organisation. But, before turning to Hegel's examination of the State, there is another important ingredient of this ethical life, namely, the informal complex of customs, habits, conventions and manners. An indication of the importance of this complex can be gleaned from the term deliberately chosen by Hegel to depict this immediate

12. Cf. J. Habermas, 'Labour and Interaction: Remarks on Hegel's Jena "Philosophy of Mind"', in his *Theory and Practice*, pp. 142 − 169. Habermas links Hegel's speculations on language here with those of Herder (p. 153), as does G. Planty-Bonjour in his Introduction to Hegel's *La Première Philosophie de l'Esprit*, p. 27 − 8.

indwelling of *Geist*, namely, *Sittlichkeit*, since it is a derivative of *Sitten* (manners).

Geist is the universal substance of a *Volk*'s way of life (Ph, 467: WL II, 290). When the individual member of the *Volk* is aware that he is only as he is because of his *Volk* (is aware, that is, of the universal consciousness as his own being and work) then this awareness is expressed in *Sitten* or acting universally as all others do. *Sitten* are thus the "inner universality of behaviour maintained in all relationships" (PR, 215 amended: WL VI, 270). The totality of *Sitten* constitutes the ethical objective context (*Sittlichkeit*) in which the individual exists. The individual when cognizant of the identity of himself with this context is fully integrated, he is at one with the (his) world. It does not confront him as an external or alien 'other', instead, it is seen as his own creation and, necessarily also, as the creation of fellow members, of his *Volk*, "I see them as myself, myself as them" (Ph, 378: WL II, 233).

It will be worthwhile to pause here to examine the significance of this understanding on a theory of human nature and habit. It was a prominent feature of the analysis of Hume in Part II that the principle of habit played a key role in both his epistemology and his political/social philosophy; a role that was based upon the constant and universal operation of the principles and springs of human nature. A consequence of this was that the process of habituation, as a universal property of human nature, was divorced from what it was that was variably habituated. The particular habits that an individual contracted did not define him. The process whereby the habits did so define was, in Chapter 7, stipulatively termed 'acculturation'. This process is one of contextualisation – what a man *is* is his habits. It is to this that Hegel subscribes. We saw, in the last chapter, how he dismissed theoretically the distinction between inner and outer and, now in his discussion of *Sittlichkeit*, we can see how he regards habitual action as fully defining the individual.[13]

There is, of course, a further dimension to the difference between Hume and Hegel here. For Hume, habit was vital because only via its operation on the imagination were the discrete particulars of experience rendered orderly and systematic. It was the fact that this entailed making causal judgments, and thence natural science, dependent on individual experience that impelled Kant to look for a necessary a priori foundation for such judgments, since they could not, in his eyes, rest on the mere contingency of individual psychology. Hegel is convinced by this point.

Indeed, in one of his few explicit references to Hume, Hegel remarks that if

---

13. Hegel does on a number of occasions refer to habit as second nature. This is generally in the context of Anthropology (subjective *Geist*). Habit is a useful and necessary process which enables the individual to 'escape' from the immediacy of feelings and fancies and it thereby prepares the ground for thinking. It thus has an important part to play in education. It is, however, only preparatory because by itself habit is enslaving and devitalising since, with nothing to oppose to it, the mind becomes inactive or stagnant and may be said to die (EG, 63, 144: WG VII, 101, 233f; PGN, 59; WL VIII, 46; PR, 108, 260, 282: WL VI, 138, 327, 353).

epistemology starts and finishes in sense perception then it is to be expected that universality and necessity will appear illegitimate – as "a subjective contingency, a mere custom, the content of which might be otherwise constituted than it is" (EL, 82 – amended: WL V, 66; cf. *Glauben und Wissen*, WL I, 299.). Furthermore, Hegel regards it as "an important corollary" of such empiricism that its treatment of legal and ethical principles reveals these as the work of chance and he charges that it is to Hume's scepticism that this conclusion is chiefly due. For Hegel, on the contrary, the relationship between the individual and his cultural context is not attributable to the play of contingency; rather, there is here objectivity and inner truth. The relationship is necessary. The relationship is that of *Geist* with itself.

Additionally, the fact that Hume's emphasis on habit was central to his internal analysis of social life (see Chapter 5) is not at all the same thing as Hegel's 'spiritual' analysis. This possibly obvious point is not without general significance. Pertinent here are the two senses of 'internality' distinguished at the end of Chapter 5. For Hegel, the context is found in *Geist*, that is, not in Nature, a merely external condition. This spiritual context, because it acculturates, is definitive or constitutive and as such its internality is societally specific. The meaning of the social practices is inherent in the actions of the practitioners. Such meaning cannot be yielded by a mere observation of their behaviour. 'Behaviour' is not the same as 'action'. The action is defined *in* the acting (signalling and not an arm raising to repeat Melden's example). There is, from this point of view, an indissoluble conceptual link that Hume's contingent repetitiveness omits. We saw that Hume's theory of human nature, whereby there are held to be common constants and uniformities present within all societies, led him to provide a formal account of social life. On the contrary, Hegel's contextualist theory of human nature leads him to give a substantive account of social life. That the corollary of Hume's social theory in his substantive theory of rationality is not echoed in Hegel with a correspondingly formal account of rationality (as in many modern analysts) will be covered in the sequel.

To return to Hegel's account of ethical life: when the individual and his world are one there is no external measure and thus in this condition (as the ancients said) "wisdom and virtue consist in living in accordance with *den Sitten seines Volkes*" (Ph, 378: WL II, 233). This "happy condition" of total integration, which Hegel sees actualised in the Greek polis, cannot endure.[14] It cannot endure because this expression of *Geist* is incomplete; it has not completed its process of coming-to-be. *Geist* here is only in its immediate truth or implicit. It is only in-itself it must become for-itself. It must, in other words, go through the triadic process, outlined in the last chapter, of differentiation and re-unification from this condition of simple unity. This is of fundamental importance to Hegel's theory of the State. The modern State 'actually' constitutes this reunification but

14. Cf. Shklar, *Freedom and Independence*, p. 69 et seq. Also her earlier piece, 'Hegel's "Phenomenology": an elegy for Hellas', in *Hegel's Political Philosophy: Problems and Perspectives*, ed. Z.A. Pelczynski, pp. 73 – 89.

only by incorporating differentiation, which means recognising the individual in his own right.

Throughout Hegel's writings on the *Volk* it is this political dimension that is of over-riding importance and significance. It is in the *Volk* qua State that *Geist* has "its substantial Rationality and immediate actuality" (PR, 212[15]: WL VI, 266). Indeed, the State can be defined as a *Volk* that is differentiated so as to comprise an "organic whole" (PGN, 96: WL VIII, 93). Since the *Volk* is a 'spiritual individual', the State can be understood in terms of the *Volksgeist*, which permeates all its institutions. Accordingly, the constitution is at one with the *Volksgeist*. It is meaningless to ask which of them comes first because each presupposes the other (EG, 268: WL V, 448); every *Volk* has the constitution appropriate to it (PR, 179: WL VI, 225). The criterion of appropriateness being the particular stage reached by *Geist* in its coming-to-be. It is this historical dimension, which provides the clearest indication of the over-riding importance that Hegel attaches to the political, because he is explicit that it is the aim of a people to become a State and to preserve itself as such. In a statement that will be elucidated in the next chapter Hegel declares that until a *Volk* has obtained the shape of a State (*Staatsbildung*) it has no history (EG, 279: WL V, 459). The corollary of this is also made explicit in *Philosophie des Rechts*, where Hegel remarks that a people does not begin by being a State; the attainment of 'Statehood' is the work of *Geist* in the guise of that people (PR, 218: WL VI, 274; cf. PGN, 134: WL VIII, 143).

Before turning to Hegel's discussion of the State in its own right mention should be made of Hegel's terminology. In the translations and paraphrases supplied above, Hegel's term *Volk* has been rendered as 'people'. Many translators often render this term as 'nation'. This is to be regretted for two reasons. One, the denotation of the latter translation is different and has led to the misapprehension of Hegel's position and, two, Hegel himself, on occasion, employs the word *Nation* thus suggesting some kind of demarcation in his mind. Such a demarcation has been put forward by Rosenzweig. He sees Hegel using *Volk* to refer to a society in its political aspect (*Staatsnation*) and using *Nation* to refer to its cultural aspect (*Kulturnation*).[16] To support this interpretation Rosenzweig supplies a number of examples,[17] such as the remark that the nation was a people without being a State (*die Nation, ohne ein Staat zu sein, ein Volk*) (PW, 147: WL VII, 8). Perhaps, the strongest support for this interpretation (though it is one that Rosenzweig does not cite) comes from the passage from the *Encyclopädie*, quoted in the last paragraph, where Hegel writes "*ein Volk ohne Staatsbildung (eine Nation als solche)*". Given, as we have here seen, the pre-eminence of Hegel's concern with the State, such an interpretation of systematic vocabulary is plausible.

15. Knox's translation here is misleading as S. Avineri points out in *Hegel's Theory of the Modern State*, p. 200: the text reads *Das Volk als Staat ist der Geist in seiner substantiellen Vernunftigkeit und unmittelbaren Wirklichkeit.*

16. *Hegel und der Staat*, Vol. 1, p. 133.

17. *Hegel und der Staat*, Vol. 1, p. 243.

However, two caveats need to be entered against it. The first concerns Rosenzweig's suggested interpretation of *Nation* as 'cultural'. A better, less ambiguous, term would be 'ethnic' – meaning to emphasise by this the 'naturalness' of the union. It is here, perhaps, that the distinction between *Nation* and *Volk* lies. The *Nation* is natural entity compared to the *Volk* as the work of spirit. Such a demarcation would accord with Hegel's concentration on *Volksgeist* and the political (State qua *Geist*). In addition, the etymological connexion between 'nation' 'native' and 'nature' is one that appealed to Hegel, who was fond of drawing attention to such 'facts'. In one place, indeed he does link together *natio* and *nasci* when delimiting the extent of "natural influence" on the *Volksgeist* (PGN, 56: WL VIII, 42). Thus, as examples of this association, we can find Hegel remarking that the family expands into a "people (*Volk*) that is a nation (*Nationen*), which *thus* has a common natural origin" (PR, 172: WL VI, 154 – my emphasis). Again, exploiting the etymological connexion, Hegel comments that a people is born a nation ("*Nation ist ein Volk als geborenes*") (WL VIII, 180). It is as a natural entity (*Nation*) that a people is subject to the effect of climate and other physical causes; an effect that helps constitute national character (EG, 46: WG VII, 73). Further, Hegel uses the term *Nationalgeister* to refer to differences, like those between the different races, that belong to the realm of the 'natural soul' (EG, 35: WG VII, 55). Finally, all these possible grounds for such a demarcation, can be seen in the following

The philosophy of history. . .has for its subject-matter the world-historical significance of *Völker* [the translator here gives 'races'!], that is to say, if we take world-history in the most comprehensive sense of the word, the highest development to which the original disposition of the national character attains, the most spiritual form to which the natural mind indwelling the nations (*Nationen wohnende Naturgeist*), raises itself. (EG, 46: WG VII, 73)

But the second caveat should now be introduced. This demarcation should not be pushed too far because it is difficult to sustain the argument that Hegel did have a rigorously consistent demarcation in view. On many occasions he uses the two words inter-changeably in the same context; thus to give just one example (which also illustrates the practice of the translator) – "the fate of Jesus was that he had to suffer from the fate of his people (*Nationen*); either he has to make that fate his own. . .or else he had to repel his nation's (*Volkes*) fate from himself" (TW, 285: TJ, 328).

Regardless of the solution of this issue, we must now turn to Hegel's discussion of the State, for in the last resort, as Kenneth Minogue pithily puts it "Hegel's thought is concerned not with the nation but with the State".[18] It is probable that of all the aspects of Hegel's thought none has excited more comment and controversy than his view of the State. In the light of this wealth of literature it is as well that the precise significance of this subject to this study be stated at the outset. It would be futile and irrelevant to consider every aspect of Hegel's

18. *Nationalism*, p. 63.

theory. Here the focus will be on the relationship held by Hegel to subsist between the individual and the State, which, as we have established, is one aspect of our basic concern – the relationship between human nature and society. This focus is deliberately narrow; much of the detail of Hegel's view of the State will not be discussed.

The necessary first step is to locate or 'place' Hegel's discussion of the State within his system. The State constitutes the acme of Objective *Geist*. This location has two dimensions; one, the place of Objective *Geist* in the system as a whole and, two, the place of the State within Objective *Geist* itself. Objective *Geist* is the middle term between Subjective and Absolute *Geist*. As follows from the discussion in the last Chapter, this means that Objective *Geist* is the realm of differentiation and externalisation. *Geist* is at first only in-itself, only potential; this is the realm of Subjective *Geist*. Yet *Geist* is active – it has already overcome (*aufgehoben*) Nature. This overcoming takes the form of *Geist* attaining self-consciousness through recognising itself in Nature. This attainment, the relation of self to self and the absence therefore of dependence on an Other, has been achieved by thought and, since "it is in thought that freedom directly inheres" (EL, 45 – my translation: WL V, 57), then the "substance of *Geist* is freedom" (EG, 15: WG VII, 15). Subjective *Geist* is thus the realm of the free spirit in the form of self-relation (EG 20: WL V 335).

This implicitly active free spirit must become explicit; its potential must be actualised. Objective *Geist* is this actualisation; it makes itself (its freedom) 'objective' in the world. Here is the place of the State. But, the State, though the supreme objectification of freedom, is not the final resting-place of *Geist*. *Geist* needs to return to itself, to a reunion with itself as a unity enriched by this objectification. This re-unification is the work of Absolute *Geist* – of art, religion and philosophy. There are two crucial points about Hegel's theory of the State that should be borne in mind as a consequence of seeing it in this dimension. Firstly, its premise is that of freedom and, secondly, it is not the ultimate location of purpose or meaning but provides the conditions that enable art, religion and, above all, philosophy to flourish.

The second dimension concerns the place of the State within the realm of Objective *Geist* itself. This dimension Hegel spells out most thoroughly in the *Philosophie des Rechts*. In an important passage he makes clear the scope of the book – "the system of right is the realm of freedom made actual" (PR, 20: WL VI, 27). The book, as he states in the Preface, is designed to explicate the Moments of *Geist's* progress – it is "nothing other than the endeavour to apprehend and portray the State as something inherently Rational" (PR, 11: WL VI, 15).

As is to be expected these Moments fall into three phases – Abstract Right, Morality and Ethical Life – corresponding to the three general phases of the immediate concrete particular, the abstract universal and the concrete universal. Inside Ethical Life the same phases are to be found in the guise of the Family, Civil Society and State. Just as Ethical Life is the union at a higher level of Abstract Right and Morality, so the State is the union at a higher level of the Family and

Civil Society. As the dialectical process of *Geist* this arrangement is Rational and not temporal. But, phenomenologically (in history) there has been a development through the family to civil society to the Rational State and, in this regard, it mirrors Hume's account of the development through the family to families to civil society to government. Yet, as the work of *Vernunft* it mirrors Aristotle's depiction, in Book 1 of the *Politics*, of the household, village and polis, where the polis is accorded priority.[19] The State as the dialectical fulfilment of *Recht* thus contains within itself what has gone before. This, as we shall shortly see, is of crucial importance in a correct apprehension of the relationship between the individual and the State.

This two-dimensional placing of the State now makes it possible to appreciate the significance of its general characterisation, as outlined by Hegel. Above all else the State is spiritual. Given that the meaning of the world is constituted by *Geist*'s coming-to-be then this general characterisation of the State entails that its existence is no mere accidental contingency but, rather, that it is a decisive Moment in *Geist*'s self-actualisation. It is because the State has this focal role to play that Hegel feels able to talk about it in terms that have brought this aspect of his philosophy such notoriety. Thus, on several occasions, he says (or his students or editors say he says) that the State is God in the world and, perhaps most notoriously of all that the State's existence is God's progress in the world (*Es ist der Gang Gottes in der Welt dass der Staat ist*)[20] (PR, 279: WL VI, 349; cf. PR, 283, 165, 166: WL VI, 355, 207, 209).

The State as the work of *Geist* (as spiritual) partakes of its characteristics: as *lebendiger Geist* the State comprises an organised whole (EG, 265: WL V, 349). The imagery here is familiar from the last chapter. The State is a whole or individual totality (PGN, 118: WL VIII, 121); it is an entity in its own right and it is as such (as an individual – see next Chapter) that it partakes of its world-historical role. But, it is a totality of a specific type: it is alive, it is organic – "The State is an organism" (PR, 282: WL VI, 353). This alone indicates that it consists of mutually inter-dependent parts, which can only be understood in their necessary inter-relation. To attempt to examine these parts in isolation is to dismember it; to treat the living organism as a corpse.

We saw in the previous Chapter, that it was the hallmark of *Verstand* to study things in isolation, to see them (at times appropriately) as discrete particles of machinery, whereas it was the prerogative of *Vernunft* to appreciate the vitality of the organism. It is because an organism is a teleologically functioning whole that it is an appropriate image or *Vorstellung* for *Geist*'s own process. Accordingly, this organicism reflects the operation of Hegel's metaphysics. The State is not merely an organism, it is also actual. As *Geist* the State "sunders itself into

---

19. Cf. H. Paolucci who regards Hegel's system (omitting the *Phänomenologie*) as "essentially Aristotelian" and who sees this division of Ethical Life as an updating of the *Politics*, 'Hegel: Truth in the Philosophical Sciences of Society, Politics and History', in *Beyond Epistemology: New Studies in the Philosophy of Hegel*, ed. F.G. Weiss, pp. 98 – 128.

20. On the various translations of this sentence see Avineri, *Hegel's Theory*, p. 177.

the particular determinations of its concepts" (PR, 281: WL VI, 351), but, also as *Geist*, these particulars have a precise relationship to the whole and it is this relationship that is definitive of actuality — "actuality is always the unity of the universal and the particular, the universal dismembered in the particulars which seem to be self-subsistent although they really are upheld and contained only in the whole" (PR, 283: WL VI, 353 – 4). In the case of the State this means that "the interest of the whole is realised in and through particular ends" (Ibid). This, as we shall see, is the proper premise for understanding the place of the individual in the State.

To say that the State is actual is also to say that it is Rational. We have noted already that the purpose of the *Philosophie des Rechts* is to exhibit this Rationality. This can be done as long as the State is viewed Rationally, which is to say using *Vernunft*, because only in that way can the true organic actual character of the State be evidenced. This accounts for the mode of argument in this work. Hegel is presenting (as it were) the Rational template of contemporary society. This template can only be discerned by *Vernunft* and thus any theory of the State which utilises *Verstand* will be inadequate because it will merely describe the observable (quantifiable) surface. This inadequacy is most acutely felt in the distinction that Hegel draws between the State and Civil Society. This can be appreciated by briefly looking at Hegel's understanding of *Sittlichkeit* as it is set out in the *Philosophie des Rechts*.

Ethical Life, as noted above, has three Moments — Family, Civil Society and State. The Family is the 'ethical substance' in its immediacy. It is dominated by natural feeling or love. An individual is characterised by his familial relationship; he knows himself only as a member of a family. But the 'logic' of *Geist* is to break free of this immediacy and, here, this takes the form of the children of the family growing up. This process of growing-up entails, firstly, the growth of personality, an awareness on the individual's part that indeed he is an individual distinct from the other members of the family and, secondly, the setting up, by these 'persons', of a family of their own, that is, by them leaving the original setting.

This process leads the individual into Civil Society. Here he acts as a self-conscious agent pursuing his own ends. As each has his own ends their interaction is on the basis of the reciprocal satisfaction of needs. It is a market society. It is the realm of differentiation that has arisen out of the unity and immediacy of the Family. *Verstand* identifies Civil Society with the State (PR, 123: WL VI, 155) but this is a misconception (seen most patently in the theories of the Utilitarians). The differentiation must be united — not a primitivistic return to the simple unity of the immediacy of the Family but a union which incorporates (dialectically) the personality, the subjective self-seeking, that is the hallmark of Civil Society. Though Civil Society itself develops practices (the consequences of the division of labour) and institutions, which promote common, or, in the Civil Servant's case, universal ends, it is in the State that this union is achieved consciously.

The State is "the actuality of the ethical idea" (PR, 155: WL VI, 195), that is, it contains within itself the unity of the Family along with the self-conscious differentiation of Civil Society. This fusion (*Aufhebung*) is the key to the modern State.[21] The State is the necessary union of the particular and the universal. The individual still has private ends but he also has self-consciously public ends and in the modern State the public and the private are one. This point Hegel makes over and over again. The freedom of subjectivity, the particular, is one with the universal. In this unity lies the State's inherent Rationality —

Rationality concrete in the State, consists (a) so far as its content is concerned, in the unity of objective freedom (i.e. freedom of the universal or substantial will) and subjective freedom (i.e. freedom of everyone in his knowing and in his volition of particular ends); and consequently, (b) so far as its form is concerned, in self-determining action on laws and principles which are thoughts and so universal. (PR, 156: WL VI, 196)

This brings us to a discussion of the understanding of the individual's place in the State. The State, to repeat, is the ethical substance (the context) within which the individual finds himself. Though the State is treated after the Family and Civil Society it is their presupposition or ground (PR, 155: WL VI, 194). Since the State, as the highest moment of Ethical Life, is thus the ultimate constitutive and definitive context of the individual this has important repercussions on Hegel's theory of human nature and its relationship to society. We shall elucidate this theory by examining the two chief theoretical positions that Hegel is concerned to refute — Social Contract theory and Political Romanticism (together with the Historical School of Jurisprudence).

Hegel's rejection of the Social Contract provides not only a clear expression of his understanding of relationship between the individual and the State but also, when viewed in conjunction with Hume's rejection, it is a good illustration of the change in the conceptual appreciation of human nature that occurred between their writings. In other words, we can discern in Hegel's anti-Contractarianism another expression of his espousal of the contextualist theory of human nature.

The following passage contains Hegel's position in a nutshell — "Since the State is *Geist* objectified, it is only as one of its members that the individual himself has objectivity, genuine individuality and an ethical life" (PR, 156: WL VI, 196). What makes the individual what he is, that is, a spiritual, acculturated, concrete universal, is his membership of the State. This definitive constitutive emphasis on the State follows, of course, from Hegel's conception of the State as a Moment in *Geist*'s process. Accordingly, Hegel is able to say that "only in the State does man have a Rational existence" for as a "knowing being, he has spiritual actuality only in so far as his being, that is, the Rational itself is his object and possesses objective and immediate existence for him; only as such does

21. This is the theme of Avineri's *Hegel's Theory* — see Preface — "Hegel can be seen as the first major political philosopher of modern society" (p. x). Similarly, T.M. Knox — "Hegel's rational State, then, is a description of the essence of modern political life", 'Hegel and Prussianism', in Kaufmann, *Hegel's Pol. Phil.*, p. 22.

he possess consciousness and exist in an ethical world within the legal and ethical life of the State" (PGN, 94: WL VIII, 90). As we have brought out in earlier discussion, the individual as a spiritual universal can only be 'at home' in the spiritual universality of the *Volk* or State, since they are all ultimately the work of *Geist*. It is because Hegel attributes such significance to the State (God's progress in the world) that he exploits this conception even further by concluding that "Man must therefore venerate the State as a secular deity" (PR, 285: WL VI, 357). But, because man himself is an agent of *Geist* this relationship must pay heed to man's 'quality': a point that will acquire greater significance when Hegel's attack on Romanticism is considered later.

As is to be expected from his view of the State as an organic totality many of Hegel's comments on the individual/State relation employ this particular metaphor. Although this metaphor has been utilised so often by so many writers (particularly in the phrase 'members of the State') without any intention to subscribe to the view that the State is an organism, in Hegel it is deliberate.[22] Thus the citizens are said to be 'distinct moments like those of organic life" (PGN, 95: WL VIII, 91). The thrust behind the metaphor is that the parts are inter-dependent and that they cannot subsist outside the whole that enlivens and defines them. This is an image (*Vorstellung*) that conveys the germ of the theoretical underpinning of Hegel's contextualism in his concept of actuality as the unity of inner and outer. Such a conception is contrary to a means/end relation; but it is such a relation that is implied by Contractarianism.

Hegel's chief objection to the notion of the Social Contract is that it operates with an abstract, acultural or non-contextual view of man. That is to say that the idea of a Social Contract has cogency only because it assumes that the individual (the inner) can be separated from the State (the outer), so that, from this putative separateness, membership of the State can become optional and a matter of voluntary choice. This means that the State's existence now depends on the individual's capricious will (*Willkür*) through his individually given consent (PR, 156 – 7: WL VI, 196 – 7).

Thus for Hegel, the State is not based upon a contract since that presupposes arbitrariness in the sphere of necessity (the State's actuality as a Moment in *Geist's* coming-to-be). The legitimate arena for Contract is in the Moment, within Objective *Geist*, that Hegel terms Abstract Right. Here the relationship between the contracting parties is contingent or arbitrary, for the object of such contracts is "a single external thing" (PR, 58: WL VI, 75). The Contractarians have endeavoured to assimilate the relationship between the individual and the State (where will is universal) to this superficial level (where will is merely 'common'). By operating at the level of *Verstand* they have misapprehended the true (dialectical) relationship of the parts to the whole: instead, they have operated

---

22. Commentators who studiously ignore Hegel's organicism simultaneously ignore an important and informative aspect of his thought, for, as we have seen, his espousal of organicism is directly related to his metaphysic – see E. Fackenheim, *The Religious Dimension in Hegel's Thought*, p. 47; G.D. O'Brien, *Hegel on Reason and History*, p. 132.

with isolated individuals and judged the State as a means to their end (recall Locke's location of the end of government in the preservation of property: another institution appropriately treated in the arena of Abstract Right). Indeed, given Hegel's theory of the State as an agent of contextualisation, theorists like the Contractarians (and Natural Lawyers – see Chapter 11), who deal with the individual simply as a bearer of rights, are bound to hold an inadequate understanding of human nature.

More particularly, Hegel is, here, utilising his distinction between the universal and the common. The former is not a "mere sum of features common to several things" rather it is, as befits an attribute of *Begriff*, at home in its negation (EL, 292: WG VI, 321). Significantly, Hegel goes on to illustrate this difference between the truly universal and mere common-ness by referring to Rousseau's distinction, in *du Contrat Social*, between *la volonté générale* and *la volonté de tous*.[23] However, as we shall see, Hegel is still in fundamental disagreement with Rousseau.

The Contractarians, for Hegel, have obscured the true relationship between the individual and the State. Nor is this a harmless philosophic error because, to Hegel, this particular misconception lay behind the French Revolutionary programme of which the Terror was the inevitable product. The 'logic' here is spelt out in a celebrated chapter in the *Phänomenologie*. *Geist* at this point appears in the shape of the absolute certainty of self-consciousness to the extent that "the world is for it absolutely its own will and this will is universal will" which is moreover "concretely embodied" as the "will of all individuals as such" (Ph, 600 – 1: WL II, 380). No division is thus recognised because this will, as the will to universal freedom, can only realise itself as the work of the whole. But this universal can only operate by becoming concrete, that is, by becoming specific in particular self-consciousnesses. Yet such particularity sets up division so that anything that is done cannot, by definition, be the true act of universal self-consciousness; it becomes immediately, as soon as it acts, the work of a faction. There can be, therefore, no representation or mediation, no organic structure (*Glieder*). All that there can be are atoms existing in their spendid isolation. The upshot is that since nothing positive can be done "there is left only negative action: it is merely the rage and fury of destruction" (Ph, 604: WL II, 382). As Hegel chillingly puts it on the following page "the sole and only work and deed accomplished by universal freedom is therefore death".

The philosophical errors of the Jacobins here are basically two-fold. This will is, in fact, a common will. It is the product of discrete independent selves; the very conception of such selves emanates from separating the inner from the outer; from thinking that it is possible to conceive of men independently of their State. This is the same basic error as that of the Contractarians. From their premises the State becomes an association that proceeds from mutual independence so that it can only consist of a casual tie, which is far removed from seeing the political (intra-State) relationship as "objective, necessary and in-

---

23. Cf. Hegel's fuller treatment of Rousseau in GP III, 462: WL XIX, 528.

dependent of choice and whim" (PW, 281: WL VII, 197). The Contractarians' principles lack the necessary concreteness that stems from not appreciating that the part (the contracting individuals) only makes sense in terms of a specific whole, which makes the individuals what they are in the first place and gives them thereby the ideas and sentiments (the content) for their theorising. The principles of '89 are similarly abstract in the double sense of being extracted from specific context and being empty formalisms (PHS, 469 – 70: WL VIII, 921).

Secondly, by remaining at the level of *Verstand* the Revolutionaries fail to see the world in terms of inter-relationships. *Geist* differentiates itself as it comes-to-be. Hegel stresses, again and again, in his own positive delineation of the State's Rationality, the role of institutions and practices that act as mediators between the individual and the whole – "The constitution is essentially a system of mediation" (PR, 292: WL VI, 365). Thus, Rousseau's conviction that *la volonté générale* cannot be represented betrays his insensitivity to modernity – the Greek polis has gone forever and cannot be recreated, as Rousseau, himself, perhaps realised in his pessimistic passages.

It is Hegel's emphasis upon mediation that also explains his hostility to popular suffrage. Such a practice conceives of the electorate abstractly, that is, as a mere agglomeration of atoms (PR, 202: WL VI, 254; cf. PW, 262: WL VII, 175). Atomism characterises Contractarianism, indeed, Hegel goes so far as to remark that atomic theory is now more evident in political than in physical science (EL, 182: WL V, 119) but in both sciences it spells "death to every Rational concept, organisation [*Gliederung*] and life" (PW, 263: WL VII, 177). A consequence of conceiving the electorate in such atomistic terms is that it is counter-productive for having merely one vote amidst a multitude of electors can only engender electoral indifference (PR, 203: WL VI, 254; cf. PW, 318: WL VII, 309). By contrast the organic structure of the State should be followed. Participation in the State should be mediated by the various branches of society; Hegel cites trade and manufacture (the Corporations of Civil Society)[24] as examples. Each branch represents a particular interest in society and it is thus guaranteed a voice in the State by not being dependent on the capricious lottery of popular election. Hegel is here advocating what is generally known as 'functional representation'. The important point in all this is that the individual must be conceived concretely. His universal consciousness unless mediated remains empty and, as we have seen, ultimately destructive. By being mediated it acquires a content, or becomes concrete, and this mediation takes the form of membership of the Family or one of the institutions of Civil Society so that thereby "the single person attains his actual and living destiny for universality" (PR, 201: WL VI, 252). In sum, the atomic, abstract individual does not appear as such in the State for the State is an organisation each of whose members is itself a group (PR, 198: WL VI, 249) and it is the cardinal error of the advocates of popular

---

24. For an informative discussion see G. Heiman, 'The Sources and Significance of Hegel's Corporate Doctrine', in Pelczynski, *Hegel: Problems and Perspective*, pp. 111 – 135.

suffrage to over look this structural mediation.[25]

We saw in Part II that Hume rejected Contract theory. But, although Hume and Hegel share this animus, Hume is operating with assumptions that Hegel refutes in his own argument. There is thus a profound gulf between their respective positions and, because this centres on their respective views of human nature, it will be germane to compare these refutations. In addition, in this comparison, attention will be drawn, in passing, to a reformulation of Contractarianism that took place between their writings.

Hume rejected Contractarianism on two fronts — historical and philosophical — but these are essentially complementary because they both have their basis in his theory of human nature. History reveals the 'uniform principles' and 'regular springs' of human nature and historical knowledge is only possible because of the constancy implicit in human action. Thus, despite his admission that there is no record of the origin of government (it "preceded the use of writing"), nevertheless, he affirms that "we can trace it plainly in the nature of man" (E (OC) 454). Given what we know of human nature together with what is known about the various but contingent conditions of social life, reasonable conjecture is permissible. Similarly, the 'philosophical' argument, utilising the distinction between natural and artificial virtues, only works in its required way because it consists of universal propositions. Justice proceeds necessarily (naturally) from the juxtaposition of 'confined generosity' and scarcity and the source of virtue, natural and artificial, is a constant quality of mind (approbation in that which 'pleases'). The significant point in this, for present purposes, is that this theory of constantly uniform human nature is that also upheld by his Contractarian opponents.

However, as we argued in Chapter 5, Hume's attack can be viewed as a de facto dismissal of an essentially, though ambiguously formulated, de iure theory as manifest in the focus on the *Original* Contract. Later in the eighteenth century, in the work of Rousseau and Kant, a reformulation of Contract theory took place. These reformulations 'disambiguated' the seventeenth-century versions of Hobbes, Pufendorf, Locke etc. by putting forward the Social Contract as a de iure theory pure and simple. Rousseau uses the notion of a Social Contract to answer the question of how I can be free and yet be subject to social regulation, that is, it becomes a criterion of legitimacy. Rousseau's answer to this question in the form of the sovereignty of *la volonté générale* need not concern us here. This interpretation of the Social Contract is even clearer in Kant, for in Rousseau it is at least disputable if he is assuming that such a contract between the citizens takes place (the *Je suppose* at the opening of Book 1, Chapter 6, in the *du Contrat Social*, is perhaps crucial). Kant employs his technical notion of a regulative Idea (see Chapter 3). The Social Contract is such an Idea —

---

25. The need that Hegel saw for such mediation is stressed by C. Taylor and it forms a persistent theme in his interpretation of Hegel and his contemporary significance; thus "This [alienation and ecological disaster] puts us in a dilemma not unlike that of Hegel and the Romantic age", *Hegel*, p. 461; also see the long concluding chapter.

we by no means hold that this contract. . .actually exists as a fact for it cannot possibly be so. . .it is merely an idea of reason which nonetheless has undoubted practical reality; for it can oblige every legislator to frame his laws in such a way that they could have been produced by the united will of a whole nation (*Volks*) and to regard each subject. . .as if he had consented within the general will (*Willen mit zu sammen*). This is the test of the rightfulness of every public law.[26]

Social Contract theory, therefore, can be seen to have been put forward in the seventeenth century as an ambiguously historical and philosophical idea, which was rejected as history in the eighteenth century, but then this rejection was made redundant by a purely theoretical reformulation later in the century. Hegel's position can now be seen as a rejection of this theory. That Hegel is dealing with a *theory* is evident from his remark that 'origins' are philosophically irrelevant (PR, 156: WL VI, 196). Hegel's specified opponent in the *Philosophie des Rechts* is Rousseau, though he does also refer to Fichte[27] (PR, 157: WL VI, 197). Rousseau, by seeing that 'will' is the basis of the State, does mark an improvement on theories such as Hume's (and other 'sociological' versions) which base the State on 'natural' principles like sociality.[28] But, the important point is that it is Rousseau's *theory* that Hegel rejects, because, as we have elucidated, this is based upon a faculty bifurcation of man and society. The point at issue here, though, is that this rejection of Rousseau is grounded in principles that also constitute a rejection of Hume's position.

We can illustrate both the gulf between Hume and Hegel and the extent of Hume's 'overlap' with his opponents. Hume whilst rejecting the Contract nevertheless says originally submission must be understood as a form of contract or voluntary consent (E (OC) 454, 460; cf. E (OG) 37). When Hegel (in one version of his introductory lectures to the philosophy of history) mentions the origins of a State he locates this in "domination on the one hand and instinctive obedience on the other. But obedience and force, fear of a ruler, is already a connection of wills" (VG, 60: WJ XI, 29).[29] Although these two arguments seem similar, to

26. *Theorie und Praxis*, tr. H. Nisbet, in Kant's *Political Writings*, ed. H. Reiss, p. 79: *Werke* VIII, 297.

27. The criticism of Fichte is the same as of Rousseau and Kant, because he, like they, talks of freedom in the shape of an "isolated individual" and does not apprehend accordingly the true essence of the State (GP III, 503 – 4: WJ XIX, 638 – 9).

28. Cf. M. Riedel, 'Nature and freedom in Hegel's "Philosophy of Right"', in Pelczynski, *Hegel: Problems & Perspective*, who quotes from a manuscript version of Hegel's lectures – "The impulse toward sociability which philosophy formerly accepted as the basis of the state is something indefinite and abstract which can only furnish some of the necessary conditions for the vast and highly structured state, and which appears excessively thin beside the phenomenon it is meant to explain", p. 148.

29. Cf. JR II, 245 – 6, where Hegel rejects the original contract and sees the origin of all states in the actions of *Grosser Menschen*. They establish their position as leaders not through their strength for (as Hume had also pointed out) the many are always stronger than the individual but through something in their character of personality (*Zügen*) which extracts obedience. In fact, by expressing the absolute will these men constitute and uphold the State's unity as absolute *Geist*. Similarly, though the State may originate in violence it does not rest on it for in the State the individual obeys a universal – he recognises others as free persons like himself (EG, 172: WG VII, 277).

Hegel this argument only shows that since the State must be seen as a totality, as an organic whole, it cannot be understood by abstracting a part and considering it in isolation. Hence, in obedience it is not the isolated individual wills that prevail but the 'general will', the concrete cultural complex. The individual cannot be separated from his State.

Hume's theory, however, in principle, allows for just such a separation and thus from Hegel's perspective, he also has a faulty view of the relationship between man and society. Hume's anti-Contractarianism still assumes a view of human nature that is non-contextual; as in principle intelligible outside the specificity of a society. Hume's frequent practice of portraying or conjecturing what it is 'natural' for man to do in certain circumstances reveals just that assumption. Thus, although both Hume and Hegel reject Contractarianism their rejections involve a different conception of man. For Hegel, to repeat, the individual only is what he is by virtue of his context; by virtue of being a member of a State (society). Outside his specific society the individual is a meaningless abstraction. The universality that Hume attributes to human nature is merely what is common; in contrast, Hegel's universality is concrete. There is no 'human nature', that can be turned to irrespective of any specific society, by which to understand, and criticise, any particular society. Hume in his criticism of Contract theory, just as much as the Contractarians in their avowal of it, is working with a specious, indeed, pernicious, notion.

Though anti-Contractarianism is an important 'clue' to Hegel's view of human nature implicit in his conception of the individual/State relationship it requires augmentation. This can be provided by looking at this conception from a different perspective; a perspective neatly encapsulated in his understanding of the French Revolution not as the product of mistaken theories but as the completion of the Reformation (see next Chapter) and, more pertinently here, as the "struggle of Rational constitutional law (*vernünftige Staatsrecht*) against the mass of positive law and privileges by which it had been stifled" (PW, 282: WL VII, 198). It is central to Hegel's theory of the modern State that it pay heed to the demands of self-conscious freedom; demands, which in the guise of the realisation of human ideals and opinions, are (have their meaning in) *Geist's* own work. These demands, which necessarily therefore bear the hallmark of Rationality, are not recognised by those like the Romantics, who glorify the Middle Ages, nor by those who advocate a 'historical' jurisprudence.

An example of the former is Adam Müller. In his *Die Elemente der Staatskunst* (1809) he also rejects the idea of a Social Contract because it promotes the illusion that man can be thought of outside the State (an illusion that has, moreover, produced the catastrophe of the French Revolution). In addition, Müller defines the State as "the totality of human affairs, their union into a living whole",[30] which is contrasted, in a markedly Burkean fashion, with the State

---

30. In Political Thought of the German Romantics, tr. A. Hayward, ed. H. Reiss, p. 157: *Elemente*, ed. J. Baxa, Vol. 1, p. 51.

as a utilitarian device, as a factory, farm or commercial undertaking.[31] This jux-taposition is interesting for two reasons, both of which demonstrate the dif-ference between Müller and Hegel. Firstly, this image of the State as a factory is a 'modern' one and it is to be contrasted with an earlier ideal as manifest in a Medieval community, with its harmony reflected in an unqualled reciprocity be-tween power and obedience, liberty and authority.[32] Secondly, it is symptomatic of this rejection of 'modernity' that Müller deems it appropriate to criticise Adam Smith. Smith's view ignores the organic harmony of the State, which can-not be comprehended as an economic unit. Thus Müller is critical of Smith for mistaking 'wealth' for 'riches', for ignoring spiritual factors, and most crucially of all for his construction of a system based on 'economic man', who, as an extra-social abstraction, infringes one of Müller's basic propositions, namely, "man cannot be thought of outside the State".[33]

Hegel is explicit that such Medievalism fails to comprehend the action of *Geist* in the world; and fails simultaneously to have an historically adequate view of human nature. Earlier in this chapter we quoted from one of Hegel's essays that the imagery of medieval Germany was no longer appropriate and, in another ear-ly essay (*Die Verfassung Deutschlands*, 1802), the political dimension of this re-jection is spelt out. In this essay Hegel acknowledges that the foundation of *Volk's* union was originally to be found in the identity of manners, education (*Bildung*) and language but this is no longer the case. Moreover, it need no longer be the case because the modern State coheres by virtue of "the spirit and art of *Staatsorganisation*" (PW, 158: WL VII, 25). The *Philosophie des Rechts* reiterates and reinforces this conviction. In that work Hegel declares, "the great advance of the State in modern times is that nowadays all the citizens have one and the same end, an absolute and permanent end; it is no longer open to in-dividuals, as it was in the Middle Ages, to make private stipulations in connexion with it" (PR, 242: WL VI, 305).

This means in direct opposition to Müller[34] that the Medieval State was not an organism; it was rather an "aggregate" (PR, 180: WL VI, 226). The same point is made a little later when Hegel remarks that in feudal monarchies the State was divided on mechanical principles (PR, 188: WL VI, 236). Conversely, to attack Adam Smith's theories as anti-organic betrays a misunderstanding of the necessary differentiation and diversity that constitutes an integral part of the modern State's organicism. Hegel was familiar with the work of the Scottish economists – Smith and Steuart in particular – and the whole conception of

31. Reiss edition, p. 150: Baxa edition, Vol. 1, p. 37. For the impact of Burke on Müller see Meinecke, *Cosmopolitanism*, p. 100ff.

32. Baxa edition, Vol. 1, p. 283.

33. Reiss edition, p. 145: Baxa edition, Vol. 1, p. 31. For a discussion of Müller's economic theory see G.A. Briefs 'The Economic Philosophy of Romanticism', *JHI* (1941) 279–300.

34. Heiman, 'Sources and Significance', is thus in error when he remarks that Hegel's theory of the State is "not too far removed" from Müller's, p. 113n. G.A. Kelly is clear that the differences be-tween Hegel and Müller are "striking", *Hegel's Retreat from Eleusis*, p. 123.

Civil Society as a Moment in Ethical Life owes much to his acceptance of their reading of 'modernity'.[35] The term 'Civil Society' itself, Rosenzweig suggests, Hegel appropriated from Adam Ferguson's *Essay on the History of Civil Society*, which had considerable impact in Germany from Herder and Lessing onwards.[36]

Müller's medievalism is part and parcel of a general rejection of political and legal rationalism. This rejection found its most celebrated exposition in the writings of Savigny and the other members of the Historical School of Jurisprudence. Savigny saw the law as necessarily connected with the whole matrix of a *Volk's* existence (which he later termed *Volksgeist*). Law was an integral and developing part of the *Volk*.[37] In this regard, it was frequently and persistently compared to language; both were intrinsically social products emanating from the *Volksgeist* as such, and not from any separate, identifiable, specific souce.[38] Given that the law has no separate existence, it follows that it cannot be studied in a vacuum; rather, it must be studied historically, focusing less on the

35. Hegel cites Smith in his Jena writings (at JR II, 239 – for example he quotes the famous example of the pin-making process) and in 1799 he wrote a commentary (now lost) on Steuart's *Political Economy*. The debt of Hegel to Steuart has been stressed by P. Chamley (see 'Les Origins de la Pensée Economique de Hegel', *Hegel-Studien* (1965) 225 – 261) and he is followed by R. Plant (*Hegel*, p. 64ff.). Much, though not all, of Steuart's doctrine is, however, stock eighteenth-century theorising which Hegel could have got from Rousseau, Herder, Ferguson etc. In addition, though Plant regards Steuart's notion of the 'Statesman' as "having an enormous influence upon Hegel"(p. 68, cf. p. 168) and, though, to Chamley (p. 251 – 5), Hegel found in Steuart, rather than in Adam Smith, more insights into the dialectics of economics, nevertheless, much of Hegel's discussion in the *Philosophie des Rechts* can be seen to have Smithian roots. For example, the 'other side' of the division of labour manifest in the distress of those restricted to particular tasks and in their inability to enjoy the mental (*geistigen*) benefits of Civil Society (PR, 150: WL VI, 188) is found in Smith's discussion of the division of labour in Book 5 of the *Wealth of Nations* as producing "torpor of the mind" (Everyman Edit., Vol. II, p. 264). Again, Smith's remedy for this in education provided by government acton (II, 265 – 6) can be seen in Hegel's demand that society must furnish public education (PR, 148: WL VI, 187). Further, the actions that Hegel sees public authority performing (street-lighting bridge building, pricing of necessities, public health) (PR, 276: WL VI, 346) are those that Smith advocated (II, 211ff) and for the similar reason that they are 'public goods', that is, socially advantageous but not such that it would repay any one individual the cost of establishing them. Finally, there is considerable literature on Adam Smith's theory of 'alienation', based on the above passages from Book 5, which compares this theory with that of Marx. Marx, indeed, obtained his conception of alienation from Hegel (see Chapter 11 infra) but it should be stressed that Smith's discussion and Hegel's are not identical. Smith's is rather to be seen in its admittedly complex relationship to the classical question of 'virtue' whilst Hegel's theory presupposes a theory of human nature far removed from Smith's basically Humean account.

36. *Hegel und der Staat*, Vol. II, p. 118.

37. The following account is gleaned from Savigny's *Vom Beruf unserer Zeit für Gesetzgebung und Rechtswissenschaft*, tr. in Reiss, *Pol. Thought German Romantics*, & from Vol. 1 of Savigny's *Geschichte des Römischen Rechts im Mittelalter*, 2nd Edit. (1834).

38. Cf. H. Kantorowicz, 'Savigny and the Historical School of Law', *Law Quarterly Review* (1937) 310f. who sees the influence of J. Grimm as here decisive.

codified edicts of legislators than on the customs and traditions of the *Volk*, who are the vital source of all law. It was a consequence of this approach that any attempt to codify or rationalise such customs, as Napoleon had done in France and as was threatened in parts of Germany, was a mutilation of the living tissue of law.

It was this antipathy by Savigny to the codification and rationalisation of law that prompted Hegel's opposition. In a clear reference to Savigny's pamphlet *Vom Beruf unserer Zeit für Gesetzgebung und Rechtswissenschaft* (1814) Hegel calls the denial that peoples have a vocation to codify their laws an insult (PR, 272: WL VI, 340). But further, it is a mistake to juxtapose customs and codes as if they were antithetical since the laws of a people do not cease to be customs by being written down. Uncodified law, as evidenced in England, represents a "monstrous confusion" (PR, 135: WL VI, 171). What the English lack, as Bentham also from his own very different perspective ceaselessly tried to demonstrate, is the scientific remodelling of law (PW, 300: WL VII, 289). Despite their misguided actions and ideas, the French Revolutionaries, by overthrowing the feudal incubus, nevertheless "succeeded in creating the new ethical world-order" (EG, 49: WG VII, 79) and, for Hegel, the Rationality thereby actualised demands that the law be put on a Rational footing.

It is on these grounds that Hegel supports the King in his dispute with the Württemberg Estates. The King wished to bring the constitution "within the ambit of Rational constitutional law" but the Estates defended their ancient (feudal) privileges by committing themselves to the retention of the existing positive law. Hegel remarks sardonically that the situation here is the reverse of that in France in 1789, because in Württemberg it is the King who is progressive and the Estates that are 'reactionary', since, as he puts it, "they seem to have slept through the last twenty-five years possibly the richest that world history has had and for us the most instructive, as it is to them that our world and our ideas (*Vorstellungen*) belong" (PW, 281 – 2: WL VII, 197 – 9).

Now the hallmark of Rationality is universality and so the law should be *known* by all. Savages are governed by impulses and feeling but as the vehicles of *Geist's* self-actualisation in the world, human nature changes (see next Chapter) so that the previous accidental quality of law passes over into the comprehension of right as right. To codify or systematise law is to elevate the customary hodgepodge of regulations and feudal survivals into a coherent universal system, a comprehensive complete whole. The introduction of *Geist* here also helps pinpoint the difference between Hegel's and Savigny's use of *Volksgeist*. For Hegel, since the *Volksgeist* is *Geist*, it is necessarily Rational and not, as in Savigny, a 'quality' that defies rationalisation by virtue of it being the work of unconscious social interaction. Moreover, for Hegel, such work over time, through history, is the self-same work of *Geist* so that it is Rational and not, as Savigny's position implies, the product of chance.[39]

39. Cf. H. Marcuse, *Reason and Revolution: Hegel and the rise of social theory*, 2nd Edit., p. 237. Avineri in Kaufmann, *Hegel's Pol. Phil*, comments "in Hegel's thought the *Volksgeist* underwent a

It is his definite espousal of modernity (the underlying theory of history here will be covered in the next Chapter) that accounts for Hegel's hostility to both Müller and Savigny and their respective followers. The modern Rational State requires (for it is the principle of the modern world) "freedom of subjectivity" (PR, 286: WL VI, 358). The union of the universal and the particular, in the Idea of the State, is only possible if subjectivity attains "its full and living development"; only then is the State "genuinely organised" (PR, 280'; WL VI, 351; cf. EG, 290: WL V, 472). My particular end should be identified with the universal end but the State is only actual (is what it has it in it to be) when in so doing its particular members have a feeling of their self-hood (PR, 281: WL VI, 352).

This has practical consequences for Hegel's conception of the State as a political entity (*politische Staat*).[40] It entails the presence of certain institutions, such as public trials (PR, 142, 275: WL VI, 179, 344), freedom of press and opinion (PR, 205: WL VI, 258) and open competitive entry to the civil service (PR, 190: WL VI, 239). In short, in general, the universal end of the State cannot prevail "except along with particular interests and through the co-operation of particular knowing and willing" (PR, 160 – 1: WL VI, 202). The modern State is a unity enriched by the incorporation of differentiation, unlike the relatively impoverished medieval ideal of Müller, which submerges the individual rather than preserving (*Aufhebung*) him. This is the source of its strength – it allows "the principle of subjectivity to progress to its culmination in the extremes of self-subsistent particularity and yet at the same time brings it back to the substantive unity and so maintains this unity in the principle of subjectivity itself" (PR, 161: WL VI, 202). The State is a concrete universal which, as befits its status as the objectification of *Geist*, is able to incorporate the individual by defining him, and thus Contractarianism is wrong, whilst enabling him to act and express himself as an individual, and thus Romanticism and Savigny are wrong.

To summarise: Hegel's theory of human nature, as a spiritual universal, entails that an individual can only subsist in a spiritually universal context. This is the most important fact about his theory of the *Volk* and, more especially, of his much criticised theory of the State. They are concrete (contextual) universals (spiritual). Hegel, by his articulated omni-explanatory metaphysic, has elevated the theory of human nature as a social product into a cohesive, integral element of his theory. Human nature is what it is because it is found in a specific context; outside this context nothing appropriate or meaningful can be known about it. Hegel, in his theory of the State, clearly enunciates this conception. Human

profound process of rationalisation", p. 123, and for comparison with Savigny see p. 124 but when Avineri says (p. 126) that the analogue between language and law is rejected by Hegel, since, whilst one legal system can be superior to another, "it would be nonsense to say anything like this about languages", he is in error because Hegel does say this about the inferiority of Chinese to European languages, see EG, 216: WG VII, 399.

40. The distinction between the strictly political state and State as the highest Moment of Ethical Life is emphasised by Pelczynski, 'The Hegelian Conception of the State', in Pelczynski, *Hegel: Problems and Perspective*, pp. 1 – 29.

nature, the premise of Hume's science of man, can no longer be looked upon as a societally-indifferent universal by which to gauge different societies. But, Hegel, does not eschew trans-societal universalism and evaluation and the next chapter will examine how a contextual theory of human nature is yet made non-relativist.

10. SOCIAL DIVERSITY AND THE MEANING OF HISTORY

The contextualist theory of human nature holds that Man as such does not exist, only particular men in particular societies. From this premise a relativist conclusion can be drawn. Since a contextually defined human nature is integrally particularised by its societal setting, and since there are a considerable number of different societies, then human nature cannot function as a trans-societal constant. What one society, in its practices and institutions assumes to be 'human nature', and thereby imputes to it universality, need not be the case for another society with different practices and institutions, and thence with a different assumption. Given the acceptance of the widespread view that any society's definition of 'man' reflects that particular society's perspective and values, then for these values to be used to judge other societies (with their own standards) is merely an expression of parochiality; each is valid in its own terms, there is no over-arching schema of evaluation. Thus it is that along these, or similar, lines the contextualist theory can be said to 'invite' relativism.

We saw in Chapter 2, how Herder's celebration of the 'primitive', and his critique of the cultural arrogance of the historians and aestheticians of the Enlightenment, led him to a conception of the *Volk* as the autonomous bearer of its own values; it should be judged in its own terms. But, Herder was no relativist, because he endeavoured, in his concept of *Humanität*, to retain a universalist perspective, whilst still doing justice to the intrinsic worth of the various *Völker*. Hegel also endeavours to harmonise his own brand of contextualism with universalism. This harmonisation is effected through the concept of *Geist*.

Man for Hegel is a concrete spiritual universal. This means, amongst other things, that any universalism based on man's physical capacity to enjoy pleasure and dislike pain, such as that of Hume and the Utilitarians, is abstract and uninformative; it is the product of *Verstand*. Moreover, man is not an animal and it is because this is the case that the context in which he lives is not an externally given environment, but his own creation. It consists, so to speak, not of 'bricks and mortar' but of 'houses', that is, of purposively built and designed artifacts, which as such, embody thought. Man, since his ultimate definition is thought, thus, cannot be separated from his society, so that, although thought is universal, this universality, as the previous Chapter established, is 'concrete'. But, it is because man and his society are both, as universals, expressions of *Geist* that this contextualism is inseparable from the ultimate universality – the world's progressively actualised meaning.

This meaning is *Geist's* process of coming-to-be. It is a *process* and it is *this* which constitutes the history of the world. Here is to be found Hegel's account of, and explanation for, social diversity. *Geist's* process consists of its becoming for-itself what it is in-itself. As we have outlined in earlier Chapters, this process takes the dialectical form of differentiation from simple unity before self-completion in an enriched reunion. Since it is *Geist's* activity that is the world's meaning this differentiation necessarily partakes of this meaning. The experience and evidence of the multiplicity and diversity of the societies that exist and have existed, each with their own intrinsic values, can thus be judged historically as Moments in *Geist's* process. Hegel's explanation of social diversity is thus historical. It is because societies are the work of *Geist* that this is the appropriate perspective, since "world history as a whole is the expression of *Geist* in time" (PGN, 128: WL VIII, 134). In fact, time itself is nothing other than *Geist's* self-completion (Ph, 800: WL II, 515).[1]

Moreover, the historical perspective is appropriate because the geographical location of societies concerns their 'natural', as opposed to their 'spiritual' dimension ("Nature is the expression of the Idea in space" (PGN, 128: WL VIII, 134)). Societies, as natural entities enter into a passive relationship with *Geist*, but as spiritual entities, the activity of *Geist* is directed to an object which is itself active (EG, 13: WG VII, 22). Nature has no history (Ph, 326: WL II, 196), it consists of repetition (one generation of pigs is like all other generations of pigs), but the activity of the spiritual signifies progress, and it is this that simultaneously constitutes the history of the world and imbues it with universal meaning. Given that the *Volk* and, preeminently, the State are spiritual, then it is to be expected that the history of the world is constituted by their activity. Given further that this activity is man's own activity, so that he is contextually self-defined by his membership of his *Volk* and State, then the progressive history of the world necessarily entails the progressive history of man. Man, to repeat the essential point, is spirit and thus progressive. Human nature is no passive ahistorical constant, but as *Geist's* vehicle, it is the active historical subject; it is radically historicised.

History is, by definition, progressive but to regard, as the relativist does, every State (each with its own self-authenticating values) that has existed as on a par, is to deprive the events of the past of meaning. Relativism is thus, on this understanding of history, necessarily ahistorical.[2] World history, as the work *Geist*, is a unity. W.H. Walsh, however, from the correct observation that Hegel saw history as a single process, misconceives Hegel's basic position, when he says

1. For a discussion of the place and problem of time in Hegel's system see N. Rotenstreich, *From Substance to Subject*, pp. 64 – 70, 98 – 105.

2. Cf. G.D. O'Brien, *Hegel on Reason and History*, p. 68, 158.

that Hegel missed the main point of Herder's work, which picked up the diversity of human nature and the 'independent interests of distinct civilisations'. Walsh even goes so far as to remark, "I think it is true that Hegel retained something of the eighteenth-century belief in a common human nature, and that he had little use for the extreme historicism or historical relativism which was coming into fashion".[3] Hegel is no relativist but his argument which supports this position is the same argument that engenders contextualism and, as we demonstrated from Hegel's own writings in Chapter 8, this is far removed from the typical eighteenth-century approach.

Hegel's philosophy of history is a systematisation of his conception of world history as a unity. Since the meaning of world history is *Geist's* process, then this history "is governed by an ultimate design": it is, as he declares on numerous occasions, a "Rational process" (PGN, 27 – 9: WL VIII, 5 – 7). This is the perspective from which the history of the world should be viewed. Hegel is careful to spell out that this commitment is not a licence to introduce a priori fictions (such as the notion of an *Urvolk*) into history. We must, he emphasises, "take history as it is: in other words, we must proceed historically and empirically" (PGN, 29: WL VIII, 7). But, such a procedure is not as straightforward as some historians like to believe. It is to the end of demonstrating this point that Hegel produces his well-known three-fold categorisation of types of history (PGN, 12 – 24: WL VIII, 166 – 177). There is first of all Original history, which is written by contemporaries, then Reflective history, whereby the historian brings to the past his own ideas, principles and assumptions, and, finally, there is Philosophical History.

This last category has the history of the world for its subject-matter – it is universal but it is also concrete. This, as G.D. O'Brien has noted,[4] provides the best clue as to the relationship between these three categories – they are dialectical. Philosophical history is the preservative supersession of the other categories. This can be seen from Hegel's later (1830) depiction of the perspective of a philosophical history of the world as, "not just one among many general perspectives, an isolated abstraction singled out at the expense of the rest. Its spiritual principle is the sum total of all possible perspectives. It concentrates its attention on the concrete spiritual principle in *Völker* and their history and deals not with individual situations but with a universal thought which runs throughout the whole" (PGN, 30: WL VIII, 9). Philosophical history elicits the Rational core – the 'universal thought' – of history. Thus it requires the use of *Vernunft*; for, just as the State presents a Rational 'face' when studied Rationally so too does the world assume a Rational aspect when looked at Rationally (PGN, 29: WL VIII, 7). All historians bring interpretative perspectives to bear on

3. W.H. Walsh, 'Principle and Prejudice in Hegel's Philosophy of History', in Z. Pelczynski (ed.), *Hegel's Political Philosophy: Problems and Perspectives*, p. 193. In an earlier work Walsh saw relativism as the logical outcome of Hegel's historical approach, though Hegel himself, it is acknowledged, did not recognise this. *Hegelian Ethics*, p. 11, 52.

4. O'Brien, *Hegel Reason & History*, p. 16ff. Cf. B.T. Wilkins, *Hegel's Philosophy of History*, who holds that the types of history are "Hierarchical not merely taxonomical", p. 44.

their material and thus it is that historians are misled if they think that the 'facts' can speak for themselves. The philosophical historian brings to history the philosophically accredited and established principle that "Reason governs the world" (PGN, 27: WL VIII, 4).

The diversity among the *Völker* and States that have existed in the world, when thus viewed to the end of eliciting the Rational movement of *Geist's* coming-to-be, can be adjudged to be of differential value. Such a judgment requires a criterion. This criterion is Rationality, that is, the extent to which *Geist* has actualised itself in them. Though this constitutes (in our own terminology) Hegel's substantive theory of rationality, to which we shall return, the criterion Hegel evokes, above all, is that of freedom. We have seen that Hegel regards thought as the essence of freedom. Man, as a spiritual universal constituted by thought, is necessarily a free agent. The reasoning behind Hegel's use of freedom as the criterion is the same as that which underlay his theory of the State, namely, the actualisation of Objective *Geist*. The implicit active freedom of Subjective *Geist* is embodied or actualised in the 'world', ultimately in the State. This is the basic reason why States are the agents and units of world history and, since States are the embodiment of freedom, then, they are most appropriately evaluated in terms of freedom.

Before discussing the periodisation of world history that Hegel derives from the application of this criterion, it is important to grasp the relationship of *Geist* with *Völker* and States. It was emphasised in the previous Chapter that this relationship was an internal one, that is, was of *Geist* with itself. In his discussions of the historical dimension to this relationship Hegel introduces the term *Weltgeist*. The *Weltgeist* is the substance of history and while it remains always one and the same, it "discloses this nature in the existence of the world" (PGN, 29: WL VIII, 6). This disclosure takes the form of the various *Volksgeister*: "the *Geist* in history is an individual which is both universal in nature and at the same time determinate" (PGN, 51: WL VIII, 36). There is accordingly a bifocality attributable to a *Volksgeist* and State. This is spelt out most clearly in the *Philosophie des Rechts*. "The State in its actuality is essentially an individual State and beyond that a particular State. Individuality is to be distinguished from particularity. The former is a moment in the very Idea of the State, while the latter belongs to history" (PR, 279: WL VI, 350).

It is important to appreciate the relationship here expounded between the individual and the particular. The *Weltgeist* has no form other than its existence in a *Volksgeist* or State. In no way is it transcendent, because transcendence would reduce the significance of the world, when it is Hegel's concern, above all, to vindicate the world's meaning*ful*ness. *Geist* is, as *Weltgeist*, variously throughout history, a world-historical *Volk*; there is no residue – *Geist's* becoming "presents a slow procession and succession of spiritual shapes (*Geistern*), a gallery of pictures, each of which is endowed with the *entire wealth* of Spririt" (Ph, 807 – my emphasis: WL II, 520). Similarly, it is part and parcel of *Geist's* concreteness that it actualises itself in the world, in concrete form. Now these various concrete forms (the States and *Völker*) do differ, by virtue of their concreteness, one from another. This is their particularity. It follows from this, as we shall develop later, that the States are self-complete entities, which cannot, as concrete particulars, be united. But, from the perspective of the *Weltgeist*, there is a unifying dimension (an "essential connection") because, as individuals, they are Moments in the becoming of *Geist* (PGN, 65: WL VIII, 52). A State's or *Volk*'s individuality (the dialectical unity of particularity and universality – see Chapter 8) is thus its identity with the *Weltgeist*. The *Weltgeist* is necessarily progressive and the different concrete *Völker* are its creation. This provides the periodisation into which the history of the world falls.

The history of the world is periodised because there have been through history different societies. If the *Weltgeist* had confined itself to one *Volk*, then that *Volk* alone would have borne the meaning of the world. But, the 'rise and fall of civilisations' that comprise the record of history, which Hegel cannot discount (because there is no transcendent meaning, so that meaning inheres in the world and its 'experience' – hence Hegel's injunction that 'we must proceed empirically') tell against this. When a *Volk*'s particular concreteness is the form that *Geist* manifests in the world (or more accurately when it *is Geist* – for *Geist* is what it does) then it is an individual, but this is transient, because *Geist* moves on to embody itself in another *Volk*'s particularity. Each *Volk* has a life of its own, its concrete particularity, but the whole of its life is merely as one individual in the course of world history (PGN, 62: WL VIII, 50).

Hegel, as might be expected, explicates this process by organic analogy. *Völker*, as we pointed out at the beginning of this chapter, have a natural as well as a spiritual dimension.[5] As a natural entity, a *Volk* "blossoms, flourishes, fades and perishes" (PGN, 58 – amended: WL VIII, 45). Its high point is its coincidence with the *Weltgeist*, when its particularity is simultaneously its world-historical individuality. When the *Weltgeist* moves on so the *Volk* returns to its particularity and begins to fade, though it need not die; the world still has within it *Völker*, such as the Chinese, whose role in world history is long past. This point is a further indication why Hegel's explanation of social diversity is historical, because we cannot explain the diversity that *now* exists by synchronic categories. Such, of course, was also the position of the eighteenth-century theorists, who plotted the course of social development in terms of four basic economic modes of production.

This distinction between individuality and particularity leads to a further factor responsible for periodisation. Just as the seed can only grow into its 'programmed' plant, so a *Volk* cannot 'go beyond' its self-conception. Each *Volk*, as a spiritual universal, creates its own determinate 'social order' – religion, customs, art – culminating in its Statehood. These creations constitute its identi-

5. It is a weakness of O'Brien's sympathetic and enlightening account of Hegel's philosophy of history that he dismisses Hegel's organicism out of hand in his endeavour to establish a decisive break between natural teleology and Hegel's sense of historical individuality. Nature does have a positive role to play simply because it is dialectically differentiated from *Geist*, and it is not just a "careless use of biological metaphors" on Hegel's part. *Hegel, Reason & History*, p. 146.

ty (the *Volk* is what it does). Yet, if a *Volk* could continue to play its role, or play another role, in world history, it would mean that it had progressed beyond its principle, had somehow transcended its identity. This progress or transcendence (*Aufhebung*) is properly the prerogative of *Geist* itself; accordingly, "in world history, a *Volk* can be dominant only once because it can have only one task to perform within the spiritual process" (PGN, 148: WL VIII, 163).

The various societies that have existed are thus 'plotted' or 'placed' by the course that the meaning of the world has taken. This meaning is progressively realised and, consequently, this 'placing' is necessarily simultaneously a judging. The societies are not all on a par. A society whose individuality is 'richer' than another's is, by virtue of that fact, also superior to it. The criterion chiefly employed by Hegel to adjudicate between societies is, as mentioned above, the extent to which freedom has been actualised. On this basis Hegel divides the history of the world into four epochs or 'worlds' − the Oriental, Greek, Roman and Germanic. The relationship between them is expressed pithily by Hegel on several occasions, "The East knew and to the present day knows only that One is free; the Greek and Roman world that some are free; the German world knows that All are free" (PHS, 110: WJ XI, 150; cf. PR, 220: WL VI, 296; PGN, 39, 54: WL VIII, 136, 130; GPG, 303: WJ XVII, 134). It should be noted that though there are four epochs, these are nevertheless reducible to the basic triplicity that characteristics all the movements of *Geist*. The first epoch is still immersed in the simple unity of Nature, the second and third epochs represent the differentiation of *Geist*'s separation from Nature and the fourth epoch is that of *Geist*'s enriched reunion. Each of the epochs exhibits internally the expected triadic dynamism. Thus, the dialectic of one-some-all occurs *within* the Oriental epoch in the form of the absolute exclusivity of the Chinese despot,[6] the relative hierarchical exclusivity of the Indian caste system and the legalism (and hence incipient universalism) of the Persian monarch. The transition from one *Volk* to the next is the internal progression of *Geist*, though it is manifested externally in conquest, as in the defeat of the Persians by the Greeks.

There is no need to rehearse the details of Hegel's account but it will be profitable to examine his treatment of the Greeks and the Germans. The general significance of the Greeks to Hegel we have already had occasion to mention. The most decisive aspect of his treatment and understanding of the Greeks is his emphasis on their historicity. They *were* a world-historical people, but *Geist* has moved on. It has *progressed* and thus the Greek experience has been improved upon, so it cannot be an exemplar to the modern world. Hume, in contrast, in his subscription to the 'neo-classical' ideal of imitation, rejects the idea that "the strains of ancient eloquence are unsuitable to our age" and that they should not therefore be imitated (E (El) 102). It is the concreteness of Hegel's conception of *Geist* which entails that the Greek *Volksgeist* is all of a piece and thus even its art, expecially its poetry and drama, cannot function as contemporary models. In-

6. The association between the Orient and despotism was made by Montesquieu and had been taken up by many subsequent writers, see F. Venturi, *Italy and the Enlightenment*, p. 41ff.

deed, the fact that a deep understanding of the Greeks can be gained through their drama serves to demonstrate the cultural specifity of this art (hence Hegel's frequent and elaborate use of the drama of Antigone).

At its acme, the *schönste Blute* (PHS, 276: WL VIII, 641), there occurred, especially in Athens, as perfect a union between the citizen and the State at was possible in the Greek world (EG, 47: WG VII, 75) and Periclean culture was permeated and animated by the Spirit of Beauty. But, though the Greek spirit has escaped from Nature it still needs it. Nature is transformed into Art but the material is still inhibiting and limiting, that is, in Greek life *Geist* is not yet acting upon itself through and through. Spirituality here is thus not absolutely free (PHS, 248: WL VIII, 571).

This general characterisation necessarily pervades the whole *Volksgeist*. Thus the Greek's conception of the Divine is humanly conditioned. Individualities such as Athene are the gods of the Greeks. They are revered in festivals, games, song etc.; this is the experience of the *Kunstreligion* depicted in the *Phänomenologie* (Ph, 709: WL VII, 452). These individualities are qualitatively different from the natural 'objects' of worship of the Oriental World. Hegel, indeed, interprets the myth of the defeat of the Titans by Zeus as symbolising the defeat of Natural gods by *Geist* (PHS, 254: WL VIII, 583). But, though banished, the Natural gods retain their rights (PRel II, 232: WJ XVI, 103) because the natural is still present in the shape of Zeus; he is no abstraction, rather he (and the other Greek gods) is a concrete individuality who loves and hates, who partakes, in other words, of all man's natural traits – his needs, habits, passions etc. (PRel II, 257: WJ XVI, 127). This retention of natural elements by the Greeks, as seen also in their dependence on oracles and the like, is indicative of their dependence on the external. Greek thought is limited. The Greeks are unable to universalise *Geist*; there is no consciousness of the infinite subjective activity of man (PRel II, 259: WJ XVI, 128).

This decisive limitation means that man as such was not accorded absolute value. Politically this expresses itself in the presence of slavery. It was a necessary feature of the 'classical' democratic polis, with its active participatory citizenry, that these citizens should be relieved of many of the necessary but time-consuming tasks required to supply the satisfaction of basic needs. These tasks were performed by slaves (PHS, 265: WL VIII, 610). In comparison with the Oriental World, the Greek World has enlarged the scope of freedom but this enlargement of freedom for a few is self-contradictorily based on the unfreedom of many. Contradiction, as we have seen, is the 'motor' of *Geist*, so that a contradictory situation must 'give way'. This 'half-way house' of the Greeks between freedom for one and freedom for all (the universal recognition of the right of subjectivity) mirrors *Geist*'s emancipation from Nature, whilst still 'utilising' it in its own activity; thus whether or not a particular man was a citizen or a slave depended on the contingent natural factor (accident) of birth.

Since the Greek ideal, even at its own Periclean high point, cannot constitute *Geist*'s self-completion, it must give way. The seeds of its downfall are to be found within, because as the Greek spirit directs itself outwards it becomes unfaithful to its principles at home and internal dissension or corruption commences. This first exhibits itself in the Peloponnesian War between Athens and Sparta. However, the root cause of the Greek decline is not 'civil' war but the introduction of the principle of free thought (WL VIII, 638). The Greek ideal is one of beautiful harmony between the citizen and his polis – this, as discussed in the previous Chapter, is the original *Sittlichkeit* depicted in its profoundest guise in the *Phänomenologie*. This harmony is, however, unreflective and can only survive by suppressing any spirit of individualism (Ph, 467: WL II, 310). But, the emergence of subjectivity or individualism is the work of *Geist* and cannot be suppressed. It is in Socrates that the principle of subjectivity, of the inherent independence of thought, first attained expression (PHS, 281: WL VIII, 644). The customary morality of Antigone is now a thing of the past, for with subjectivity comes reflection, and from that comes judgment of the status quo. Though the decay sets in at this time this second period of Greek history is only terminated by the death of Alexander the Great and the disintegration of his Empire. Now the Greek World is in ruins and it is in this condition that the next world-historical people – the Romans – appear on the scene.

It is important to the general argument of this study, to grasp the significance of this treatment of the limitations of the Greeks for a theory of human nature. Hegel is here quite clearly saying that the Greeks lacked certain conceptions and this is put down to their historical situation. The Greeks thought what they did because they were Greeks, not because of any of the external factors, such as mode of economy, the connivance of priests, lack of leisure, etc., that Hume and the eighteenth century generally evoked to explain differences. In Hegel, human nature is regarded as a historical product which differs contextually from epoch to epoch. The Greeks are not men just like us in the eighteenth century but who happen contingently to experience different social and cultural circumstances. It is because these circumstances are different that the Greeks are different from us (inner and outer are a conceptual whole). Thus, for example, the Greeks' polytheism cannot be explained by universal propensities in human nature (pace Hume cf. N 51) or to put their worship of Zeus and the other Olympians down to vulgar superstition is radically to misunderstand the Greeks. More generally, "to get a grasp" of the history of religions means to acknowledge what is "horrible, dreadful and absurd" in them. We do not accept them but we justify them, for they are human creations and "therefore there must be *Reason* in them" (GR, 200: WJ XV, 94 – Hegel's emphasis). The history of religion reveals the history of the human mind.

It is Hegel's conception of *Geist* as a process of self-completion responsible for the world, and its meaning, that permits him to emphasise and grasp the historicity of human nature. Man in his universality *is Geist* and, because, to repeat, the essence of man is thought, is spirit, then man can have a history. This history, comprising the history of man's thought, and thence of his culture, *is* this process of self-completion. *Geist* functions as the ultimate context at any particular historical epoch. A man exists inside such a context and what he *is* is determined by it or (in the terminology used earlier) he is thereby radically acculturated. Another man, who dwells within another context, is in all important (spiritual) aspects a different man.

Additionally, these contexts are progressive, so that Hegel is able to say that one manifestation of human culture is superior to, because it is in *Geist*'s actualisation subsequent to, another. Thus, for example, Greek culture is superior to Persian and the Persian itself occupies a "higher" stage than the other Oriental *Völker* (PHS, 231: WL VIII, 512). This normative use of time necessarily also holds for the individual (he and his *Volk* are one). It is testament to the progressiveness of human nature that knowledge (thought), which was at one time the prerogative of the leading minds, is subsequently, as *Geist* (qua human thought) moves on, the material for school exercises (PhK, 44: WL II, 20). This testament signifies a real change in human nature, because man *is* thought, and, as such, this view is to be profoundly distinguished from Hume's account, since to him knowledge merely affects the 'tempers' of men; the passions (to which reason is subservient) remain ever the same. This same point will recur later in the Chapter.

The third stage, wherein *Geist* frees itself entirely from Nature to come-home-to-itself is the work of the German *Völker*. The decisive turn that inaugurates this third synthesising Moment is the birth of Christ. The Germanic World is thus also the Christian world (PGN, 131: WL VIII, 137) and the German *Völker* are the bearers of the Christian principle (PHS, 354: WL VIII, 763). This world is the world of completion for in it *Geist* can achieve its goal. The Christian God is not empty, but as Triune is concrete – is *Geist* (GR, 155: WJ XV, 48; cf. WL VIII, 721; PRel III, 111: WJ XVI, 318). Hegel explicitly states, in one version of his lectures, that this Christian recognition of *Geist* is the start and finish of history (*Bis hieher und von daher geht die Geschichte*) (WJ XI, 410; cf. PHS, 331). The Christian revelation provides the "key to world history. For we have here a definite knowledge of providence and its plan" (PGN, 41: WL VIII, 23).

In Christianity, the Natural (the external) is finally overcome because now *Geist* is working upon itself, since in Christ there is a Man who is God and God who is Man (PHS, 336: WL VIII, 725). The unity of Man with God thereby established is an internal unity within *Geist*. The "essential end" of Christianity is the redemption of the individual as an individual (and not merely as a species) (GR, 143: WJ XV, 35); in shorthand terms, Hegel here sides with Herder and against Kant in their dispute over this issue. This redemption occurs through the individual's participation in the realm of *Geist*. In Christ, God has become man on earth and this has given to subjectivity henceforth "the absolute moral justification by which it is subjectivity of infinite self-consciousness" (PRel II, 274: WJ XVI, 142). The individual now has what was lacking in the Greek and Roman Worlds, namely, infinite value. Man is now completely free; slavery is incompatible with Christianity. But, slavery was not immediately abolished and the task of the Germanic World is the actualisation of this implicit universality.

This actualisation not unsurprisingly falls into three phases. It commences with the appearance of the Germanic *Völker* in the Roman Empire and their conversion to Christianity and lasts until Charlemagne. The second phase, the Middle Ages, sees the birth of States and the clash between Church and State. The Reformation, however, resolves the truth of this conflict with its embodiment of universal but concrete freedom.

Though the Germanic World is thus necessarily connected with Christianity, and cannot without gross misrepresentation be identified with an espousal of German nationalism, there is within this World progression. The essence of the Reformation is that man in his very nature is destined to be free; it actualises Christian freedom (PHS, 433 – 4: WL VIII, 882). Luther's translation of the Bible is a decisive event for it became a *Volksbuche* and, as such, represented a means of deliverance for all from all spiritual slavery (WL VIII, 883; PRel III, 81: WJ XVI, 290). This originated in Germany (*Deutschland*) and took root only in *den rein germanischen Völkern* (PHS, 437: WL VIII, 885), that is, only in Scandinavia and England outside Germany.

The Roman Catholic peoples did not adopt the Reformation. Hence, although most of the European states originated in the Germanic *Völker*, as successors to the Roman Empire (PW, 202: WL VII, 92), there has been progress and there can be no doubt that Hegel does hold the Protestant States to be superior to the Catholic ones. This superiority is not to be put down to religious reasons alone but also because the modern Rational State can only be built on the emancipation of conscience that the Reformation signals. It is true that religion can oppress liberty of spirit and corrupt political life but this oppression is overcome and accommodated to political life in the form of Protestantism so that "the constitution and the code as well as their several applications embody the principle and development of the moral life, which proceeds and can only proceed from the truth of religion. . . The ethical life of the State and the religious spirituality of the State are thus reciprocal guarantees of strength" (EG, 291: WL V, 473). It is foolish, therefore, to attempt to implement constitutions independently of religion. In Catholic states political principles are divorced from the "internal justice and ethicality" that "the more profound principle of Protestantism embodies" (PGN, 104: WL VIII, 103). This lack is exemplified in the failure of the French Revolution. The ancien regime was Catholic and "therefore" the concept of freedom (Reason embodied in law) did not obtain (PHS, 466: WL VIII, 926), and thence the Revolution was foredoomed; there cannot be a revolution without there first being a Reformation (PHS, 472: WL VIII, 932). Whilst Avineri is thus correct to separate Hegel's notion of the Germanic World from that of German nationalism,[7] he is himself misleading when he equates this World with Western Christendom as such without allowing for its internal *qualitative* development – "The best state is that in which the greatest degree of freedom prevails" (PGN, 119: WL VIII, 122).

This tie-up between Protestantism and the modern State, as the culmination of world-history, helps to throw more light on Hegel's pronouncements, discussed in the last Chapter, that the State is God on earth. The religious dimension in Hegel's theory of history cannot be overemphasised. To provide a secular

---

7. S. Avineri, Hegel's Theory of the Modern State, p. 228.

reading of Hegel's philosophy of history as O'Brien does might possibly produce a coherent Idealist philosophy but it cannot pretend to be an accurate interpretation of *Hegel*.[8] Löwith is much closer to the mark when he observes that "the history of the world is to Hegel a history BC and AD not incidentally or conventionally but essentially. Only on this presupposition of the Christian religion as the absolute truth could Hegel construct universal history systematically from China up to the French Revolution".[9]

It is important in other words to take seriously Hegel's own pronouncements that his view of world history constitutes a Theodicy. There is such a thing as world history because the world as a whole has meaning. World history is a whole since its components are all the work of a *Weltgeist*. This *Weltgeist* explicitly "corresponds to the divine spirit which is absolute *Geist*. Since God is omnipresent, he is present in everyone and appears in everyone's consciousness" (PGN, 52 – 3: WL VIII, 37). Such a view of history as God's work is used by Hegel to emphasise its meaningfulness. He closes his lectures by declaring that world history, understood as the development and actualisation of *Geist*, is the "true Theodicaea, the justification of God in history" and "only this insight", namely, that "what has happened and is happening everyday is only not without God but is rather essentially his own work", can reconcile God and the world (PHS, 477 – slight amendment: WL VIII, 938). Nor can this sentiment be put down to concluding rhetoric since this precise wording is repeated elsewhere (PGN, 42: WL VIII, 24 – 5; EL, 269: WG VI, 294; GR, 206: WJ XV, 100).

The view that history exhibits God's meaning is scarcely a view unique to Hegel. Indeed, in the guise of Providentialism it is commonplace. Hegel's relationship to theories of Providence is distinctive. In one respect he is critical of Providentialism but this is not because it is out of place, but, rather, because it is typically incoherent. That is, Hegel is critical of any theory of Providence that refrains from seeking a comprehension of the necessity in what has happened. This diffidence, to Hegel, not only degrades Providence by making it responsible for "blind and irrational caprice" (EL, 269: WG VI, 294) but also such an interpretation of Providence, as the inscrutable and indeterminate (PGN, 37: WL VIII, 18), glorifies ignorance, licenses an unfettered imagination and assumes God is knowable apart from the world. It thus devalues the world by not seeing it verily as God's work. The world is Rational, and, as such, it is amenable to Reason. Men as Rational beings are themselves in their history the bearers of *Geist*'s process. Their Reason *is Geist*; their discovery of meaning in history is *Geist*'s *self-discovery*. The history of mankind (human nature through time) is the self-same process of *Geist* coming-to-be or, in appropriately 'theological' language, *Geist* is incarnate in Man.

---

8. *Hegel, Reason & History*, p. 53 *et passim* (To be fair O'Brien's book does carry the subtitle "A Contemporary Interpretation" (presumably meaning 'modern')). Similarly unacceptable is W. Kaufmann who puts down Hegel's references to God to the presence of Schleiermacher as a rival lecturer, and claims that these references are "mere frills", *Hegel*, p. 265.

9. K. Löwith, *Meaning in History*, p. 57.

However, the Providentialist view is correct in seeing meaning in the world's events – "world history is nothing more than the plan of providence. The world is governed by God and world history is the content of his governance and the execution of his plan" (PGN, 67: WL VIII, 55). This evocation of Providence is often associated with (and the notion of a Theodicy invariably associated with) the problem of unhappiness, conflict or evil generally. That is, if history is truly ruled by Reason, is God's work, then how is irrationality, in all its dimensions, possible? Hegel has no hesitation in recognising that history is not a record of untroubled happiness, that it can be even contemplated as "an altar at which the happiness of peoples and the wisdom of States and virtue of individuals are slaughtered" (PGN, 69: WL VIII, 58). But, this recognition is immediately followed by the rhetorical question – to what final purpose has this happened? The answer in the shape of the increasing consummation of freedom we already know, but the important point is the asking of the question in the first place. To acquiesce in the historical record with all its suffering is to absolve the world of all meaning. Yet the progressively actualised inherent meaning of the world must thus take heed of these 'historical facts'. It is in this context that Hegel's notions of the Cunning of Reason, the world-historical individual and the role of war are to be placed. Each of these can be examined briefly to indicate the scope and nature of the meaningfulness of history and thence of social diversity.

The inter-relationship between conflict, progress and Providence is not confined to Hegel.[10] It figured, for example, in the thought of two at least of his recent predecessors. One of the more noteworthy features of Adam Ferguson's *Essay on the History of Civil Society* (1767) is his exposition of 'conflict' theory.[11] Ferguson sees conflict as inherent, since men "appear to have in their minds the seeds of animosity". But this propensity to strife in fact produces a number of useful consequences; thus, for example, "the sense of common danger and the assaults of an enemy have been frequently useful to nations by uniting their members more firmly together", indeed, "without the rivalship of nations and the practice of war, civil society could scarcely have found an object or form". Nor are these useful consequences confined to the social level but also provide, on the individual level, "a scene for the exercise of our greatest abilities". Whilst it is true that much of Ferguson's analysis is conducted in purely social (sociological) terms he does at the end, significantly, of this chapter on 'War and Dissension', remark that "these reflections [on the pro-social outcome of seemingly anti-social behaviour] may open our view into the state of mankind; but they tend to reconcile us to the conduct of Providence, rather than to change our own".

Kant's essay on *Idee zu einer allgemeinen Geschichte* (1784) also, as we remarked in Chapter 3, contains similar sentiments albeit that the structure and

10. Cf. M. Ginsberg, 'The Idea of Progress: A Revaluation', in his *Essays in Sociology and Social Philosophy*, p. 81.

11. All quotations are taken from the edition of D. Forbes (1966) Pt. I, Sect. iv, 'Of the principles of War and Dissension', pp. 20–25.

assumptions of the argument is different. It is only through the urgings of Nature that man's desire to live comfortably is overcome and that, although these urges produce unsociableness, it is through them that man's capacities are developed. Thus war itself is perhaps ultimately an enterprise of "supreme wisdom" in man's progress toward international law and perpetual peace.

The particular question of the role of conflict here is part of the recognition of the wider phenomenon of 'unintended consequences'. Thus, although there is little 'conflict theory' in Hume, his own theory (and practice) of history, as we demonstrated in Part II, is replete with instances of the historical importance of the unintended. Hume did not believe that the advancement of freedom was the prime motive in history but, rather, he held that it was the outcome of local preoccupations. On this precise limited point Hegel is saying the same. Individual men or societies did not intend to promote freedom but through their actions (qua agents of *Geist*) freedom, and consciousness of it, has come about. There is, however, a decisive difference between the fully articulated arguments of Hume and Hegel.

For Hume, freedom is a contingent feature of the historical record. It is a corollary of the growth of cultivation (knowledge), leisure and commerce. There is nothing guaranteed about their continuance; Man has not changed – knowledge, as we recalled above, affects the 'temper' not the constitution of man. For Hegel, on the contrary, the growth of freedom is identical with *Geist*'s process of self-completion. But, since this process constitutes the meaning of the world, freedom is a necessary constituent of this meaning. This, of course, is the nub of Hegel's programme. What men are, namely, beings who live their lives on the assumption that their lives have a purpose, or on the assumption that problems have solutions (for how else would we come to know of a 'problem'?) is itself testament to cosmic meaningfulness. To assume that mankind, and the totality of its experience, has meaning or purpose is warranted because the meaning or purpose of mankind, and of the world's existence, involves the warrant for making that assumption. The circularity here, for Hegel, is not vicious but, rather, is the very self-authenticating structure of the Absolute.

It is then because the world (actuality) is self-authenticating or purposeful that its history – the growth of freedom – is necessary. For Hume, retrogression is always possible; enthusiasm and superstition can, as ever present propensities of human nature, undermine the tenuous establishment of liberty. For Hegel there can *actually* be no retrogression. He is not saying that history presents a straightforward uncomplicated progress, for there have been, as he acknowledges, cultures whose "enormous gains" have been destroyed. But such retrogressions will be regarded erroneously as "external contingencies" as long as history as a whole is not seen to have within it meaning, to possess a necessary structure (PGN, 127: WL VIII, 133).

This structure, the growth of freedom, is necessary because it is the work of *Geist* and it is in terms of *Geist*, and not in terms of the deliberate aims and purposes of individual men, that the history of the world proceeds. This dissonance between the aims of individuals (and societies) and the progressive actualisation of *Geist* is the thrust behind Hegel's notion of the Cunning of Reason (*List der Vernunft*).

Perhaps, the most celebrated example of the evocation of the role of unintended consequences in history is Adam Smith's "invisible hand". As H.B. Acton points out Hegel's early references to *List* occur, in the Jena writings, in the context of consumption and production, and he further remarks, that "there is nothing far fetched in linking this with Adam Smith's 'invisible hand'".[12] More precisely, Lukacs[13] draws attention to the teleological dimension and the particular use to which Hegel here puts the notion of *List* in the utilisation of Nature by man (through tools or labour) in making Nature's own blind activity purposive; permitting it to act on itself, so that the tools themselves partake of activity (JR II, 198 – 9). These points are echoed in his later system. Thus, in the second part of the *Encyclopädie*, through the Cunning of his Reason man is said to be enabled "to preserve and maintain himself in the face of the forces of nature, by sheltering behind other products of nature, and letting these suffer her destructive attacks" (EN, 5: WG VIII, 10). Earlier, in the first part of this same work, *List* is regarded as an intermediary, whose action consists in letting active objects follow their own bent and work upon each other as they thereby carry out its end (EL, 350: WG VI, 382; cf. SL II, 397: WL IV, 387 – 8).

The full context here is a discussion of the teleological or purposive relationship between end and means, whereby the end is realised through the placing of an object between itself and the object that is the means. Through the interaction and destruction of these objects the end is promoted and preserved (*aufgehoben*). This is its power (*Macht*) (EL, 350: WG VI, 382) or force (*Gewalt*) (SL II, 387: WL IV, 397). The pertinence of this discussion is that in the *Encyclopädie*, Hegel immediately follows this exposition with the declaration that "with this explanation, Divine Providence may be said to stand to the world and its process in the capacity of absolute cunning. God lets men do as they please with particular passions and interests; but the result is the accomplishment of – not their plans, but His, and these differ decidely from the ends primarily sought by those whom He employs".

This passing comment is developed in the lectures on World-History. There Hegel glosses 'passion' as "human activity which is governed by particular interests, special aims or, if you will, by selfish intentions". Moreover, this is all-embracing, no other interest is possible (PGN, 72: WL VIII, 62). Particular men's actions are thus localised but it is through these actions that a *Sittlichkeit* and State are constituted. It is through their passions that men come into conflict and history resembles a *Schlachtbank*. But, this is the Cunning of Reason, since through this passion-induced conflict the world progresses whilst the 'unit' of progress – *Geist* itself – is preserved (PGN, 89: WL VIII, 83).

---

12. 'Distributive Justice, the Invisible Hand and the Cunning of Reason', *PS* (1972) 430 – 1.

13. *The Young Hegel*, p. 345. Lukacs, too regards Hegel as "decisively influenced by Adam Smith's conception of labour" and that he "was an adherent of Adam Smith" (p. 321, 323) though he repeats Marx's mistake that Ferguson was Smith's teacher here.

This general position raises two further issues – the impact of individuals 'in fact' on history and the place of war or conflict in the relationship between States. Individuals are warranted a role because the individual as such is of worth – this is the truth of Christianity. Since the truth is an immanental whole (see Chapter 8) then it must find expression in the world. This expression was necessarily absent in the Greeks and it is central to Hegel's justification of the monarch in the modern Rational State that he, in his very individuality, gives "objective existence" to the role and importance of the individual within the State (PR, 288: WL VI, 360). In similar fashion (cf. PR, 218: WL VI, 274) in the history of the world the actions of individual human beings, finite spiritual subjects, find their 'objective existence' in the actions of 'world-historical individuals'. The status of these individuals within Hegel's theory has been the subject of much debate.

For example, Shlomo Avineri, on the one hand, regards Hegel's various pronouncements as inconsistent, since, in one place, the world-historical individual is wholly conscious of the idea of history and its development, in another place, is instinctively conscious of it and, in yet another place, is totally unaware of it.[14] But, Charles Taylor, on the other hand, noting Avineri's discussion, remarks that these positions all come from lectures, and not from a work Hegel himself published, so that (it is seemingly held to be inferable) they can be reconciled "around the notion that world-historical individuals have a sense of the higher truth they serve, but they see it through a glass darkly".[15] The only examples Hegel gives of world-historical individuals are Alexander, Caesar and Napoleon. What do these three have in common?

The context where all three are cited together is to the effect that their whole lives were spent in toil in achieving their purpose, and that this did not bring happiness; rather, to the contrary, one dies young, one was murdered and one was exiled (PGN, 85: WL VIII, 78). That alone is not sufficient to demarcate them. What they shared in addition was the fact that their own particular purpose was also *Geist*'s purpose – that in prosecuting their end they were actualising a stage in *Geist*'s progress (Ibid.). Thus in the ensuing historical narrative Alexander was responsible for the final triumph of the Greek World over its Persian predecessors. He presents the ideal of Hellenic existence and he bequeathed a noble and brilliant union (PHS, 285: WL VIII, 652–3). Caesar effected two objects – he calmed internal strife and originated a new one, for by extending Rome beyond the Alps he thereby enlarged the scope of world history and introduced the next world-historical people, the Germans (PHS, 324: WL VIII, 712). Napoleon is not treated at the same length. He is merely said to have restored France as a military power and, knowing how to rule, he settled France's internal affairs. But, from that base he then subjected Europe and diffused his liberal institutions yet they were powerless against recalcitrant Catholic peoples

---

14. *Hegel's Theory*, p. 233; cf. similarly J. Plamenatz, *Man and Society*, Vol. 2, p. 205.

15. *Hegel*, p. 393n. I have discussed this issue more fully in my 'Hegel on the World Historical' in *History of European Ideas* (1981) 155–162.

(PHS, 471: WL VIII, 930 – 1); Hegel cites as an example his failure to establish a new constitution in Spain.

What conclusions can be drawn from these instantiations? One point that Hegel makes frequently is that they were great men, they did achieve great things. It is in this context that Hegel is critical of the pragmatic psychologising historians, who endeavour to trivialise their actions in terms of their subjective interests like ambition and avarice (EL, 256: WL V 280; WG, 42: WL VIII, 80; cf. Chapter 8 supra).

Given that Alexander, Caesar and Napoleon were great in what did their greatness consist? The clue to the answer here is that world history is the history of States as the embodiments of freedom. To be a world-historical individual means to be great in this arena; all three were political heroes. This explains why neither Luther nor Socrates qualify as heroes.[16] In contrast to the worldly political deeds of these three heroes Socrates was a teacher and Luther a "simple monk" (PHS, 431: WJ XI, 522). Their significance lies elsewhere for as Hegel says explicitly of Socrates "the world of thought was his true home" (PHS, 281: WL VIII, 645). There is, however, more than being political to the specific identification of these three heroes as being world-historical. Their world-historicality stems from the further fact that their heroism operated at transitional stages in history.

Caesar is the best example of the transitional hero, but Alexander did sum up Greek superiority over the Orient and out of the ruins of his Empire the Romans emerged into dominance, and Napoleon demonstrates, through his internal reforms and their diffusion, the true message of the French Revolution. On this criterion, it is understandable how William the Conqueror does not have world-historical status, for, although he introduced feudalism into England, this was not an inauguration of universal significance (PHS, 422: WL VIII, 866). Charlemagne is rather more problematic. He is a political actor since he formed a systematically ordered State, which given the theoretical importance of the State for Hegel is a truly significant achievement (PHS, 376: WL VIII, 800). Furthermore, his reign forms the conclusion to the first period of the Germanic World and it is thus transitional. The fact, moreover, that his Empire soon fragmented is no different than Alexander's. But, what is a difference is that from the fragmentation of the Alexandrine Empire, arose the next epoch in world history, whereas, out of Charlemagne's all that occurred was the "infinite falsehood" of the Middle Ages (PHS, 380: WL VIII, 804). More pointedly, though Charlemagne was a man of power, greatness and nobility of soul, his rational constitution depended solely on his own strength of character, and not on the *Geist des Volkes*. It was, in short, like Napoleon's constitution for Spain, an external imposition (PHS, 383: WL VIII, 808). For a transition to be world-historical, therefore, it must be identifiable as integral to *Geist*'s self-

---

16. This difference in dimension is obscured by Walsh (in Pelczynski, *Hegel: Problems and Perspectives*, p. 189) when he remarks that Socrates and Luther are the two 'heroes' of greatest importance, overwhelming Caesar and Alexander.

actualisation. The aims of these three heroes are also world-historical processes (PGN, 83: WL VIII, 76). This is why *they* are world-historical individuals.

This sheds light on the problematic issue of the extent to which these individuals were conscious of the import of their deeds. This consciousness is the prerogative of the philosopher, from his retrospective vantage-point. The hero does not share this perspective. The very fact that he is "created by his age just as much as he creates it" (EG, 13: WG VII, 22), or that he can "put into words the will of his age" (PR, 295: WL VI, 368), or, yet again, that it is the hero "who expresses what the age requires" (PGN, 84: WL VIII, 76), means that as a contemporary he lacks the requisite 'distance' for philosophy. Heroes are "men of practice" (PGN, 831: WL VIII, 76). Thus when they are said to seize the higher universal or to have "inner vision" or "insight" into what is needed and "to know" the necessary next stage in the world's progress (PGN, 82 – 4: WL VIII, 75 – 6) this cannot (given Hegel's articulation of the role of philosophy) be consciousness of actuality; of Reason in the rose of the cross of the present (PR, 12: WL VI, 16); for then the Cunning of Reason would not operate.

We can now turn to Hegel's delineation of the relationship between States. *Geist* manifests itself progressively in its identity with various *Volksgeister*, which culminate in their formation of States. States are particulars for it is only by virtue of their particularity that they become qua individual the agents of *Geist* and universal vehicles of self-consciousness and freedom. States in the arena of world history are, therefore, autonomous entities. It is only through awareness of itself as a unit distinct from other units that a State can attain awareness of self-consciousness (PR, 208: WL VI, 261). The relationship between States is thus a relationship between self-validating entities, between two 'rights' (PW, 210: WL VII, 101; cf. PR, 34: WL VI, 43 – 4). On this level there can be no resolution. States might make treaties (contracts) one with another but when there is disagreement, there is no international legal order to adjudicate. The desire for such an order – Hegel explicitly refers to Kant's notion of a League to establish 'perpetual peace' – is merely an ought-to-be (PR, 212 – 3: WL VI, 266 – 9; cf. PW, 208: WL VII, 199; EG, 276: WL V, 456). If States continue to disagree then the matter can only be settled by war.

Hegel's view of war is another highly contentious aspect of his thought. Like much of the debate concerning his political philosophy this has taken the form of restatements of Hegel's position which seek to place his view in its full context and which, more generally, aim to vindicate his argument against misinterpretation or prejudice.[17]

Hegel's view on war will here be looked at simply from the perspective of his theory of history and its relationship to its status as a Theodicy. History is meaningful as the process of *Geist*'s self-completion and war has been a persistent ever-present 'fact' of history. War, accordingly, partakes of this meaning; it is not, Hegel says, to be regarded as an "absolute evil" (PR, 209: WL VI, 262).

17. See, in particular, in this context, Avineri, *Hegel's Theory*, Chap. 10 & D. Verene, 'Hegel's Account of War', in Pelczynski, *Hegel: Problems and Perspectives*, pp. 168 – 180.

Note that it is an evil; Hegel is not denying the cold reality of war with its death and suffering. But, more generally, this signifies the appropriateness of the teleological perspective, so that when war is looked upon philosophically (Rationally) then its necessity (meaningfulness) can be discerned.

As in Adam Ferguson, this meaningfulness is to be found at both the individual and social level. Individually, it 'brings home' the debt and the dependence owed to the State. To sacrifice one's life for one's State is to achieve that fully self-conscious recognition that the State is indivisible from oneself (PR, 211: WL VI, 265). The State is not a means to an end, if it was then it would be rational (as Hobbes — the theorist supreme of the State as Civil Society — acknowledged) to flee.[18] Socially, it invigorates "the essential moment of the ethical substance" by preventing its fragmentation into isolated atoms (Ph, 474, 497: WL II, 294, 310); domestic unrest is checked and the State becomes as one (PR, 210: WL VI, 264).

However, the true place of war (conflict) is to be found explained in the overall context of world history as Theodicy. We have seen that it is common trait of Providentialist views that they take their very raison d'être from reconciling the presence of evil within a benignly inspired plant. In Hegel, this takes the distinctive form of the completely immanental progressive actualisation of *Weltgeist*. The *Weltgeist* is the common thread between all the individual States of history and, because this is progressive, it forms of world history a court of judgment (PR, 216: WL VI, 270; EG, 277: WL V, 457).

This is the decisive ingredient in Hegel's anti-relativism, in his distinctive conjoining of a substantive theory of rationality with a substantive theory of social life. Hegel's contextualist theory of human nature means that a man must be understood within his particular social setting, since, outside it, all that pertains are empty, formalistic, abstract universals. However, each society, though its own bearer of meaning, need not be compared with another in terms of a minimal empty notion of rationality, because there is a substantive principle of rationality that warrants the making of cross-cultural, trans-historical judgments.

The individual States of history, though having a history of their own, nevertheless are actually participants in the dialectical process of world history (EG, 277: WL V, 457). From the perspective of *Geist*, the various diverse forms of social and political life fall qualitatively into order. As we have seen the Greeks are *better* than the Persians, the Germans are *better* than the Romans, the Protestant States are *better* than the Catholic ones. At any time in the history of the world one people is (objectivises) *Geist*. At that time, that people is dominant and vis-à-vis it other peoples are *Rechtlos* (PR, 218[19]: WL VI, 273), that is, can make no claim against, it, since in the court of world history they have, at this

18. Cf. Avineri, *Hegel's Theory*, p. 135.

19. As. D. Germino points out Knox translates this as 'without rights' — 'Hegel as a Political Theorist', *JP* (1969) 907n — when the context is the role of distinct *Völker* as the progressive bearers of *Recht*.

time, 'been ruled against'. This justifies "civilised nations" in treating as "barbarians" those that lag behind them, for their 'rights' are unequal to its own (PR, 219: WL VI, 275). Such is not regarded, by Hegel, as a question of "mere might", by which he means a pointless irrationality, because, as representatives of different stages of freedom and self-consciousness, the superiority of one people over another in the history of the world, is the necessary progress of *Geist* to self-completion (PR, 216: WL VI, 271).

This superiority is not exhibited merely in terms of political conflict but pervades the whole, since States are concrete universals. As such, they develop their own forms of artistic expression, religious worship, science and philosophy. *Völker* differ one from another in all these aspects. But, the difference is not superficial: it involves their "basic import" (*Gehalt*), the "most important difference of all, that is, of Rationality" (PGN, 143: WL VIII, 156). Thus, to cite the example Hegel himself gives here, though there are numerous criteria by which the Indian epics can be rated as highly as Homer's, these are merely formal considerations and the works remain "infinitely different in their import". The content of the work of art (just as with a man or State) is not something separate from its form. The whole (form and content) is the point of reference and the whole embodies a societally – specific expression but, crucially in Hegel's account, an expression that is differentially (progressively) valued.

To say that the Indian epic is as great a work of art with reference to its own culture, as Homer's is to his, and thus there is nothing to chose evaluatively between them, is, for Hegel, to deprive history of meaning. Hegel is well aware that differences in aesthetic standards suggest that they are culturally relative (see especially GA 74: WJ XII 75). but such thinking is derived from using a formal criterion, like imitation. This now makes the beauty of what is to be copied subsidiary to whether or not it has been correctly copied. This, in turn, degenerates into a question of subjective taste[20] as the criterion for deciding what is worthy of imitation (GA 73: WJ XII, 74 – 5). Art, for Hegel, is a matter of form and content and its end is the "revealing of truth in the form of sensuous artistic shape" (GA, 87: WJ XII, 89). The diverse forms of aesthetic expression are also thus open to the absolutist trans-historical cross-cultural perspective of *Geist*'s process to self-coincidence. The Greeks are an *improvement* on the Indians, the Iliad is *better* than the Epic of Gilgamesh.

It is, therefore, by virtue of his conception of the concrete universal that Hegel marries substantive accounts of society and rationality. Hume's theory possesses substantive rationality, that is, the ability to judge diverse social practices, at the cost of a superficial acknowledgment of the import of diversity on a proper understanding of these practices. Conversely, those modern social theorists, such as Peter Winch, who, as a part of their anti-causalism (Humeanism), emphasise the societally-specific character of human action have done so at the cost of an etiolated notion of rationality. Hume's theory is universal but abstract whereas

20. For Hegel's critique of eighteenth-century theories of 'taste' (Kames is singled out as an example) see GA, 73: WJ XII, 74 – 5.

that of his opponents is concrete but particular. Hegel's contextualism entails his rejection of the abstractness of Hume's universalism and his all-important conception of *Geist* entails the rejection of the particularity of the anti-Humeans' concreteness. But, in both Hegel rejects the contingency they attribute to society. In Hume the particular society in which a man lives is a contingent variable in that human nature is constant and uniform. On the other hand, to see all social experiences as internally validated 'forms of life' is tantamount to seeing all the diverse forms of social life as contingent and their very diversity as meaningless. Hegel's philosophy of history demonstrates, in his own eyes, that there is within history a progressive actualisation of freedom – absolute significance. This significance is inseparable from the Christian revelation and Hegel's view of history as a Theodicy is no mere rhetorical sop to his audience, but is fundamental to his vision and system as a whole.

This can be borne out, in conclusion, by noting the relationship between the religious dimension in his philosophy of history and his presentation of Absolute *Geist*. There can be no actual retrogression in world history, because in Christianity we have the perfect religion, where *Geist* is for itself, where "the Universal *Geist* and the particular *Geist*, the infinite *Geist* and the finite *Geist* are inseparably connected" (PRel II, 330: WJ XVI, 193 – 4). In short, there is an Absolute. This, since it is an internally differentiated dynamic whole, gives meaning to the world as such for "without the world God is not God" (PRel I, 200: WJ XV, 210).

This bears directly on the significance of world history. World history, as the actualisation of *Geist*, constitutes the realm of Objective *Geist*; religion is a Moment in Absolute *Geist*. Absolute *Geist* has the Absolute, the eternal, for its content; it is absolute self-knowledge (Subject and Substance are one). This eternal self-knowledge is mediated through men (finite spirits) who are conscious of this content sensuously in Art, representatively or figuratively (as *Vorstellungen*) in Religion and 'thought-fully' in Philosophy. The content is one and the same in each case, for the Truth is the whole, but it is apprehended in an increasingly adequate form. Since man, as a spiritual universal, is such because he possesses thought or Reason, then, the most adequate form of apprehension is Philosophy, which can be briefly defined as the "thinking about thinking" (PGN, 143: WL VIII, 156).[21] Through Philosophy *Geist* achieves knowledge of itself, so that, ultimately, in truth, philosophy is not a transaction or product of men, but the work of the Absolute Subject itself coming to knowledge of itself as Substance.

Two brief points can be pertinently made. Firstly, in the Christian religion, consciousness (qua *Vorstellungen*) of the Absolute (that is, as Father, Son and

---

21. See the quotation from Aristotle's *Metaphysics* that Hegel chooses to conclude the entire *Encyclopädie* (EG, 315) – "Now thought does think itself because it shares in the intelligibility of the object. It becomes intelligible by contact with the intelligible, so that thought and the object of thought are one" (Everyman Edit, p. 346). For Hegel's interpretation of this passage, and his discussion of it in *GP* see H.G. Gadamer, 'Hegel und antike Dialektik', in his *Hegels Dialektik: Fünf hermeneutische Studien*, p. 25 – 6.

Holy Ghost) is attained by all (PRel III, 11 – 12: WJ XVI, 228). However, the Absolute still needs to be grasped philosophically in thought. Philosophy thus constitutes the dialectical supersession of Religion, but this is, as such, in essence, preservative as well as successive, for the truth of Philosophy and Religion are one.[22]

Secondly, this philosophical grasp is the final (dialectically synthesised) encapsulation of the 'meaning' of what has happened. It is, by virtue of this, necessarily retrospective. Thus the meaning of Objective *Geist*, as we noted when discussing the world-historical individual, is only fully grasped by the philosopher, whose thought is ipso facto *Geist*'s thought. Accordingly, the history of philosophy is "a revelation of what has been the aim of *Geist* throughout its history; it is therefore the world's history in its innermost signification" (GP III, 547: WJ XIX, 685). In the State and in history *Geist* comes to objective consciousness of itself, but it is only in Religion and ultimately only in Philosophy that *Geist* knows itself as the Absolute – "this content which the knowledge of absolute *Geist* has of itself is the absolute truth, is all truth, so that this Idea comprehends the entire wealth of the natural and spiritual world in itself, is the only substance and truth of all that constitutes this world" (PRel I, 206: WJ XV, 217).

The State and its historical progression in the world thus exists in order that *Geist*'s absolute self-comprehension can take place. Christianity is of decisive importance to that end for with it (to employ a non-Hegelian metaphor) the 'eternal present' of the Absolute is enmeshed with its historical presentation.[23] By providing a Theodicy Hegel is providing the philosophical encapsulation of the truth of the modern Protestant world, which, given that the latest philosophy dialectically preserves within it those which precede it (GP III, 532: WJ XIX, 690), is simultaneously the provision of the meaning of world history.

22. Cf. G.R.G. Mure, 'Hegel, Luther, and the Owl of Minerva', *Philosophy* (1966) 130, and the admirably rigorous argument of E. Fackenheim, *The Religious Dimension in Hegel's Thought*.

23. *Cf.* G.A. Kelly, *Idealism, Politics and History: Sources of Hegelian Thought*, p. 318f. for identification of two general categories of history (of the absolute and of the world) in Hegel. Also S. Rosen, *G.W.F. Hegel*, who refers to the "reconciliation" of God (eternal wisdom) and man (finite historical individuals) in human history, p. 12 – 13, 33 – 34.

11. SELF AND SOCIETY

This concluding Chapter will discuss Hegel's conception of, what was termed in Part II, socio-psychical dynamics, namely, the inter-relations between a theory of self and society. Many commentators have drawn attention to what John Plamenatz called the shift from a preoccupation with rationality in the eighteenth century to one with self-consciousness.[1] To appreciate this shift both a long-term and short-term perspective is needed.

Whilst there is something approaching consensus that it is meaningful to say that the sixteenth and seventeenth centuries saw the emergence of man as an individual, there is extensive debate as to the reasons for this, whether, for example, the emergence of labour upon the market, the rise of the bourgeoisie or the post-Reformation conviction that every man was his own priest, etc. Evidence as to this burgeoning individualism is diverse, from the development of portrait painting, the emergence of autobiography as a genre distinct from memoirs and later the 'rise of the novel' and finally, the most famous (itself a species of evidence) of Polonius' lines in *Hamlet*, "This above all: to thine own self be true".[2] Alongside these there are the various movements and events, noted in Chapter 1, which coalesced into forming the distinctive eighteenth-century view of man, society and nature; a view, which Hume's endeavour to establish a 'science of man' fairly represents, to extend to society, and to man himself, the order and regularity that the cosmos as a whole had been recently seen to possess. We sketched in Chapter 2 how this attempt to the Enlightenment to reduce men and his 'products' to abstract regularity was rejected by thinkers conveniently labelled as Romantics.

This brings us to the short-term. Here two names, in particular, stand out as significant and pertinent – J.J. Rousseau and I. Kant. Almost all of Rousseau's writings provided a stimulus to his successors, Hegel included, but here it is one of the most remarkable of all his works – the *Confessions* – that is of especial importance. The celebrated opening sentences set the tone,

---

1. *Karl Marx's Philosophy of Man*, p. 67.
2. Cf. L. Trilling, *Sincerity and Authenticity*, Chap. 1, itself a synthesis of such 'trends'.

I have resolved on an enterprise which has no precedent. . .My purpose is to display to my kind a portrait in every way true to nature, and the man I shall portray will be myself. Simply myself. I know my own heart and understand my fellow man. But I am like no-one in the whole world.[3]

The distinctiveness of the enterprise is its intended completeness – the aim being that the reader should judge the 'true' Rousseau from the 'full' evidence he brings forward, Rousseau had what was by all accounts a pathological preoccupation with self-assessment and with the dissonance between this assessment and the assessment made of him by the rest of humanity (the *Confessions* was, of course, only the first of his self-revelations).[4] In the prosecution of this intent to make his "soul transparent to the reader's eye" Rousseau relates not only all that has happened to him and all he has done but also "all that I have felt".[5]

That Rousseau's project marks an important stage in the articulation of a theory of the self we can illustrate briefly by a comparison of the design, detail and intent of his autobiography with that of Hume's. Hume wrote a short sketch on 'My Own Life'. This opens defensively; it is perhaps a mark of vanity to write an autobiography at all, and so this performance will be short and confined to little more than the 'History of my Writings' (E (M OL) 607). What follows is essentially a catalogue of the chief events of his career. His disappointment and chagrin at the immediate failure of his early writings upon their publication is recorded but not analysed. Indeed, when juxtaposed with his sentiments as they appear in his correspondence, the autobiography is studied in its equanimity. The sketch does conclude with some self-analysis but even this ("a man of mild dispositions, of command of temper, of an open, social and cheerful humour, capable of attachment but little susceptible of enmity and of great moderation in all my passions" – of which the "ruling" was "love of literary fame" (615)) is scarcely revelatory. This detached and dispassionate, virtual 'third-person', view of his own life is part and parcel of Hume's general outlook and, with some licence, of the Enlightenment's emphasis on order and regularity. Hume, as near as is possible, has given a 'scientific' self-portrait. Rousseau, on the other hand, and here is his importance for our purposes, glories in the passionate, impressionistic revelation of his innermost feelings.

It was for Rousseau's creation of a genuine work of art out of the resources of his own inner experience alone that Dilthey saw in his work the first stirrings of the new literary epoch of Romanticism.[6] Certainly, it is one of the hallmarks of that protean movement that it shifted the emphasis from external, impersonal regularities to internal, personal feelings. The artist, the poet, holds the stage. Aside from the semi-autobiographical works, such as Goethe's *Werther*, there

3. Penguin Books edition; tr. J. Cohen, p. 17: *Oeuvres Complètes* (Pléiade Edit.) Vol. 1, p. 5.

4. This preoccupation by Rousseau has given rise to numerous 'psychological' and 'psychoanalytical' studies; the most notable of these is J. Starobinski, *J.J. Rousseau: la Transparence et l'Obstacle*.

5. *Confessions*, p. 169: Vol. 1, p. 175.

6. *Das Erlebnis und Dichtung*, 14th edit., p. 152–3.

were the explicitly self-revelatory autobiographies of de Quincey and, perhaps most notably of all, of Wordsworth in his great poem *The Prelude*, subtitled the 'growth of a poet's mind'.

This concern with the self and its harmony or otherwise with its environment is, of course, closely linked to the identification of the 'phenomenon' of alienation. Nor is it coincidental that it is in Rousseau's thought that many of the themes that were to be labelled 'alienation' first make their appearance. However, much of the literature concentrates on the Marxist and sociological import of the term and, consequently, a high proportion of it (including its treatment of Hegel) is retrospective from Marx.[7] Much of Hegel's own treatment of alienation − of man's non-recognition of his one-ness with *Geist* − is, nevertheless, prompted by the sense of fragmentation in man and society that provides one of the leitmotifs of Romanticism.[8]

Alongside this literary exploration of the self − the journey of the artist to the interior − is the Kantian 'revolution' and the development of German Idealist philosophy. The thrust of this 'revolution' as we outlined it in Chapter 3, was to locate the principles responsible for providing a structured coherent account of experience in man himself. Just as he argued for the necessary presence of synthetic a priori principles, in order for there to be experience at all (an explanation that Hume's epistemology could not provide), so Kant also, as we briefly discussed, showed the necessary presence of an 'I think' (again something that Hume's theory notoriously found problematic). Kant's 'rescue' of necessity from Human contingency involved the distinction between the phenomenal world of things-as-perceived and the noumenal world of things-in-themselves. Man's freedom, and hence morality, meant complete independence from natural motives, such as the desire for happiness. Moral action resulted from subscription to the Categorical Imperative, from action that is universalisable and autonomous, and which can, as such, only be the product of self-imposition by a rational being.[9] That this

7. For example, R. Schacht (*Alienation*) deals with Hegel, Marx and their successors. I. Meszaros (*Marx's Theory of Alienation*, Chap. 1) and Plamenatz do draw attention to Rousseau's importance, and Meszaros also refers to Diderot, whose *Neveu de Rameu* (popularised in Germany by Goethe), as Trilling discusses, had deep impact on Hegel's depiction of *der sich entfremdete Geist* in the *Phänomenologie*. M. Berman (*The Politics of Authenticity*) provides a general interpretation of Rousseau's thought, in which Rousseau's central concern is held to be with a world in which men were alienated not only from themselves but from each other; a concern which is said by Berman to prefigure Marxism in many way.

8. The debt that Hegel owes to Schiller's *Briefe über die ästhetische Erziehung des Menchen* (1794/5), which Hegel declared to be "a masterpiece" on its appearance (*Briefe*, ed. J. Hoffmeister, Vol. I, p. 25 [to Schelling, 16 April 1795]), is often pointed out in this regard. More generally, R. Plant (*Hegel*) sees as the key to the identity of Hegel's thought the twin themes of personal fragmentation and social division (p. 28) and the role Hegel allots to philosophy to harmonise these fissures (p. 88).

9. *The Moral Law* (*Grundlegung zur Metaphysik der Sitten*), ed. & tr. H.J. Paton, p. 80; *Werke* (Akad. Edit.) Vol. IV, p. 412.

definition of freedom echoes that given by Rousseau in *du Contrat Social* is not coincidental.[10]

Kant's philosophy, with its twin themes of a self-structured reality and freedom, thus comes together with the Romantic's emphasis on internality and its outward expression. But, Kant's dichotomisation between the phenomenal and the noumenal, and in particular his application of this to the self, for this is only 'known' phenomenally on Kantian principles, proved unacceptable. In Chapter 3 we noted how Herder's all-pervading organicism was used to overcome this dichotomy. But Herder belongs to the pre-Romantic generation and we can cite Fichte as an example of this new philosophical attentiveness to the self.

In his popular Introduction (1797) to his *Wissenschaftlehre* (1794) Fichte, having demonstrated that Idealism was the only possible philosophy (dogmatism being the only alternative), declares the object of Idealism to be the 'self in-itself'. Pointedly, this actually occurs as something real in consciousness and not as a thing-in-itself (which is a pure invention and the fundamental principle of dogmatism).[11] The nub of Fichte's position can be said to be his enunciation of the principle of self-conscious activity. To Fichte, we cannot abstract from the self, for "to everything thought as occurring in consciousness, the self must necessarily be appended in thought".[12] But, whilst for Kant (according to Fichte) all consciousness was merely "conditioned" by self-consciousness, which means that its content can be something outside self-consciousness, in Fichte's own system, by contrast, consciousness is "determined" by self-consciousness, that is, everything that occurs in consciousness is the product of self-consciousness.[13] Thus, without self-consciousness, there is no consciousness whatever. Crucially, for Fichte, self-consciousness is consciousness of activity; to think of oneself is to act upon oneself – "The thought of himself is nothing other than the thought of this act, and the word 'I' nothing other than the designation thereof".[14] This self-activity is the basic postulate of Fichte's system proper –

The source of all reality is the self, for this is what is immediately and absolutely posited. . . But the self exists because it posits itself (*sich setzt*), and posits itself because it exists. Hence self-positing and existence are one and the same. But the concepts of self-positing and activity in general are again one and the same. Hence all reality is active and everything active is reality.[15]

10. The link between Kant and Rousseau is explored in several writings of E. Cassirer but as a useful corrective to an overly Kantian reading of Rousseau see R. Derathé, *Le Rationalisme de J.J. Rousseau* & J. Shklar, *Men and Citizens: A Study of Rousseau's Social Theory*, Chap. 2.

11. All references are to the edition of the *Wissenschaftlehre with First and Second Introductions*, ed. & tr. P. Heath & J. Lachs and to *Werke*, ed. I. Fichte (1845): thus p. 10: Vol. 1, p. 428.

12. *Wissenschaftlehre*, p. 71: Vol. 1, p. 501.

13. *Wissenschaftlehre*, p. 50: Vol. 1, p. 477. Fichte is concerned not so much to refute Kant as to render him consistent. Thus he quotes Kant's treatment of the 'I think' as a unity of apperception and holds that implicity within Kant's treatment is the concept of the pure self exactly as put forward by Fichte himself; pp. 48 – 50; Vol. 1, pp. 475 – 6.

14. *Wissenschaftlehre*, p. 77: Vol. 1, p. 462.

15. *Wissenschaftlehre*, p. 129: Vol. 1, p. 134.

That reality is active is, of course, a lynch-pin of Hegel's system, though he thought Fichte had not gone far enough in 'deducing' the entirety of human knowledge out of self-consciousness. However, more immediately, Fichte's 'deduction' was perfectly attuned to the emphatic interiority of the Romantics. The Romantics took over Kant's revolution, with its centrality placed in the self, but in so doing, they broke free of the limitations that Kant had meticulously built into his philosophy. Fichte's philosophy provided the key precedent and instrument; but it was subject to "poetic exaggeration" and essentially "caricatured".[16] The creative freedom of the self, which for Fichte meant selfhood in general, was applied to the individual empirical self. To Novalis, for example, Fichte had invented a whole new way of thinking for which language was inadequate and to F. Schlegel, Fichte's *Wissenschaftlehre*, together with Goethe's *Wilhelm Meister* and the French Revolution, was one of the three great portents of the century.[17] Fichte himself, however, always philosophically remained a 'Rationalist' and he became increasingly critical of the Romantics.

It is against this very general background that we are to place Hegel's concern with the self and its inter-relation with society. Hegel is writing, in his maturity, after the Kantian revolution and the self-expressionism of the Romantics and, much as his own system is critical of these two 'events', nevertheless, because they undergo a process of *Aufhebung* in his system, this criticism is not a total rejection.

We have outlined in the previous Chapters, how Hegel's theory of human nature is contextual and yet, by being placed within an Absolutist perspective, have also seen that this theory is anti-relativist. The key to this distinctive position we have identified as the notion of the concrete universal. Man, as a spiritual, thought-defined, being, partakes of the universality that is *Geist*, which is the ultimate explanation of reality; but, because *Geist* is thus reality, then this universality is at one with it, is concrete. Hegel's account of socio-psychical dynamics works from this same premise. We discussed in Chapter 9 the role that language plays in Hegel's theory of self-consciousness and we shall here confine our elucidation of this account to two particular discussions – the dialectic of self-consciousness (master/slave) and the theory of property.

The most celebrated account of the master and slave occurs in the *Phänomenologie* but it is also broached in the *Encyclopädie* as well as explored in his early Jena writings. This replication, especially in his mature writings, is not without significance, for it helps to place this particular discussion in its proper context; a context from which it is often torn by commentators. In both the *Encyclopädie* and the *Phänomenologie*, self-consciousness is the middle-term between Consciousness and Reason. This dialectical triad, as the *Encyclopädie* makes clear, occurs within the Moment of Subjective *Geist*. Its particular location here should always be borne in mind.

16. Cf. X. Léon, *Fichte et son temps*, Vol. 1, p. 450 & H. Korff, *Goethe und der Goethezeit*, Vol. 3, p. 258.

17. Léon, *Fichte*, Vol. 1, p. 459, 453.

Man uniquely is self-conscious, because man uniquely qua spiritual universal is free. This means that there is a radical disjunction between man (*Geist*) and Nature. As we have seen, *Geist* (Subjective *Geist*) is at first immersed in Nature. This constitutes Anthropology – the study of *Geist* in its corporeity. But, *Geist* raises itself above Nature and becomes conscious. The 'I' is differentiated from the 'Other', but at first this 'I' is an empty abstract subjectivity; it is in-itself and not yet for-itself, because it still relates to the Other. This constitutes Phenomenology – the study of *Geist* as it appears. The 'I' now fills itself with content and becomes self-conscious. In so doing it attains universality and becomes Psychology – the study of *Geist* subjectively in and for-itself (EG, 27 – 8: WG VII, 43 – 5). The relationship between Anthropology, Phenomenology and Psychology is dialectical. This means that self-consciousness is the truth of consciousness – "all consciousness of another object being as a matter of fact also self-consciousness" (EG, 165: Wl V, 375).

This echoes the Fichtean critique of Kant. There is no thing-in-itself (cf. Ph, 212 – 3: WL II, 112). But the Fichtean formula of self-consciousness, that I = I, is motionless tautology, which, as static, lacks reality for it makes the 'Other' the merely passive creation of the I. This 'I' is essentially self-sufficient; like Kant's unity of apperception (see Chapter 3), it pertains regardless of, and independent of, society. Instead, truly to appreciate self-consciousness as movement (Hegel's Faustian bent according to Lukacs)[18] it is necessary that the Other have life or being, that is, exist for itself (Ph, 222: WL II, 118). This, at the same time, as we shall see, is to regard self-consciousness as necessarily social.

The dialectic of self-consciousness commences with the relationship between the self and this living Other. It commences with appetite or desire. This is a consequence of the contradiction between the self-conscious agent, knowing itself as identical to the external object, and yet being confronted by its independent externality. The possession of this object, the negation of its independence, is the satisfaction of desire. Through this satisfaction, the self-consciousness affirms its identity with the object, it acquires thereby the certainty of its own self as true certainty. Desire however is limited. It is essentially animalistic for it is characteristic of *all* living beings that they are impelled by contradiction. Further, self-certainty attained through gratification of a desire is still conditioned by the object of gratification. It stands in a negative relation to it, which means that the object or the Other is not overcome (*aufgehoben*) but, through being so conditioned, is ever reproduced, along with the desire (Ph, 225: WL II, 121). Less abstractly, the most transparent example of this relationship is the gratification of hunger by food. By consuming the Other (the independent external) its identity with the self is attained and the desire is satisfied, but once hunger is felt the whole process commences once more.

All animals as living beings feel hunger and are impelled to assuage it. Men, however, are not merely animals and therein lies the decisive step to self-consciousness proper, for, as Kojève remarks, animal desire might be a necessary

---

18. G. Lukacs, *Goethe and his Age*, p. 175ff.

condition of self-consciousness but it is not a sufficient condition.[19] For human desires to be *human* they must have as their object another human, since "self-consciousness attains its satisfaction only in self-consciousness" (Ph, 226: WL II, 121). This is the first decisive step that will lead ultimately to recognition of a self as one with *Geist*.

Self-consciousness proper therefore subsists only by being acknowledged or recognised by another self-consciousness. This is an integral part of Hegel's analysis. To attain full consciousness of ourselves it is necessary that we are recognised by our fellows. We can state here two important consequences of this for our study. First, as the earlier discussion brought out, men are radically social beings (contextual), we need other men to know ourselves and, second, from these premises about the attainment of self-consciousness, Hegel's conception of socio-psychical dynamics can be seen to be clearly differentiated from Hume's, despite the superficial similarity that might seem to flow from Hume's remark, inter alia, that men are mirrors to one another (see Chapter 7).

It is when self-consciousness proper, or *das anerkennende Selbstbewusstsein*, has been attained that the master/slave dialectic commences. When the Other is another self-conciousness, then I not only see myself (for what I am depends on the Other's acknowledgement of me) but also I see another Ego, absolutely independent of me. Again there is contradiction and again I must strive to overcome it. But, unlike the objects of desire, another self-consciousness is not passive; rather, it is a source of independent activity and to treat this Other as a natural passive object is to deprive myself of recognition. I am certain of myself as 'above' Nature but, until I am certain of the Other as also above Nature (as an active 'agent' capable of bestowing recognition), my self-certainty is without truth (Ph, 232: WL II, 125). I need to achieve identity with it (consume it on the natural plane). I am 'above' Nature because I am a spiritual or free agent. An animal, by contrast, is not free; it is a natural being impelled by desires which are for its self-preservation, for food, for shelter, etc. An animal, therefore, cannot maim or destroy itself; a man can, he can so act as to put his preservation at risk (PR, 43: WL VI, 56). Here is the evidence of the radical break between man and Nature. Thus by my risking my life I demonstrate that I am above Nature. This whole process is reciprocal, hence the two self-consciousnesses in order to attain certainty of themselves in truth enter into a struggle, which, since it is a struggle for certainty (identity), is a struggle for life and death. Only in this way is freedom attained for only in this way does a man demonstrate his spirituality, his transcendence of the animalistic requirements of "bare existence" (*das Sein*) (Ph, 233: WL II, 126).

When self-consciousness in truth is attained, when freedom is actualised, then the first steps toward the apprehension of *Geist* have been taken (Ph, 227: WL II, 122). Man, then, is not a creature of pain and pleasure as Hume, Locke and the Utilitarians would have it. Men qua spiritual beings need to be recognised. Only this can explain why men can compete and struggle for more than appetitive

19. A. Kojève, *Introduction à la lecture de Hegel*, 2nd Edit., p. 11.

satisfaction, mere biological survival.[20] We cannot understand *human* interaction in terms of the pleasure and pain calculus. It is true that Hobbes, for example, identified glory, whereby "everyman looketh that his companions should value him at the same rate he sets upon himself", as one of the sources of conflict.[21] However, the whole of man's behaviour according to Hobbes, is governed by the pursuit of what each perceives to be his best interest or, in terms of his basic 'scientific' model of man as matter in motion, by the impulsion of the 'animal motions'. This conflict over "reputation" is thus thought by Hobbes to be deducible from man's necessarily self-interested desires (his continuance in motion and avoidance of rest – death). Moreover, such conflict is not divorced from the basic question of survival, because men will destroy each other upon "signes of contempt or undervaluing".

Similarly, Hume never doubts that the explanation of human action is, in principle, identical with the explanation of natural phenomena. There is nothing 'special' about men as intentional agents. Since human nature is uniform in its 'principles' and 'springs', then, regardless of location or an individual's own understanding of his situation, it is amenable to 'scientific' investigation; to the uncovering of its operant causes. Thus, although Hume is aware (as we documented in Part II) that men are susceptible to, and wish to conform to, the actions and opinions of their fellows, that they associate and sympathise with them and that they habituate prevailing norms to establish and preserve social cohesion, he does not say that men act so as to achieve recognition of themselves in the actions of others, or so as to realise, 'live up to' or variously effectuate an image of themselves. Such a concern, which Hegel works up systematically, is the joint-offspring of the (post-Humean) Romantic preoccupation with self-authenticity and the Idealist redrawing of the cognitive map.

To return to Hegel and the dialectic of self-consciousness; we have seen that the particular dynamic of self-consciousness is the search for recognition. But, if this life-and-death struggle in which men mutually witness their freedom, ends in the death of one of the parties, then the dynamic is thwarted; their interaction loses its defining human quality. Accordingly, proper self-consciousness requires life. The interaction should be dialectical in that there must be preservation as well as success. This is achieved by the losing party in the struggle preferring life to death. The option is made for biological survival, but this is at the cost of surrendering the claim for recognition as an equal since he recognises the victor as superior. The victor is the master, who is independent and for-himself; the vanquished is the slave, who is dependent and exists for the other. Hegel now proceeds with the dialectic, whereby the slave, by working on nature for the master, attains via this activity universal self-consciousness – the next and higher stage of *Geist*'s actualisation. Whilst the master achieves only the recognition of a dependent consciousness not that of equal, the slave, on the contrary, by his work, comes to an awareness of himself as an independent being. A made

20. Kojève, *Introduction*, p. 14, 169.
21. *Leviathan* (1651) (Everyman Edit.) p. 64.

object is *his* and in it, and its endurance, he can attain consciousness that he exists in his own right (Ph, 239: WL II, 130 – 1). There occurs then in this way a reversal of the relationship between dependence and independence.

Extensive commentary on this dialectic is not necessary, save to emphasise the specificity of the discussion. In the *Zusatz* to the discussion in the *Encyclopädie* Hegel cautions that this struggle for recognition belongs to the natural state and pertains to single individuals (EG, 172: WG VII, 277 – 8). In the *Phänomenologie*, too, the 'journey' is still that of a single self-consciousness. Of course, Hegel provides a historical reading of the situation and it is this that has captured the attention of many commentators.

Thus, on the resolution of the struggle in the master/slave relation, Hegel comments that "we see, on their phenomenal side, the emergence of man's social life and the commencement of political union" (EG, 173: WL VII, 378) and, given the link-up between Hegel's philosophy of history and the emergence of the political order that we outlined in the last chapter, Kojève has some warrant for identifying the course of history with the interaction between master-warriors and slave-workers.[22] Further, as we also discussed in the last Chapter, it was a leading characteristic of the Greek and Roman Worlds that freedom there was not universal but confined, in a slave-based culture, to a few. Yet, because these *Völker* were, at their due time, of world-historical import, it does mean that the discipline of slavery is a necessary preparatory stage (just as discipline is in the initial stages of education) since, by its restraining of self-will, it permits the development of freedom (EG, 175: WG VII, 282). Slavery has a particular locus, namely, in man's transition from the state of nature to genuinely ethical conditions, that is, in a world, as Hegel puts it paradoxically in the *Philosophie des Rechts*, "where a wrong is still right" (PR, 239: WL VI, 301).

Man, as single self-consciousness, struggles for recognition and the resolution of this struggle initiates the development of social, essentially human, life. Society and history belong to the realm of Objective *Geist*. Men as spiritual universals are, as we have emphasised in earlier Chapters, only 'at home' in a spiritual context and 'objectively' this context reaches its fulfilment in the State. Through equal membership of the rational State, men are, by virtue of their very membership, accorded recognition. This is manifest in participation in the institutions of Civil Society and by rational self-conscious obedience to the law. This, because it is Rational and universal, actualises freedom and gives genuine objectivity, which means that the individual "behaves therefore toward others in a manner that is universally valid, recognising them – as he wishes others to recognise him – as free, as persons" (EG, 172 – 3: WG VII, 278).

Though it is as a citizen of the State that the individual is both concrete and universal, he exists analytically as a legal person and bearer of rights in the initial

22. Kojève, *Introduction*, p. 172. But Kojève's further claim that this interaction ceases with Napoleon and the creation by him of the universal state is to stretch this warrant unacceptably. For pertinent comment see G.A. Kelly, 'Notes on Hegel's "Lordship and Bondageaa"', in *Hegel: A collection of critical essays*, ed. A. MacIntyre, pp. 189 – 218.

Moment of Objective *Geist*, namely, Abstract Right. This is the dialectically simplest Moment of Objective *Geist* but it has as its premise the fully actualised Subjective *Geist*. We have noted that it is the slave who, through his labour, is the progressive element in the master/slave relation. The progressive quality of labour stemmed from its objectification of the slave's will so that he was able to attain independence by recognising himself in his products. In the realm of Objective *Geist*, this objectification takes the form of property. It is first of all in his property that the individual achieves recognition in the Objective or socio-historic world.

Hegel's theory of property provides another clear illustration of the account of socio-psychical dynamics that is to be found in his writings and of the distinctiveness of his account vis-à-vis that of Hume. It is for these two reasons that the topic can be fruitfully explored but that this discussion occurs in the limited legal sphere of Abstract Right should always be borne in mind. Whilst the emergent self-conscious belongs to Subjective *Geist*, it enters the sphere of Right (Objective *Geist*) as personality, that is, as consciousness of oneself as an abstract ego, as free – for I know I can through thought abstract myself from every concrete restriction (PR, 37: WL VI, 48 – 9). This constitutes man's universality. It is, however, perfectly abstract or empty and needs, therefore, to be objectivised or externalised. In order that this freedom should be more than potential it must be actualised for it is only as actualised that man can enter the Objective realm of Right, that he can exist as Idea or Reason (PR, 40: WL VI, 52). Property is the initial agent of this objectification. This, crucially, is its function and justification.

How does this objectification take place? That which differentiates man from things and animals is, as we have seen, his spirituality; more particularly, with regard to Right, it lies in his free will – "the will is free, so that freedom is both the substance of right and its goal (*Bestimmung*), while the system of right is the realm of freedom made actual" (PR, 20: WL VI, 27). By putting his will into "any and everything" man thereby makes it his, for things possess no will of their own. This is the right of appropriation. Through this process of objectification, "I as free will am an object to myself in what I possess and thereby also for the first time am an actual will, and this is the aspect which constitutes the category of property" (PR, 42: WL VI, 54). It follows from this that property is necessarily private, for it is the individual will that is existent (*Dasein*) or objectivised in property. I am only an 'object to myself' when I can say of a particular 'thing' that it is mine.

Like Locke, Hegel extends this analysis to the body. For Hegel, this is a corollary of man's ability (though not his unqualified right (PR, 242: WL VI, 304 – 5)) to kill himself, to withdraw his will from his body (PR, 43: WL VI, 56). That Hobbes' theory allows of no difference between human and animal behaviour (which from the Hegelian perspective is further proof of its inadequacy) is apparent in his inability to recognise that a man can sanely put an end to his life (stop moving). Although the individual can be free in himself whilst enchained Hegel does not subscribe to the Stoic's idea of *apatheia*, where the body belongs to the realm of 'things indifferent'; because, as Fichte had earlier also argued,[23] from the point of view of *others* I am my body and to restrict my body is to curtail my freedom.

Though property-bearing occurs at the level of Objective *Geist*, and thus presupposes recognition by others, nevertheless, that a particular thing is my property, having been appropriated by my will, is purely an inward idea, and it is necessary that others recognise *that* particular as mine. This is achieved in general terms through occupancy which is an "external activity whereby we actualise our universal right of appropriating natural objects" (PR, 45: WL VI, 58). This activity takes on various guises, which constitute the modifications in the relationship between the will and the thing.

Hegel specifies three general modifications (PR, 46 – 57: WL VI, 60 – 73). First, there is taking possession. This progresses through mere physicality, to 'forming', where possessions have a degree of independence, as in the case of plant cultivation, to possession in idea alone, that is, symbolically through marking. The second modification is by use. This involves the change, destruction or consumption of the thing, whether singly, intermittently or persistently. The final modification is by alienation. This entails the withdrawal of the property-defining will, though this by the very definition of property can only refer to externalities. Hegel does, however, remark, in a passage which hindsight imbues with great significance, that the alienation of the whole of my work would mean that "I would be making into another's property the substance of my being, my universal activity and actuality, my personality" (PR, 54: WL VI, 69).

What this last statement indicates, above all, is the basis of Hegel's theory. Property as the initial embodiment of freedom is a "substantive end" or end in itself, for freedom is the 'substance of right'. Property of itself is freedom; it needs no functional justification. To attain freedom it is necessary that I have property, for in my property I become an 'object to myself'. Not to have a sphere of property that is one's own is to fail to attain self-conscious knowledge of oneself as free. To have property, therefore, follows necessarily from the very premise of man's spirituality, his free will. To regard property merely as a contingency, as a means to an end, such as the satisfaction of needs, is to misapprehend its significance (PR, 42: WL VI, 54).

Here we confront the polemical aspect of Hegel's theory. Part of the general thrust of the entire section devoted to Abstract Right is to criticise partial theories of the State, in particular, at this point, to criticise Natural Law theories.[24] It was a common tenet of Natural Law doctrine that the emergence of private property, from a state of commonality, is to be explained by the occurrence of a compact. Though Locke rejected this tenet (common to both Grotius and Pufendorf) his own theory that each man has property in his own person (*Second Treatise*, para. 27) was firmly in the Natural Law tradition.[25] Despite the fact that this theory

23. *Grundlage des Naturrechts nach Principien der Wissenschaftlehre*, tr. A.E. Kroeger, p. 163: *Werke* Vol. III, p. 114.

24. Cf. P.G. Stillman, 'Hegel's critique of Liberal Theories of Rights', *APSR* (1974) 1086 – 92.

25. K. Olivecrona notes that Locke's term 'property' or 'propriety' is a translation of Grotius'

might suggest that property is an end in itself the Lockean theory is effectively instrumentalist.

Men are God's creatures (they are His property (para. 6)) and their property in their own person is not theirs to destroy (paras. 23, 135). Men, accordingly, are duty-bound to preserve themselves and, to achieve this end, God gave to mankind in common the Earth and all its fruits. A man now has the right to use or to appropriate (that is, to make his 'own' or his property), by labour, whatever he requires "to the best advantage of Life and convenience" (para. 26). This, for Locke, is the "original Law of Nature for the beginning of property" (para. 30), and, in this way, he has explained, and justified, private ownership without recourse to compact. Property exists for man's use or enjoyment. That this is the case is apparent from the further injunction of Natural Law that proscribes unlimited accumulation, since a man is only entitled to appropriate so much as "he can make use of to any advantage of life before it spoils" (para. 31).[26]

Hegel takes issue with such an instrumentalist reading. 'Use', for Hegel as we have seen, is one of the *modifications* of property and is, as such, secondary to its basis in the owner's will. It is a weakness of the State of Nature theorists that, by failing to make this distinction, they look upon any property as derelict when it is not in use (PR, 49: WL VI, 63). Hegel is here pre-empting the radical theory that if something (especially land) is not being used by the owner then his title to it is forfeit. Use as a modification of the basic will is an event in time and so long as the will continues to express itself, the 'thing' remains my property. This durational element is prescription (PR, 52: WL VI, 67). The fact that property thus rests internally on will, and not on use or some other externality, seems akin to Hume's theory of property as an internal relation. We can now briefly compare Hume's and Hegel's theories of property with an eye to elucidating their respective notions of socio-psychical dynamics.

Whilst Locke's theory of property is couched in the language of Natural Law, in the Utilitarians the instrumentality of property is clearly advocated. To Bentham, "the idea of property consists. . . in the persuasion of being able to draw such or such advantage from the thing possessed".[27] Property is not an end in itself.[28] It is true that a person's property does take on a "value of affection", so that it "becomes part of our being and cannot be torn from us without rendering us to the quick".[29] But, as this last phrase suggests, this is put forward as the explanation of the pain that results from the loss of our property. Hence, the first

'suum'. 'Appropriation in the State of Nature: Locke on the Origin of Property', *JHI* (1974) 218.

26. See also *First Treatise*, para. 92 — "Property, whose original is from the right a man has to use any of the inferior creatures for the subsistence and comfort of his life, is for the benefit and sole advantage of the proprietor, so that he may even destroy the thing that he has property in by use of it, where need requires".

27. *Theory of Legislation*, ed. R. Hildreth, p. 112.

28. J.S. Mill puts this unequivocally, "property is only a means to an end, not an end in itself", *Principles of Political Economy*, Bk. II, Chap. 2, para. 4 (Pelican edit.) p. 376.

phrase of that same quotation should not be misconstrued, there is no hint of a theory of self-consciousness. The further explanation that Bentham proffers to account for the connexion between pain and loss of property is based on his adoption of Hume's theory. This adoption is beyond dispute, since Bentham defines property as –

nothing but a basis of expectation; the expectation of deriving certain advantages from the thing we are said to possess, in consequence of the relation in which we stand towards it. There is no image, no painting, no visible trait, which can express the relation that constitutes property. It is not material, it is metaphysical; it is a mere conception of the mind.[30]

All that is missing from this definition is the reference of causation. Hume, it will be recalled from Chapter 5, had depicted property as a 'species of causation'. The thrust of this depiction was two-fold. It not only denied the Lockean idea of natural property by bringing out the conventional origin of property, from which it followed, on Hume's premises, that it was instituted to promote utility (M, 31 – 2). But also, secondly, it emphasised the separability of man and his possessions; the 'internal satisfaction of our minds' is distinct from the 'enjoyment of such possessions as we have acquired by our industry and good fortune'. The former cannot be taken from us, the latter can and thus constitutes the major source of social instability.

For Hume the relationship between a man and his property is contingent. But, it is the decisive factor, in Hegel's theory that this relationship is necessary. A man's will and its objectification, like the 'inner' and 'outer', are a conceptual whole. Just as Hume's theory of property deliberately parallels his theory of causation so the same parallel can be seen between Hegel's concepts of property and cause. Hegel's account of cause is, in fact, the locus classicus for objections to Hume's own classical analysis; it is at the root of Collingwood's account for example. Hegel remarks that the cause and the effect are commonly conceived as two independent existences but this is the typical product of the approach of *Verstand*, because, philosophically approached, though the two terms are distinct they are also identical, as a simple example illustrates – "The rain (the cause) and the wet (the effect) are the self-same existing water. With respect to form the cause (rain) collapses into the effect (wet): but now the outcome can no longer constitute an effect, since without the cause it is nothing and only the indifferent wet remains" (EL, 267 – amended: WL V, 152).

The crucial difference over causation is representative of the basic difference between Hume's and Hegel's philosophies. This can be seen, in the present context, in their respective responses to Locke's theory of property. Both reject Locke's extreme individualism. In Hume the property relation is artificial in that it depends on prior social convention – on the existence of justice and sentiments of morality that give us 'a sense of duty' in abstaining from an object. In

29. Bentham, *Theory of Legislation*, p. 115.
30. *Theory of Legislation*, p. 111 – 2.

Hegel, the property relation intrinsically depends on mutual recognition. In both Hume and Hegel there is an implicit distinction between possession and property. For Hume, property is 'stable possession', but the stability is the result of justice and, for Hegel, possession is only property when it is imbued with my will, and when my will therein is recognised by others.[31] But, just as with the Social Contract, though Hume and Hegel both reject Locke that does not make their own positions identical. The crux of their divergence is the intrinsic connexion, in Hegel's account, of property with personality; a connexion that is absent in Hume. We can, in conclusion, examine this difference since it points up their very distinct accounts of socio-psychical dynamics.

Property, is said by Hume to produce pride (T, 309). Pride itself is an indirect passion, whose object is the self (or "that connected succession of perceptions") (T, 277). This relation between pride and the self is "determined by an original and natural instinct", and it is an "original quality" of pride that it is a "pleasant sensation' (T, 286). But man's susceptibility to pleasure is a Newtonian 'ultimate' in the 'science of man'. Such susceptibility constitutes what Hegel would call an 'abstract universal', which signifies, in other words, that Hume's man is not contextually defined and, indeed, Hume explicitly states that "in all nations and ages" the same factors give rise to pride (T, 281).

It is against this backcloth that Hume's remark that we can get pleasure when others esteem our property should be placed, and, given this backcloth, this remark cannot be construed properly as constituting a *theory* of self-consciousness (Hume simply states, we are always intimately conscious of ourselves). Humean men, regardless, temporally or spatially, of specific location, interact principally to attain that security of external goods which is endangered by the conjunction of scarcity and 'confin'd generosity'. By establishing the inflexible general rules of justice, society is able to cohere, since men are now enabled to form expectations that others will 'perform the like'. It is clearly an economic or market model of society (recall the long quotation (from U, 98) supplied in Chapter 5). As such it corresponds to what Hegel terms Civil Society, where men interact to satisfy mutual needs. Such interaction does not involve any question of identity. For Hegel, when men interact merely through need satisfaction then they are only interacting as externals, but where each reciprocally recognises the other as a spiritual being and a free agent then "this freedom of one in the other unites men in an inward manner" (EG, 171: WG VII, 276). By establishing this inward dimension, Hegel is able to include the self dynamically in social interaction.

It is true, however, that Hume's theory is not simply a question of the interaction of self-interested atoms. Man is a social animal and it was because of this and because, more particularly, of his use of the concept of sympathy that Hume could be said to have an awareness of socio-psychical dynamics (so the esteem

---

31. This distinction between possession and property is made by Hegel in his early writings – property is a universal and appertains to Spirit not Nature (JR II, 206). Fichte had also distinguished property and possession in terms of recognition – *Grundlage*, p. 182: Vol. III, p. 130.

from others that the rich man enjoys is 'one of the principal recommendations' of his riches). But, whilst this awareness distinguishes Hume's theory from that of his individualist predecessors and Utilitarian successors (see Bentham's critique of sympathy in his *Principles of Morals and Legislation*) it must be understood in terms of his own premises and assumptions.

Thus, though Hume allows that the individual's behaviour might be modified through his interaction with his fellows in ways more complex than economic transaction, nevertheless, because human nature is, in principle, uniform, the comprehension of this behaviour is independent of any particular pattern of interaction. Similarly, universally valid self-comprehension can be attained by introspection, since the social setting, in which the particular self is ineluctably found, is, for such purposes, a contingent variable. Again, as we argued in Chapter 7, the sympathetic process itself can only operate on the observation of similarity and, Hume believes, though this operation is indeed facilitated by similarity in habits, customs etc., it operates in principle equally well with those dissimilar in such respects; with strangers as well as friends. This is guaranteed by the very constancy and uniformity of the principles and springs of human nature. The presence of these constancies gives to Hume's account of socio-psychical dynamics a non-definitive, non-constitutive, character vis-à-vis the self.

Whilst these dynamics do not, therefore, in Hume involve an active or dynamic theory of the self, in Hegel, on the contrary, they are intrinsic to such a theory. As the premises of his theory of property establish, the Hegelian self is directly involved with its surroundings and its definitive contact with other selves. The self (human agent) changes, it is self-modifying; it can transform itself in the light of (in accord with its knowledge of) experiences.[32] It is defining man as a spiritual being that Hegel gives to him a dynamic. In so much as the Humean self is a constant that is 'activated' by externally variable sources of pleasure and pain, it stands outside any 'learning process' in the sense of internal development. Human nature does not change; the self might be conditioned in its responses but such conditioning is necessarily 'external'. The governing principles in the human mind are no different in kind from those in nature as a whole. However, the Hegelian self is developmental because it is thought-constituted and its interactions are all mediated by this fact.

In short, in sum, Hume's theory of human nature and society places them firmly in the world of nature, whilst Hegel's theory of human nature and society places them equally firmly in the Nature-transcended realm of *Geist*.

---

32. Cf. W.H. Walsh, 'The Constancy of Human Nature', in *Contemporary British Philosophy*, ed. H.D. Lewis, p. 278.

BIBLIOGRAPHY

A – PRIMARY WORKS

ARISTOTLE   – *Metaphysics*, tr. J. Warrington. Everyman Library, London, 1956.
BACON, F.   – *Physical and Metaphysical Works*, ed. J. Devey. Bohn Library, London, 1851.
BEATTIE, J.   – *Elements of Moral Science*, 3rd Edit.. Edinburgh, 1817.
                 – *Dissertations Moral, Critical and Literary*, London, 1783.
                 – *Essay on the Nature and Immutability of Truth*, 7th Edit. London, 1807.
BENTHAM, J.   – *Works*, ed. J. Bowring. Edinburgh, 1859
                 – *Introduction to the Principles of Morals and Legislation* (1789), ed. W. Harrison. Blackwell, Oxford, 1948.
                 – *Theory of Fictions*, ed. C.K. Ogden. Routledge, Kegan & Paul, London, 1932.
                 – *Theory of Legislation*, ed. R. Hildreth. Paul, Trench & Trübner, London, 1896.
BLACKWELL, T.   – *Enquiry into the Life and Times of Homer*. London, 1735.
BLAIR, H.   – *Lectures on Rhetoric and Belles-Lettres* (1783). London, 1838.
                 – *Critical Dissertation of the poems of Ossian*, appended to *Poems of Ossian*, ed. A. Stewart. Edinburgh, 1819.
BOLINGBROKE, Ld. – *Letters on the Study and Use of History* (1735). London, 1870.
BUFFON, Cte. de – *Oeuvres Complètes*, ed. M. Flourens. Garnier, Paris, 1855.
                 – *Natural History*, tr. W. Smellie. London, 1812.
BULLET, C.   – *Mémoires sur la Langue Celtique*. Besançon, 1754.
BUTLER, J.   – *Analogy of Religion* (1736), ed. W.E. Gladstone. Oxford U.P., London, 1900.
CICERO   – *On the Commonwealth*, tr. G. Sabine & S. Smith. Bobbs-Merrill, Indianapolis, n.d.
                 – *The Offices*, tr. T. Cockman. Routledge, London, 1894.
                 – *De Divinatione*, tr. W. Falconer. Loeb Library, London, 1923.
CONDILLAC, E. de – *Oeuvres Philosophiques*, ed. G. Leroy. Paris, 1947–51.
CONDORCET, N. de – *Esquisse d'un tableau historique des Progrès de l'Esprit Humain* (1793), ed. O. Prior. Boivin. Paris, 1923.
D'ALEMBERT, J.   – *Discours Préliminaire* (1751), ed. F. Picavet. Colin, Paris, 1912.

	– *Preliminary Discourse to the Encyclopedia*, tr. R. Schwab & W. Rex. Bobbs-Merrill, Indianapolis, 1963.
DESCARTES, R.	– *Oeuvres Philosophiques*. Garnier, Paris, 1793.
	– *A Discourse on Method* (1637), tr. J. Veich. Everyman Library, London, 1960.
DIDEROT, D.	– *Oeuvres Philosophiques*, ed. P. Vernière. Garnier, Paris, 1964.
DUBOS, R.	– *Réflexions critiques sur la Poésie et la Peinture*, 6th Edit., Paris, 1755.
DUFF, W.	– *Essay on Original Genius*. London, 1767.
DUNBAR, J.	– *Essays on the History of Mankind*. London, 1780.
ENCYCLOPEDIA BRITANNICA	– 1771, repr.. Chicago, 1968.
FERGUSON, A.	– *Essay on the History of Civil Society* (1767), ed. D. Forbes, Edinburgh U.P., Edinburgh, 1966.
	– *Institutes of Moral Philosophy*. Edinburgh, 1769.
FICHTE, J.G.	– *Sämmtliche Werke*, ed. I.H. Fichte. Berlin, 1845.
	– *Addresses to the German Nation* (1808), tr. R. Jones & C. Turnbull, ed. G.A. Kelly. Harper & Row, New York, 1968.
	– *Science of Knowledge* (1794), tr. P. Heath & J. Lachs. Appleton – Century – Crofts, New York, 1970.
	– *Science of Rights* (1796), tr. A.E. Kroeger (1889). Routledge, London, 1970.
GERARD, A.	– *Essay on Taste*, 3rd Edit. Edinburgh, 1780.
	– *Essay on Genius*. London, 1774.
GOETHE, J.W.	– *Autobiography*, tr. J. Oxenford. Bohn Library, London, 1900.
HAMANN, J.G.	– *Sämmtliche Werke*, ed. J. Nadler. Herder, Vienna, 1951.
	– *Briefwechsel*, ed. A. Henkel. Insel, Wiesbaden, 1959.
HARTLEY, D.	– *Observations on Man*. London, 1749.
HEGEL, G.W.	– *Sämmtliche Werke*, ed. G. Lasson & J. Hoffmeister. Meiner, Leipzig, 1921.
	– *Werke*, ed. E. Gans et al.. Duncker & Humblot, Berlin, 1840.
	– *Werke Jubiläumsausgabe*, ed. H. Glockner. Frommann, Stuttgart, 1927.
	– *The Phenomenology of Mind* (1807), tr. J. Baillie (1910). Harper & Row, New York, 1967.
	– *Texts & Commentary*, ed. W. Kaufmann. Doubleday; New York, 1966.
	– *The Logic of Hegel* (1817/30), tr. W. Wallace. Clarendon Pr., Oxford, 1892.
	– *The Philosophy of Nature* (1817/30, tr. A. Miller. Clarendon Pr., Oxford, 1970.
	– *Briefe von und an Hegel*, ed. J. Hoffmeister. Meiner, Hamburg, 1952.
	– *The Philosophy of Mind* (1817/30), tr. W. Wallace & A. Miller. Clarendon Pr., Oxford, 1971.
	– *The Science of Logic* (1812 – 16), tr. W. Johnston & L. Struthers. G.Allen & Unwin, London, 1929.
	– *The Philosophy of Right* (1821), tr. T.M. Knox. Clarendon Pr., Oxford, 1942.
	– *Hegel's Philosophy of History*, tr. J. Sibree. Bohn Library, London, 1872.

210

- *Reason in History*, tr. R. Hartmann. Bobbs-Merrill, Indianapolis, 1953.
- *Lectures on the Philosophy of World History (Introduction)*, tr. H.B. Nisbet. Cambridge U.P., Cambridge, 1975.
- *Hegel's Political Writings*, tr. T.M. Knox. Clarendon Pr., Oxford, 1964.
- *Early Theological Writings*, tr. T.M. Knox, University of Pennsylvania Pr., Philadelphia, 1971.
- *Hegels Theologische Jugendschriften*, ed. H. Nohl (1907). Minerva, Frankfurt-am-Main, 1966.
- *Hegel on Art, Religion and Philosophy*, ed. G. Gray. Harper & Row, New York, 1970.
- *Lectures on the Philosophy of Religion*, tr. E. Spiers & J. Sanderson. Paul, Trench & Trubner, London, 1895.
- *History of Philosophy*, tr. E. Haldane & F. Simson. Kegan Paul, London, 1896.

HELVÉTIUS, C.
- *De l'Esprit* (1758), ed. P. Christian. Paris, 1843.

HERDER, J.G.
- *Sämmtliche Werke*, ed. B. Suphan. Berlin, 1891.
- *Herder on Social and Political Culture*, tr. F.M. Barnard. Cambridge U.P., Cambridge, 1969.
- *Reflections on the Philosophy of the History of Mankind* (1784 – 91), tr. J. Churchill, ed. F. Manuel. Chicago U.P., Chicago, 1968.

HOBBES, T.
- *Leviathan* (1651). Everyman Library, London, 1959.

HOLBACH, Baron d'
- *La Morale Universelle ou les devoirs de l'homme fondés sur sa Nature.* Amsterdam, 1776.

HUME, D.
- *A Treatise of Human Nature* (1739 – 40), ed. L. Selby-Bigge. Clarendon Pr., Oxford, 1946.
- *Inquiry concerning Human Understanding* (1748), ed. C. Hendel. Bobbs-Merrill, Indianapolis, 1957.
- *Inquiry concerning the Principles of Morals* (1751), ed. C. Hendel. Bobbs-Merrill, Indianapolis, 1957.
- *Hume on Religion*, ed. R. Wollheim. Fontana Bks., London, 1963.
- *History of Great Britain: The Reigns of James I and Charles I* (1754), ed. D. Forbes. Pelican Bks., Harmondsworth, 1970.
- *History of England from the invasion of Caesar to the Revolution in 1688.* Jones & Co., London, 1824.
- *Letter from a Gentleman* (1745), ed. E. Mossner & J. Price. Edinburgh U.P., Edinburgh, 1967.
- *Works.* A. & C. Black & Little Brown, Edinburgh & Boston, Mass., 1854.
- *Essays: Moral Political and Literary.* Oxford U.P., London, 1963.
- *Letters*, ed. J.Y.T. Greig. Clarendon Pr., Oxford, 1932.

HUTCHESON, F.
- *Essay on the Nature and Conduct of the Passions and Affections.* London, 1728.

ISELIN, I.
- *Über die Geschichte der Menschheit*, 5th Edit. Basel, 1786.

JOHNSON, S.
- *Dictionary*, 10th Edit. London, 1792.

KAMES, Ld.
- *Elements of Criticism*, 6th Edit. Edinburgh, 1785.
- *Sketches on the History of Man*, 3rd Edit. Dublin, 1779.

KANT, I.
- *Werke.* Prussian Academy edition Berlin, 1902 – 38.
- *Critique of Pure Reason* (1781), tr. N.K. Smith. MacMillan, London, 1929.

- *Critique of Judgment* (1788), tr. J.H. Bernard. Macmillan, London, 1892.
- *The Philosophy of Kant*, ed. C. Friedrich. Modern Library, New York, 1949.
- *Kant on History*, ed. L.W. Beck. Bobbs-Merrill, Indianapolis, 1963.
- *Anthropology from a Pragmatic Point of View* (1798), tr. M. Gregor. M. Nijhoff, The Hague, 1974.
- *Kant's Political Writings*, tr. H. Nisbet. Cambridge U.P., Cambridge, 1970.
- *The Moral Law* (1785), tr. H.J. Paton. Hutchinson University Library, London, 1962.

LESSING, G.E. — *Werke*. Kiepenheuer & Witsch, Cologne, 1962.

LOCKE, J. — *Philosophical Works*. Bohn Library, London, 1854.
- *Essays on the Law of Nature*, ed. W. Von Leyden. Clarendon Pr., Oxford, 1970.
- *Some Thoughts concerning Education*. London, 1693.
- *Treatises on Civil Government* (1690), ed. P. Laslett. Mentor Library, New York, 1963.

MACHIAVELLI, N. — *The Prince and the Discourses*, ed. M. Lerner. Modern Library, New York, 1950.

MAISTRE, J. — *Works*, ed. & tr. J. Lively. G.Allen & Unwin, London, 1965.

MILL, J.S. — *Principles of Political Economy* (1848), 1st Edit., ed. D. Winch. Pelican Bks., Harmondsworth, 1970.

MILLAR, J. — *Origin of the Distinction of Ranks*, 3rd Edit. (1779), ed. W.C. Lehmann. Cambridge U.P., Cambridge, 1960.

MONBODDO, Ld. — *Origin and Progress of Language*. Edinburgh, 1773 – 9.
- *Ancient Metaphysics*. Edinburgh, 1779 – 99.

MONTAIGNE, M. — *Apologie pour Raymond Sebonde* (1576), ed. P. Porteau. Aubier, Paris, 1937.
- *Essays*, tr. G.B. Ives. Harvard U.P., Cambridge, Mass., 1925.

MONTESQUIEU, C. — *Oeuvres Complètes*. Nagel, Paris, 1950.

MÜLLER, A. — *Die Elemente der Staatskunst* (1809), ed. J. Baxa. Herdflamme, Jena, 1922.

PASCAL, B. — *Oeuvres Complètes*. Du Seuil, Paris, 1963.

PLUTARCH — *On Superstition*. London, 1828.

PUFENDORF, S. — *On the Law of Nature and Nations* (1672), tr. C. & W. Oldfather. Classics of International Law, Oxford, 1934.

REID, T. — *Works*, ed. W. Hamilton. Edinburgh, 1846.

REYNOLDS, J. — *Discourses on Art delivered at the Royal Academy*, ed. E. Gosse. London, 1889.

ROBERTSON, W. — *Works*, ed. D. Stewart. Edinburgh, 1840.

ROUSSEAU, J.J. — *Oeuvres Complètes*. Pléiade, Paris, 1959.
- *Social Contract and Discourses*, tr. G. Cole. Everyman Library, London, 1968.
- *Emile or Education* (1762), tr. B. Foxley. Everyman Library, London, 1911.
- *Confessions* (1781), tr. J.M. Cohen. Penguin Bks., Harmondsworth, 1954.

SAVIGNY, J. — *Geschichte des Römischen Rechts im Mittelalter*, 2nd Edit. Heidelberg, 1834.

212

SCHILLER, F.	– *Werke*. National-Ausgabe Nachfolger, Weimar, 1962.
	– *On Naive and Sentimental Poetry* (1795), tr. J. Ellias. Ungar, New York, 1966.
SCHLEGEL, F.	– *Werke*. Kritische-Ausgabe Paderborn, Stuttgart, 1959.
SMITH, A.	– *Theory of Moral Sentiments* (1759), 1st Edit. Bohn Library, London, 1871.
	– *Inquiry into the Nature and Causes of the Wealth of Nations* (1776). Everyman Library, London, 1964.
	– *Lectures on Jurisprudence, Police, Revenue and Arms*, ed. E. Cannan. Oxford, 1896.
	– *Essays on Philosophical Subjects*. London, 1795. ·
STEWART, D.	– *Works*, ed. W. Hamilton. Edinburgh, 1854.
STUART, G.	– *Historical Dissertation on the Antiquity of the English Constitution*. Edinburgh, 1768.
TURGOT, A.R.J.	– *Oeuvres*, ed. E. Daire & H. Dussard. Paris, 1844.
	– *Turgot on Progress, Sociology and Economics*, tr. R. Meek. Cambridge U.P., Cambridge, 1975.
VIGO, G.B.	– *New Science*, 3rd Edit. (1744), abgd. & tr. T. Bergin & M. Fisch. Cornell U.P., Ithaca, 1970.
VOLNEY, C.	– *Oeuvres Complètes*. Paris, 1921.
	– *Ruins of Empires* (1791), ed. C. Bradlaugh. Freethought Pr., London, 1881.
VOLTAIRE, F.	– *Oeuvres Complètes*. Garnier, Paris, 1877.
	– *Age of Louis XIV and other selected writings*, ed. J. Brumfitt. New English Library, London, 1966.
	– *Candide and other writings*, ed. H.M. Block. Modern Library, New York, 1956.
	– *Philosophical Dictionary* (1764), ed. T. Bestermann. Penguin Bks, Harmondsworth, 1971.
	– *Correspondance*, ed. T. Bestermann. Institut Voltaire, Geneva, 1969 – 00.
YOUNG, E.	– *Conjectures on Original Composition*. London, 1759.

B – SECONDARY SOURCES

Books

ABRAMS, M.H.	– *The Mirror and the Lamp: Romantic Theory and the Critical Tradition*. Galaxy Books, New York, 1971.
ALEXANDER, W.M.	– *J.G. Hamann Philosophy and Faith*. M. Nijhoff, The Hague, 1966.
ALLISON, H.E.	– *Lessing and the Enlightenment*. Michigan U.P., Ann Arbor, 1966.
ANDERSON, R.F.	– *Hume's First Principles*. U. of Nebraska Pr., Lincoln, Neb., 1966.
ARDAL, P.S.	– *Passion and Value in Hume's Treatise*. Edinburgh U.P., Edinburgh, 1966.
AVINERI, S.	– *Hegel's Theory of the Modern State*. Cambridge U.P., Cambridge, 1972.
BARNARD, F.M.	– *Herder's Social and Political Thought*. Clarendon Pr., Oxford, 1965.
BECK, L.W.	– *Early German Philosophy: Kant and his Predecessors*. Harvard Belknap Pr., Cambridge, Mass., 1969.

BECKER, C.   – *The Heavenly City of the Eighteenth-Century Philosophes*. Yale U.P., New Haven, 1967 (1932).

BERLIN, I.   – *Vico and Herder: Two Studies in the History of Ideas*. Hogarth Pr., London, 1976.

BLACK, J.B.   – *The Art of History*. Methuen, London, 1926.

BONGIE, L.L.   – *David Hume: Prophet of the Counter-Revolution*. Clarendon Pr., Oxford, 1965.

BRISSENDEN, R.F. (ed.)   – *Studies in the Eighteenth-Century*. Australian National U.P., Canberra, 1968.

BRUFORD, W.H.   – *Culture and Society in Classical Weimar 1775 – 1806*. Cambridge U.P., Cambridge, 1975.

BRUNET, O.   – *Philosophe et Esthétique chez D. Hume*. Nizet, Paris, 1965.

BUTLER, E.M.   – *The Tyranny of Greece over Germany*. Cambridge U.P., Cambridge, 1933.

CAMERON, D.M.   – *The Social Thought of Rousseau and Burke*. Weidenfeld & Nicholson, London, 1974.

CASSIRER, E.   – *The Problem of Knowledge*, tr. W. Woglom & C. Hendel. Yale U.P., New Haven, 1950.
– *The Philosophy of the Enlightenment*, tr. F. Koelln & J. Pettegrove. Beacon Pr., Boston, 1955.
– *Rousseau, Kant and Goethe*, tr. J. Guttman et al. Princeton U.P., Princeton, 1963.
– *The Philosophy of Symbolic Forms*, tr. R. Mannheim. Yale U.P., New Haven, 1953.

CHAPPELL, V. (ed.)   – *Hume*. MacMillan, London, 1966.

CHURCH, R.W.   – *Hume's Theory of the Understanding*. G. Allen & Unwin, London, 1968.

CLARK, R.T. Jr.   – *Herder: His Life and Thought*. University of California Pr., Berkeley & Los Angeles, 1955.

COLLETTI, L.   – *Marxism and Hegel*, tr. L. Garner. New Left Books, London, 1973.

COOK, D.J.   – *Language in the Philosophy of Hegel*. Mouton, The Hague, 1973.

CROCKER, L.G.   – *An Age of Crisis: Man and World in Eighteenth-Century French Thought*. Johns Hopkins U.P., Baltimore, 1959.
– *Nature and Culture: Ethical Thought in the French Enlightenment*. John Hopkins U.P., Baltimore, 1963.

CUMMING, R.D.   – *Human Nature and History: A study of the development of liberal thought*. Chicago U.P., Chicago, 1969.

CURTIUS, E.   – *European Literature in the Latin Middle Ages*, tr. W.R. Trask. Harper & Row, New York, 1963.

D'ENTREVES, A.P.   – *Natural Law*. Hutchinson University Library, London, 1967.

DERATHE, R.   – *Le Rationalism de J-J Rousseau*. Presses Université de France, Paris, 1948.

DILTHEY, W.   – *Gesammelte Schriften*. Teubner, Stuttgart, 1959 – 00.
– *Das Erlebnis und Dichtung*, 14th Edit. Vandenhoeck & Ruprecht, Göttingen, 1963.

FACKENHEIM, E.   – *The Religious Dimension in Hegel's Thought*. Indiana U.P., Bloomington, 1971.

FINDLAY, J.N.   – *Hegel: A Reexamination*. G. Allen & Unwin, London, 1958.

FLEW, A.   – *Hume's Philosophy of Belief.* Routledge, Kegan Paul, London, 1961.

FORBES, D.   – *Hume's Philosophical Politics.* Cambridge U.P., Cambridge, 1975.

FRANKEL, C.   – *The Faith of Reason.* Octagon Books, New York, n.d. (1948).

GADAMER, H.   – *Hegels Dialektik: Fünf hermeneutische studien.* Mohr, Tübingen, 1971.

GAY, P.   – *The Enlightenment, Vol. 1: The Rise of Paganism.* Weidenfeld & Nicholson, London, 1967.
     – *Vol. 2: The Science of Freedom.* 1970.

GEERTZ, C.   – *The Interpretation of Culture.* Basic Books, New York, 1972.

GIARRIZZO, G.   – *David Hume: politico e storico.* Einaudi, Turin, 1962.

GILLIES, A.   – *Herder.* Blackwell. Oxford, 1945.

GINSBERG, M.   – *Essays in Sociology and Social Philosophy.* Peregrine Books, Harmondsworth, 1968.

GOMBRICH, E.   – *In Search of Cultural History.* Clarendon Pr., Oxford, 1969.

GOYARD-FABRE, S.   – *La Philosophie des Lumières en France.* Klincksieck, Paris, 1972.

GUNNELL, J.G.   – *Political Philosophy and Time.* Wesleyan U.P., Middletown, Conn., 1968.

HABERMAS, J.   – *Theory and Practice,* tr. J. Viertel. Heinemann, London, 1974.

HAMPSHIRE, S.   – *Thought and Action.* Chatto and Windus, London, 1965.

HARRIS, H.S.   – *Hegel's Development: Toward the Sunlight 1770 – 1801.* Clarendon Pr., Oxford, 1972.

HARRISON, J.   – *Hume's Moral Epistemology.* Clarendon Pr., Oxford, 1976.

HART, H.L.A.   – *The Concept of Law.* Clarendon Pr., Oxford, 1961.

HAYM, R.   – *Herder: nach seinem Leben und seinen Werken.* Gaertner, Berlin, 1880.

HENDEL, C.W.   – *Studies in the Philosophy of David Hume.* Princeton U.P., Princeton, 1925.

HONDT, J. d' (ed.)   – *Hegel et le siècle des Lumières.* Presses Université de France, Paris, 1974.

HORTON R. &
FINNEGAN, R. (eds.)   – *Modes of Thought.* Faber & Faber, London, 1973.

HOWELL, W.S.   – *Eighteenth-Century British Logic and Rhetoric.* Princeton U.P., Princeton, 1971.

HUBERT, R.   – *Les Sciences Sociales dans l'Encyclopédie.* Alcan, Paris, 1923.

HYMES, D. (ed.)   – *Studies in the History of Linguistics: Traditions and Paradigms.* Indiana U.P., Bloomington, Ind., 1974.

JENDREIECK, H.   – *Hegel und Jacob Grimm.* E. Schmidt, Berlin, 1975.

KALLICH, M.   – *The Association of Ideas and Critical Theory in the Eighteenth-Century.* Chicago U.P., Chicago, 1965.

KAUFMANN, W.   – *Hegel.* Weidenfeld and Nicholson, London, 1966.
     – *(ed.) Hegel's Political Philosophy.* Atherton, New York, 1970.

KELLY, G.A.   – *Idealism, Politics and Vision: Sources of Hegelian Thought.* Cambridge U.P., Cambridge, 1969.
     – *Hegel's Retreat from Eleusis.* Princeton U.P., Princeton, 1978.

KNIGHT, I.F.   – *The Geometric Spirit: Abbé Condillac and the French Enlightenment.* Yale U.P., New Haven, 1968.

KOJÈVE, H.   – *Introduction à la lecture de Hegel,* 2nd Edit. Gallimard, Paris, 1944.

KORFF, H.   — *Goethe und Goethezeit*. Hirzel, Leipzig, 1957.
KRIEGER, L.   — *The Politics of Discretion: Pufendorf and the Acceptance of Natural Law.* Chicago U.P., Chicago, 1965.
LAIRD, J.   — *Hume's Philosophy of Human Nature*. Methuen, London, 1932.
LASLETT, P. &
  RUNCIMANN, G.R.   — *Philosophy, Politics and Society — Second Series*. Blackwell, Oxford, 1967.
  (eds.)
LÉON, X.   — *Fichte et son temps*. Colin, Paris, 1922 – 7.
LEROY, A.   — *La Critique et la Religion chez David Hume*. Alcan, Paris, 1929.
LEWIS, H.D. (ed.)   — *Contemporary British Philosophy*. G. Allen & Unwin, London, 1975.

LIVINGSTON, D. &
  KING, J. (eds.)   — *Hume: a revaluation*. Fordham U.P., New York, 1976.
LOVEJOY, A.O.   — *Essays in the History of Ideas*. Putnam Capricorn Bks., New York, 1960.
                     — *The Great Chain of Being*. Harper & Row, New York, 1960.
LÖWITH, K.   — *Meaning in History* (1949). Chicago U.P., Chicago, 1967.
LUKACS, G.   — *The Young Hegel*, tr. R. Livingstone. Merlin Bks., London, 1975.
                     — *Goethe and his Age*, tr. R. Anchor. Merlin Bks., London, 1968.
MACFIE, A.L.   — *The Individual in Society: Essays on Adam Smith*. G. Allen & Unwin, London, 1967.
MACINTYRE, A. (ed.) — *Hegel: A collection of critical essays*. Doubleday, New York, 1972.
MANDELBAUM, M.   — *History, Man and Reason*. Johns Hopkins U.P., Baltimore, 1972.
MANUEL, F.E.   — *The Eighteenth-Century Confronts the Gods*. Harvard U.P., Cambridge, Mass., 1959.
MARCUSE, H.   — *Reason and Revolution: Hegel and the rise of social theory*, 2nd Edit. Routledge, London, 1969.
MASON, S.M.   — *Montesquieu's Idea of Justice*. M. Nijhoff, The Hague, 1975.
MEEK, R.L.   — *Social Science and the Ignoble Savage*. Cambridge U.P., Cambridge, 1976.
MEINECKE, F.   — *Die Entstehung des Historismus*, 2nd Edit. Oldenbourg, Munich, 1946.
                     — *Cosmopolitanism and the National State*, tr. R. Kimber. Princeton U.P., Princeton, 1970.
MELDEN, A.   — *Free Action*. Routledge, London, 1961.
MERCER, P.   — *Sympathy and Ethics*. Clarendon Pr., Oxford, 1972.
MERCIER, R.   — *La Réhabilitation de la Nature Humaine 1700-50*. La Balance, Villemonble, 1960.
MESZAROS, I.   — *Marx's Theory of Alienation*. Merlin Bks., London, 1970.
MINOGUE, K.R.   — *Nationalism*. Methuen, London, 1969.
MORICE, G.P. (ed.)   — *David Hume: Bicentennial Essays*. Edinburgh U.P., Edinburgh, 1977.
MORISON, S.E.   — *The European Discovery of America: The Southern Voyages 1492 – 1616*. Oxford U.P., New York, 1974.
NIDDITCH, P.H.   — *An apparatus of variant readings of Hume's Treatise of Human Nature*. Sheffield, 1976.
NISBET, H.B.   — *Herder and Scientific Thought*. Modern Humanities Research Assoc., Cambridge, 1970.
NOXON, J.   — *Hume's Philosophical Development*. Clarendon Pr., Oxford, 1973.

216

OAKESHOTT, M.   – *Rationalism in Politics and other essays.* Methuen, London, 1962.
    – *On Human Conduct.* Clarendon Pr., Oxford, 1975.
O'BRIEN, G.D.   – *Hegel on Reason and History.* Chicago U.P., Chicago, 1975.
PASSMORE, J.   – *Hume's Intentions,* rev. ed. Duckworth, London, 1968.
PELCZYNSKI, Z. (ed.)   – *Hegel's Political Philosophy: Problems and Perspectives.* Cambridge U.P., Cambridge, 1971.
PENNOCK, J. &
  CHAPMAN, J.   – *Property.* New York U.P., New York, 1980.
PLANT, R.   – *Hegel.* G. Allen & Unwin, London, 1972.
PLANTY-BONJOUR, G.   – *Introduction à la Première Philosophie de l'Esprit de Hegel.* Presses Université de France, Paris, 1969.
PLAMENATZ, J.P.   – *Karl Marx's Philosophy of Man.* Oxford U.P., Oxford, 1975.
    – *Man and Society.* Longman, London, 1963.
POCOCK, J.G.A.   – *Politics, Language and Time.* Atheneum, New York, 1973.
POMPA, L.   – *Vico: A study of the 'new Science'.* Cambridge U.P., Cambridge, 1975.
POPKIN, R.   – *The History of Scepticism from Erasmus to Descartes,* rev. ed. Harper & Row, New York, 1968.
POPPER, K.R.   – *The Open Society and its Enemies.* Routledge, Kegan Paul, London, 1962.
PRICE, H.H.   – *Hume's Theory of the External World.* Clarendon Pr., Oxford, 1940.
RANDAL, H.W.   – *The Critical Theory of Lord Kames.* Smith College Studies in Language and Literatuare, Northampton, Mass., 1941.
REDWOOD, J.   – *Reason, Ridicule and Religion: The Age of Enlightenment in England 1660 – 1750.* Thames & Hudson, London, 1976.
REILL, H.P.   – *The German Enlightenment and the rise of Historicism.* University of California Pr., Berkeley & Los Angeles, 1975.
REISS, H. (ed.)   – *Political Thought of the German Romantics.* Blackwell, Oxford, 1955.
ROBINS, R.H.   – *A short history of Linguistics.* Longman, London, 1969.
ROMMEN, H.   – *The Natural Law,* tr. T. Hanley. Herder, St. Louis, 1959.
ROSEN, S.   – *G.W.F. Hegel: An introduction to the Science of Wisdom.* Yale U.P., New Haven, 1974.
ROSENZWEIG, F.   – *Hegel und der Staat* (1920). Scientia, Aalen, 1962.
ROTENSTREICH, N.   – *From Substance to Subject: Studies in Hegel.* M. Nijhoff, The Hague, 1974.
ROTWEIN, E.   – *Introduction to Hume's Writings on Economics.* Nelson, Edinburgh, 1955.
RUNTE, R. (ed.)   – *Studies in Eighteenth-Century Culture,* Vol. 7. University Wisconsin Pr, Madison, 1978.
SAMPSON, R.V.   – *Progress in the Age of Reason.* Heinemann, London, 1956.
SANER, H.   – *Kant's Political Thought,* tr. E. Ashton. Chicago U.P., Chicago, 1973.
SCHACHT, R.   – *Alienation.* G. Allen & Unwin, London, 1971.
SCHOCHET, G.   – *Patriarchalism in Political Thought.* Blackwell, Oxford, 1975.
SCHOECK, H. &
  WIGGINS, J. (eds.)   – *Relativism and the Study of Man.* Van Nostrand, Princeton, 1961.
SELIGER, M.   – *The Liberal Politics of J. Locke.* G. Allen & Unwin, London, 1968.
SHACKLETON, R.   – *Montesquieu: A critical biography.* Oxford U.P., Oxford, 1961.

SHAPIRO, B.J.   — *John Wilkins 1614–1672: An Intellectual Biography*. University of California Pr., Berkeley & Los Angeles, 1969.

SHKLAR, J.   — *Men and Citizens: A study of Rousseau's social theory*. Cambridge U.P., Cambridge, 1969.
  — *Freedom and Independence: A study of the political ideas of Hegel's Phenomenology of Mind*. Cambridge U.P., Cambridge, 1976.

SKINNER, A. &
WILSON, T. (eds.)   — *Essays on Adam Smith*. Clarendon Pr., Oxford, 1975.

SMITH, D.W.   — *Helvétius: A study in persecution*. Clarendon Pr., Oxford, 1965.

SMITH, N.K.   — *The Philosophy of David Hume* (1941). MacMillan, London, 1964.

SMITH, R.G.   — *J.G. Hamann 1730–1788: A study in Christian Existence*. Collins, London, 1960.

STAROBINSKI, J.   — *J.-J. Rousseau: La Transparence et l'Obstacle*. Gallimard, Paris, 1971.

STEINER, G.   — *After Babel*. Oxford U.P., Oxford, 1975.

STEWART, J.B.   — *The Moral and Political Philosophy of David Hume*. Columbia U.P., New York, 1963.

TAYLOR, C.   — *Hegel*. Cambridge U.P., Cambridge, 1975.

TODD, W.E. (ed.)   — *Hume and the Enlightenment*. Edinburgh U.P., Edinburgh, 1974.

TRILLING, L.   — *Sincerity and Authenticity*. Harvard U.P., Cambridge, Mass., 1973.

TYLOR, E.B.   — *Primitive Culture*. J. Murray, London, 1871.

VARTANIAN, A.   — *Diderot and Descartes: A study in scientific naturalism in the Enlightenment*. Princeton U.P., Princeton, 1952.

VENTURI, F.   — *Italy and the Enlightenment*, tr. S. Corsi. Longman, London, 1972.

VESEY, G. (ed.)   — *The Proper Study*. MacMillan, London, 1971.

VLACHOS, G.   — *Essai sur la Politique de Hume*. Domat-Montchrestien, Paris, 1955.

VYVERBERG, H.   — *Historical Pessimism in the French Enlightenment*. Harvard U.P., Cambridge, Mass., 1958.

WADE, I.O.   — *The Intellectual Origins of the French Enlightenment*. Princeton U.P., Princeton, 1971.

WALSH, W.H.   — *Hegelian Ethics*. MacMillan, London, 1969.

WASSERMAN, E. (ed.)   — *Aspects of the Eighteenth Century*. Johns Hopkins U.P., Baltimore, 1971.

WATKINS, J.   — *Hobbes' System of Ideas*. Hutchinson University Library, London, 1965.

WEISS, F.G. (ed.)   — *Beyond Epistemology: New Studies in the Philosophy of Hegel*. M. Nijhoff, The Hague, 1974.

WHORF, B.L.   — *Language Thought and Reality*, ed. J.B. Carroll. Technology Pr., Cambridge, Mass., 1956.

WILKINS, B.T.   — *Hegel's Philosophy of History*. Cornell U.P., Ithaca, New York, 1974.

WILSON, B. (ed.)   — *Rationality*. Harper & Row, New York, 1971.

WINCH, P.   — *The Idea of a Social Science and its relation to Philosophy*. Routledge, London, 1963.

218

Articles

Abbreviations:

APSR	American Political Science Review
GLL	German Life and Letters
HT	History and Theory
JHI	Journal of the History of Ideas
JHP	Journal of the History of Philosophy
JP	Journal of Politics
MP	Modern Philology
PMLA	Publication of the Modern Language Association of America
PS	Political Studies
VS	Studies in Voltaire and the Eighteenth Century

AARSLEFF, H.
- The Tradition of Condillac: The Problem of the Origin of Language in the Eighteenth Century and the Debate in the Berlin Academy before Herder, *in* Hymes (ed.), 93 – 156.
- The State of Nature and the Nature of Man, *in* Yolton (ed.) 99 – 136.

ACTON, H.B.
- Prejudice, *Revue International de Philosophie* 6 (1952) 323 – 336.
- Hegel's conception of the study of Human Nature, *in* Vesey (ed.) 32 – 47.
- Distributive Justice, the Invisible Hand and the Cunning of Reason, *PS* 20 (1972) 421 – 431.

ASHCRAFT, R.
- Locke's State of Nature: Historical Fact or Moral Fiction, *APSR* 62 (1968) 898 – 915.

AUERBACH, E.
Vico and Aesthetic Historism, *Journal of Aesthetics and Art Criticism* 8 (1949) 110 – 118.

AVINERI, S.
- Hegel and Nationalism, *in* Kaufmann (ed.) 109 – 136.

BERGMANN, F.
- The Purpose of Hegel's System, *JHP* 2 (1964) 189 – 204.

BERLIN, I.
- Hume and the Sources of German Anti-Rationalism, *in* Morice (ed.) 93 – 116.

BERRY, C.J.
- James Dunbar and ideas of sociality in eighteenth century Scotland, *Il Pensiero Politico* 6 (1973) 188 – 201.
- Eighteenth-Century Approaches to the Origin of Metaphor, *Neuphilologische Mitteilungen* 74 (1973) 690 – 713.
- Adam Smith's 'Considerations' on Language, *JHI* (1974) 130 – 138.
- 'Climate' in the Eighteenth Century: James Dunbar and the Scottish Case, *Texas Studies in Literature and Language* 16 (1974) 281 – 292.
- On the Meaning of Progress and Providence in the Fourth Century, *Heythrop Journal* 18 (1977) 257 – 270.
- From Hume to Hegel; The Case of the Social Contract, *JHI* 38 (1977) 691 – 703.
- Property and Possession, *in* Pennock and Chapman (eds.) 89 – 100.
- Hegel on the World Historical, *History of European Ideas* 2 (1981) 155 – 162.

BEYER, C.J.
- Montesquieu et le relativisme esthetique, *VS* 24 (1963) 171 – 182.

BRIEFS, G.A.   – The Economic Philosophy of Romanticism, *JHI* 2 (1941) 279 – 300.

BURKE, J.J. Jr.   – Hume's History of England, *in* Runte 235 – 50.

CHAMLEY, P.   – Les origines de la Pensée Economique de Hegel, *Hegel Studien* 3 (1965) 225 – 261.

CHAPMAN, J.W.   – Political Theory: Logical Structure and Enduring Types, *Annales de Philosophie Politique* 6 (1965) 57 – 96.

CLARK, R.T. Jr.   – Herder's Concept of 'Kraft', *PMLA* (1942) 737 – 752.

CEIGHTON, D.G.   – Man and Mind in Diderot and Helvétius, *PMLA* 71 (1956) 705 – 724.

DUNN, J.   – The Identity of the History of Ideas, *Philosophy* 43 (1968) 85 – 116.

EDWARDS, C.   – The Law of Nature and the Thought of Hugo Grotius, *JP* 32 (1970) 784 – 807.

EMERSON, R.   – Peter Gay and the Heavenly City, *JHI* 28 (1967) 383 – 402.

FACKENHEIM, E.   – On the Actuality of the Rational and the Rationality of the Actual, *Review of Metaphysics* 23 (1969 – 70) 690 – 698.

FISCHER, K.P.   – John Locke in the German Enlightenment, *JHI* 36 (1975) 431 – 446.

FLAJOLE, E.   – Lessing's Retrieval of Los Truths, PMLA 74 (1959) 52 – 66.

FORBES, D.   – 'Scientific' Whiggism: Adam Smith and John Millar, *Cambridge Journal* 7 (1954) 643 – 670.

FORD, F.L.   – The Enlightenment: Towards a Useful Definition, *in* Brissenden (ed.) 17 – 29.

GAWLICK, G.   – Cicero and the Enlightenment, *VS* 25 (1963) 657 – 682.

GERMINO, D.   – Hegel as a Political Theorist, *JP* (1969) 885 – 912.

GILLIES, A.   – Herder's Essay on Shakespeare: *Das Herz der Untersuchung*, *Modern Language Review* 32 (1937) 737 – 752.

GOLDSTEIN, L.J.   – The Meaning of 'State' in Hegel's 'Philosophy of History', *Philosophical Quarterly* 12 (1962) 60 – 72.

GRENE, M.   – Gerard's Essay on Taste, *MP* 41 (1943) 45 – 58.
    – Hume: Sceptic and Tory, *JHI* (1943) 333 – 348.

HEIMAN, G.   – The Sources and Significance of Hegel's Corporate Doctrine, *in* Pelczynski (ed.) 111 – 135.

HENRICH, D.   – Hegels Theorie über den Zufall, *Kant Studien* 50 (1958 – 9) 131 – 148.

JESSOP, T.E.   – Some misunderstandings of Hume, *in* Chappell (ed.) 35 – 52.

KANTOROWICZ, H.   – Volksgeist und Historische Rechtsschule, *Historische Zeitschrift* 108 (1912) 295 – 325.
    – Savigny and the Historical School of Law, *Law Quarterly Review* 153 (1937) 326 – 343.

KAUFMANN, W.   – The Young Hegel and religion, *in* MacIntyre (ed.) 61 – 99.

KELLY, G.A.   – Notes on Hegel's 'Lordship and Bondage', *in* MacIntyre (ed.) 189 – 218.

KNOX, T.M.   – Hegel and Prussianism, *in* Kaufmann (ed.) 13 – 29.

LIVINGSTON, D.W.   – Hume's Conservatism, *in* Runte (ed.) 213 – 233.

LOVEJOY, A.O.   – The Meaning of Romanticism, *JHI* 2 (1941) 257 – 278.

LUCAS, P.   – On Edmund Burke's doctrine of Prescription, *Historical Journal* 9 (1968) 35 – 68.

LUKES, S.   – Some problems about Rationality, *in* Wilson (ed.) 194 – 213.

220

| | – The Social Determination of Truth, *in* Horton & Finnegan (eds.) 230 – 248. |

MACINTYRE, A.   – A mistake about Causality in Social Science, *in* Laslett & Runciman (eds.) 48 – 70.

MEEK, R.L.   – Smith, Turgot and the 'Four Stages' Theory, *History of Political Economy* 3 (1971) 9 – 27.

MEYER, P.H.   – Voltaire and Hume as Historians, *PMLA* 73 (1958) 51 – 68.

MOORE, J.   – Hume's Theory of Justice and Property, *PS* (1976) 103 – 119.

MOSSNER, E.C.   – Apology for David Hume Historian, *PMLA* 56 (1941) 657 – 690.
   – Was Hume a Tory Historian?, *JHI* 4 (1941) 225 – 232.

MURE, G.R.G.   – Hegel, Luther and the Owl of Minerva, *Philosophy* 41 (1966) 127 – 139.

ODEGAARD, D.   – Locke as an empiricist, *Philosophy* 40 (1965) 181 – 196.

OLIVECRONA, K.   – Appropriation in the State of Nature: Locke on the Origin of Property, *JHI* 35 (1974) 211 – 230.

PAOLUCCI, H.   – Hegel: Truth in the Philosophical Sciences of Society, Politics and History, *in* Weiss (ed.) 98 – 128.

PASSMORE, J.   – The Malleability of Man in Eighteenth Century Thought, *in* Wassermann (ed.) 21 – 46.
   – Hume and the Ethics of Belief, *in* Morice (ed.) 77 – 92.

PECKHAM, M.   – Toward a Theory of Romanticism: Reconsiderations, *Studies in Romanticism* I (1961) 1 – 8.

PELCZYNSKI, Z.   – The Hegelian conception of the 'State', *in* Pelczynski (ed.) 1 – 29.

PFLUG, G.   – The Development of the Historical Method in the Eighteenth Century, *HT* Beiheft II (1971) 1 – 23.

PLANTY-BONJOUR, G.   – L'esprit général d'une nation selon Montesquieu et le Volksgeist hégélien, *in* Hondt (ed.) 7 – 24.

POPKIN, R.   – Hume's Racism, *Philosophical Forum* 9 (1977/8) 211 – 226.

RAPHAEL, D.D.   – Hume's critique of Ethical Rationalism, *in* Todd (ed.) 14 – 29.

REIDEL, M.   – Nature and Freedom in Hegel's 'Philosophy of Right', *in* Pelczynski (ed.) 136 – 150.

RICHES, J.K.   – Lessing's Change of Mind, *J. of Theological Studies* 29 (1978) 121 – 136.

SALMON, P.   – Herder's Essay on the Origin of Language and the place of Man in the Animal Kingdom, *GLL* 22 (1968/9) 59 – 70.

SAPIR, E.   – Herder's Ursprung der Sprache, *MP* 5 (1907) 109 – 142.

SCHEFFER, J.D.   – The Idea of Decline in Literature and the Fine Arts, *MP* 34 (1937/8) 109 – 142.

SEADE, E.D. de   – State and History in Hegel's Concept of People, *JHI* 40 (1979) 369 – 384.

SHKLAR, J.   – Hegel's 'Phenomenology' an elegy for Hellas, *in* Pelczynski (ed.) 73 – 89.

SKINNER, A.   – Natural History in the Age of Adam Smith, *PS* 14 (1966) 32 – 48.
   – Adam Smith: an economic interpretation of history, *in* Skinner & Wilson (eds.) 154 – 178.

SKINNER, Q.   – Meaning and Understanding in the History of Ideas, *HT* 9 (1969) 3 – 53.

SPITZ, L.S.   – Natural Law and the Theory of History in Herder, *JHI* 16 (1955) 453 – 475.

STAMM, I.	– Herder and the Aufklärung: A Leibnitzian context, *Germanic Review* 38 (1963) 197–208.
STILLMAN, P.	– Hegel's critique of Liberal Theories of Rights, *APSR* 68 (1974) 1086–1092.
STOCKTON, C.N.	– Economics and the Mechanism of Historical Progress in Hume's *History*, *in* Livingston & King (eds.) 296–320.
STRAUSS, L.	– Relativism, *in* Schoeck & Wiggins (eds.).
STROMBERG, R.	– History in the Eighteenth Century, *JHI* 16 (1955) 295–302.
SWAIN, C.W.	– Hamann and the Philosophy of David Hume, *JHP* 5 (1967) 343–351.
THOMPSON, M.	– 'Reason' and 'history' in late seventeenth century political thought, *Political Theory* 4 (1976) 491–504.
VERENE, D.	– Hegel's Account of War, *in* Pelczynski (ed.) 168–180.
VIVAS, E.	– Reiterations and Second Thoughts on Cultural Relativism, *in* Schoeck & Wiggins (eds.).
WALSH, W.H.	– Principle and Prejudice in Hegel's Philosophy of History, *in* Pelczynski (ed.) 181–198.
	– The Constancy of Human Nature, *in* Lewis (ed.) 274–290.
WELLEK, R.	– The Concept of Romanticism in Literary History, *Comparative Literature* I (1949) 1–23 & 147–172.
WERTZ, S.K.	– Hume History and Human Nature, *JHI* 36 (1975) 481–496.
WILKINSON, E.	– The inexpressible and the unspeakable: some poetic attitudes to Art and Language, *GLL* 16 (1962/3) 308–320.
WINCH, P.	– On Understanding a Primitive Society, *in* Wilson (ed.) 78–111.
WOLIN, S.	– Hume and Conservatism, *APSR* 48 (1954) 999–1016.

INDEX